The Trickster i

HERMENEUTICS
Studies in the History of Religions

ROBERT D. PELTON

THE TRICKSTER
IN WEST AFRICA

A Study of Mythic Irony and Sacred Delight

UNIVERSITY OF CALIFORNIA PRESS
Berkeley · *Los Angeles* · *London*

University of California Press

Berkeley and Los Angeles, California

University of California Press, Ltd.

London, England

© 1980 by

The Regents of the University of California

First Paperback Printing 1989

ISBN 0-520-06791-6

Library of Congress Catalog Card Number: 77-75396

Printed in the United States of America

2 3 4 5 6 7 8 9

FOR ALL THOSE WHO HAVE TAUGHT ME,
ESPECIALLY THE MEMBERS OF
MY MADONNA HOUSE FAMILY

Contents

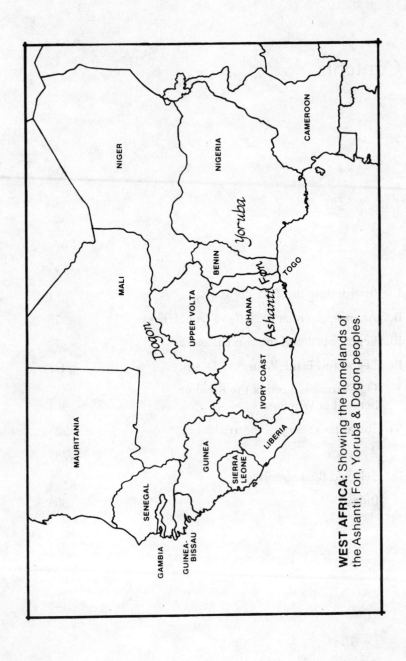

WEST AFRICA: Showing the homelands of the Ashanti, Fon, Yoruba & Dogon peoples.

CHAPTER ONE

Interpreting the Trickster

I will devise matter enough out of this Shallow to keep Prince
Harry in continual laughter.

FALSTAFF (*Henry IV*, 2: V,i)

Yes, by God, you need technique to make a good job out
of life. All you can get. You need to take necessity and make
her do what you want; get your feet on her old bones and
build your mansions out of her rock.

JOYCE CARY, *The Horse's Mouth*

LOUTISH, LUSTFUL, puffed up with boasts and lies, ravenous for foolery and food, yet managing always to draw
order from ordure, the trickster appears in the myths and folktales of nearly every traditional society, sometimes as a god,
more often as an animal. Seemingly trivial and altogether lawless, he arouses affection and even esteem wherever his stories
are told, as he defies mythic seriousness and social logic. Just
as skillfully, he has slipped out of our contemporary interpretive nets to thumb his nose at both scholarly and popular
understanding of so-called primitive peoples. Yet these peoples too know their tricksters as the very embodiment of
elusiveness.

One of the Ashanti trickster tales strikingly illustrates the
way in which Ananse, the spider-trickster, seizes the Ashanti
mind by fooling with its ordinary categories. Ananse has
promised to cure the mother of Nyame, the High God, and has
pledged his life as a forfeit if he fails. When the old woman
dies, Nyame insists that Ananse too must die. Then, as the
executioners are preparing to carry out the sentence, Ananse
plays his hidden trump. He has sent his son to burrow under

the place of judgment, and at the last moment the son cries out as Ananse has bidden him:

When you kill Ananse, the tribe will come to ruin!
When you pardon Ananse, the tribe will shake with voices!

Nyame's chief minister turns to the High God and says, "This people belongs to you and to Asase Yaa. Today you are about to kill Ananse, but Yaa, Old-mother-earth, says that if you let him go, it will be well." Nyame complies, and thus it is, the Ashanti say, that the expression, "You are as wonderful as Ananse," has gained currency among them.[1]

Tricksterlike, Ananse speaks the truth by dissembling. The Ashanti cherish him for his gall and he delights them with his tricks, but the echoes of the complex relationships between Nyame and Asase Yaa, Queen Mother and King, that float through the story hint that Ananse has become synonymous with everything amazing for deeper reasons. Somehow, his slipperiness fulfills the nation's need for healthy commerce between what is above and what is below, between male and female, between apparent and hidden order. Without him the demands of the earth will be stifled, wholeness will vanish, and the people themselves will lose their coherence.

This simple tale suggests that tricksters' tricks may not be all play and no work. Unfortunately, trickster tales have seemed either interesting but not funny, or very clever but not interesting. The second view especially has worked against understanding the trickster. It has often prevented scholars from taking him seriously, and moreover, by confusing folk humor with the sort of inconsequence we know as cuteness, it has tended to lead students of the trickster to treat his seriousness so ponderously that they have turned this most gleeful of mythic figures into a solemn philosophical statement. The difficulties that historians of religion, as well as anthropologists, have had in dealing with folklore show

1. See R. S. Rattray, *Akan-Ashanti Folk-tales*, pp. 265–67.

that the problem reaches beyond the trickster into the area of cross-cultural hermeneutics. Still, E. E. Evans-Pritchard's collection of Zande trickster tales, Claude Lévi-Strauss's attempt to fit the trickster into the categories and processes of the "savage" mind, and Georges Dumézil's study of Loki's place in the Scandinavian branch of Indo-European mythology suggest that these giants of twentieth-century scholarship came to believe that the odd, nearly omnipresent, supposedly peripheral figure of the trickster bears more weight than either anthropology or the history of religions has thus far been able to grant him.[2]

But that is just the question: how can one discover the meaning of the trickster? Or rather, how does one uncover the meaning the trickster has come to have for peoples with a rich, complex religious life, who know the trickster as a figure of the margins yet somehow of the center? The problem, I am convinced, is finally one of language. The trickster speaks—and embodies—a vivid and subtle religious language, through which he links animality and ritual transformation, shapes culture by means of sex and laughter, ties cosmic process to personal history, empowers divination to change boundaries into horizons, and reveals the passages to the sacred embedded in daily life.

By looking at the Ashanti, Fon, Yoruba, and Dogon trickster-figures in their social and mythical contexts and in the light of several contemporary ways of thinking about "primitive" religion, this book seeks to interpret the trickster's language with enough suppleness to remain faithful to it and with enough imagination to challenge our own cultural canons. This examination shows that the trickster is not an archetypal Idea, but a symbolic pattern that, like the High God or the Divine Mother, includes a wide range of individual figures. His movement between worlds, I believe, forms a human

2. E. E. Evans-Pritchard, ed., *The Zande Trickster*; Claude Lévi-Strauss, *Structural Anthropology*, pp. 220–25; Georges Dumézil, *Loki*.

world sacred both as given and as process, both as social enterprise and as divine gift. The trickster depicts man as a sort of inspired handyman, tacking together the bits and pieces of experience until they become what they are—a web of many-layered being. In symbolizing the transforming power of the imagination as it pokes at, plays with, delights in, and shatters what seems to be until it becomes what is, he discloses how the human mind and heart are themselves epiphanies of a calmly transcendent sacredness so boldly engaged with this world that it encompasses both nobility and messiness—feces, lies, and even death.

But why did I choose to study just these four West African societies and their trickster-figures? First, Africa provides a good vantage point for a new look at the trickster, because most studies have focused hitherto on North American Indian cultures. Yet Africans in general and West Africans in particular have also delighted in telling his stories and in recognizing his ties to solemn ritual, great divinities, the market, psychic structure, and other central themes of African religious thought. Furthermore, the hard necessity of making an arbitrary choice to study only certain figures (after rejecting as physically impractical and theoretically bewildering any effort to deal in depth with all African tricksters at once) is softened by the advantage of working within the geographical and cultural boundaries of West Africa. These boundaries are clear enough to make comparison possible, yet they allow sufficient room for different ethnographic methods as well as for useful variations in the trickster pattern itself.

Moreover, within West Africa the choice of which trickster-figures to study becomes much less arbitrary. Clearly, a study that chooses to make use of others' fieldwork and interpretations must look at societies which trustworthy ethnographers have dealt with reliably and imaginatively and whose tricksters are prominent enough to have been treated at length. Within this framework, then, I made the decision to examine

Ananse of the Ashanti, Legba of the Fon, Eshu of the Yoruba, and Ogo-Yurugu of the Dogon. Each of these trickster-figures is complex and intellectually provocative. The societies to which each belongs are all in some way major West African societies. And, most important of all, these societies and their tricksters have been the subject of massive and intellectually valuable research. The research often needs to be questioned; I have tried to question it and to make it question itself, but there is no doubt that the sheer volume of material available makes questioning simpler. Additionally, the Ashanti and the Yoruba have been studied almost wholly by English anthropologists, and the Fon and the Dogon chiefly by French,[3] so that the diversity among the tricksters is demonstrated by the differences in outlook, style, and aim of Bascom and Maupoil, Rattray and Griaule, or Mercier and Herskovits.

A REVIEW OF PREVIOUS THEORIES

Before moving on to Ananse, Legba, Eshu, and Ogo-Yurugu, we need to consider briefly some of the ways others have dealt with the tricksters and some of the problems they have encountered. Trickster-figures appear in all parts of the world in hunting and fishing, pastoral, and agricultural societies at every stage of religious development. Furthermore, the trickster shows himself in a baffling array of mythical masks. S. G. F. Brandon has suggested that these many "guises"—in which the trickster may be "deceiver, thief, parricide, cannibal, inventor, creator, benefactor, magician, perpetrator of

3. The work of Melville and Frances Herskovits among the Fon is a major exception. The difficulties of interpreting the fragmentary religious documents of other times and places raise many methodological issues. Pertinent treatments of these issues include Mircea Eliade and Joseph M. Kitagawa, eds., *The History of Religion: Essays in Methodology*; Eliade, *The Quest: History and Meaning in Religion* and *Patterns in Comparative Religion*; Jonathan Z. Smith, "I Am a Parrot (Red)" and "When the Bough Breaks"; Hans Penner, "The Poverty of Functionalism" and "Is Phenomenology a Method for the Study of Religion?"; and Max Gluckman, *Closed Systems and Open Minds: The Limits of Naivety in Social Anthropology*.

obscene acts"—reflect a "mythological portrayal of a kind of surd-factor, of diverse manifestation and common occurrence in human experience."[4] This is a tantalizing suggestion, but most attempts to strip away the trickster's masks fail to bring his many faces into a clear focus. These failures fall into two broad categories: those which split him into contradictory and conflicting beings and those which accept his ambiguity but seek to explain it away. Laura Makarius rejects these two interpretive tendencies for the following reasons:

If one limits oneself to examining this complex myth-structure in itself, without reference to realities lying outside it, one can only choose between two paths: to strive to explain the coexistence of contradictory traits in a single figure or to consider it as the result of the overlapping of two different figures. Those who have taken the first path have worn themselves out in psychological analyses without reaching acceptable results. The second path begins with an arbitrary assumption and ends by dissolving the mythic figure, all without explaining the figures resulting from this dismemberment or their supposed overlapping.[5]

Makarius proposes her own interpretation of the trickster, based on the assumption that his ambiguity lies in the social experience of those who speak of him in their myths and tales. A similar assumption of the importance of the trickster's social context has guided this book, and certainly Makarius's analysis of the trickster's meaning calls for a most careful examination. Here, however, her remarks simply serve to give some order to the welter of previous interpretations of the trickster, which we must look at, however briefly, before examining the four figures who are the chief subjects of this book.

Daniel Brinton seems to have been the first to give the name "trickster" to the baffling figure of North American Indian

4. S. G. F. Brandon, "Trickster," *A Dictionary of Comparative Religion* (New York: Charles Scribner's Sons, 1970), p. 623.
5. Laura Makarius, "Le Mythe du 'Trickster,'" pp. 18–19 (my translation). Cf. Angelo Brelich's observation that "to create, conserve, and reshape a figure such as the trickster, a society must have had its own reasons, needs, and aims" (my translation); "Il Trickster," p. 134.

mythology and folklore who was a gross deceiver, a crude prankster, a creator of the earth, a shaper of culture, and a fool caught in his own lies.[6] In any event, by the end of the nineteenth century, the term had become standard, and the great anthropologist Franz Boas was struggling to grasp how the trickster "combines in one personage no less than two and sometimes three or more seemingly different and contrary roles."[7] The chief problem, as Mac Linscott Ricketts saw very clearly in his important survey of the attempts to understand the North American Indian trickster, was to penetrate the "kind of logic [that] combines all these disparate elements into one mythical personality." He is

the maker of the earth and/or . . . the one who changes the chaotic myth-world into the ordered creation of today; he is the slayer of monsters, the thief of daylight, fire, water, and the like for the bene-fit of man; he is the teacher of cultural skills and customs; but he is also a prankster who is grossly erotic, insatiably hungry, inordinately vain, deceitful, and cunning toward friends as well as foes; a restless wanderer upon the face of the earth; and a blunderer who is often the victim of his own tricks and follies.[8]

The logic shaping the trickster has been a rock upon which many good scholars have foundered. Most attempts to inter-pret tricksters and their myths leave the figure himself curi-ously untouched; the many angles of approach which inter-preters have used have not come to grips with his ambiguity. Some have seen him as the degenerated remnant of a far more noble figure. Brinton sought the cause of this degeneration in a confusion and a trivialization of language.[9] Raffaele Petta-zoni, in his valiant effort to trace the historical development

6. See Daniel Brinton, *The Myths of the New World*, pp. 161–62.
7. Mac Linscott Ricketts, "The North American Indian Trickster," p. 327, an article based on Ricketts's "The Structure and Religious Significance of the Trickster-Transformer-Culture Hero in the Mythology of the North American Indians." See Franz Boas, Introduction to *Traditions of the Thompson River In-dians*, pp. 1–18.
8. Ricketts, "North American Indian Trickster," p. 327.
9. *Ibid.*, p. 328. See Brinton, *Myths of the New World*, p. 194.

of religious phenomena, has seen the trickster as a degraded, folkloricized Master of the Animals,[10] but both these hypotheses dissolve the trickster's multiformity without grasping its meaning. Others, committed not so much to a historical hermeneutic as to a certain theory of social and personal evolution, have similarly failed to grapple with the trickster as he is, but have seen him as a kind of myth on the make, a primitive construct moving toward a higher mode of sacredness. Franz Boas, Paul Radin, and Carl Jung, for instance, are convinced that the original nature of the trickster was that of the fooler-fool, and that his gathering of power and importance shows the impact of social progress, shamanic interference, or the growth of primitive man from an undifferentiated psychic state to a mature capacity for differentiation.[11] As a result, they believe, a younger, more simply heroic mythic personage has emerged from the cocoon of the older, grosser figure. Ugo Bianchi, too, despite the erudition of his analysis, looks on the trickster as an early form of gnostic dualism and thus has his eye more on Egyptian and other religious systems than on the trickster himself.[12]

Ricketts's own view, supported by extensive research, insists quite rightly that the lewd, gluttonous fool so aptly called "trickster" nonetheless establishes the world *as it is*, no matter how unthinkingly or selfishly, against the plans of the gods and the threats of monsters. He is simultaneously trickster, transformer, and culture hero, and "all these elements are integrated into one character, who, in reality, is none other

10. Raffaele Pettazoni, *The All-Knowing God: Researches into Early Religions and Cultures*, p. 370. See also Karl Kerényi, "The Trickster in Relation to Greek Mythology," pp. 186–87.

11. See Boas, Introduction to *Traditions of the Thompson River Indians*, pp. 4–11; Radin, *The Trickster: A Study in American Indian Mythology*, pp. 164–69, and "The Religion of the North American Indians"; C. G. Jung, "On the Psychology of the Trickster Figure"; and C. G. Jung and M. L. von Franz, eds., *Man and His Symbols*, p. 112.

12. See Ugo Bianchi, "Pour l'histoire du dualisme: Un Coyote africain, le Renard pâle," and "Seth, Osiris et l'ethnographie."

than Man." [13] Mircea Eliade recognizes what Ricketts means to imply by this identification:

Ricketts sees in the Trickster the image of man in his efforts to become what he must become—the master of the world. Such a definition can be accepted with the condition that the image of man be situated in an imaginary universe impregnated by sacredness. It is not a question of an image of man in a humanistic, rationalistic, or voluntaristic sense. In fact, the Trickster reflects what can be called a *mythology of the human condition*. He opposes God's decision to make man immortal and to assure him an existence somehow paradisiacal, in a pure and rich world free of all contraries. [14]

It is true that Ricketts understands the trickster to be a "myth-being," a figure belonging to the mythic time of human origins, who is not "atheistic" since he knows and recognizes the power of the High God, of spirits, and of shamans. Yet Ricketts believes that the trickster's opposition to that power is absolute. He shows man's true being: "at once noble and foolish, heroic and cowardly, daring and deceitful, often beaten but never defeated," [15] seeking to establish a "worldly religion," in which the gods exist "not to be served, but to be conquered," [16] and in which "the only experience of sacredness is of the self-transcending mind of man and its accomplishments." [17]

Thus Ricketts sees the trickster as the symbolic agent of the human struggle to make the world human, the precursor of Prometheus, Milton's Satan, Nietzsche's Superman, and the Marxist "new man." Because "the goal of all man's strivings is power," [18] the trickster, who embodies this striving, opposes the gods and mocks the shamans. In seeking this mas-

---

13. Ricketts, "North American Indian Trickster," p. 343.

14. Eliade, *The Quest*, p. 157.

15. Ricketts, "Structure and Religious Significance," p. 589.

16. Ricketts, "North American Indian Trickster," p. 350.

17. *Ibid.*, p. 345.

18. *Ibid.*, p. 344. Ricketts is referring here, I think too uncritically, to G. van der Leeuw, *Religion in Essence and Manifestation*, trans. J. E. Turner (New York: Harper & Row, 1963), pp. 339–40.

tery of the world and the creation of a secular sacredness, the trickster often fails. In his failures he becomes a joke, yet in laughing at him men are set free, for "they are laughing at themselves. He endures their ridicule like a suffering savior, and in the end he saves them, through their laughter." [19]

These conclusions and the reasoning on which they are based weaken Ricketts's sense of the celebratory purpose of the trickster and undercut his argument that in the trickster's very open-endedness lies his true coherence. [20] By defining religion too narrowly as the will to power, Ricketts has enlisted the trickster too quickly in the post-Renaissance war between heaven and earth. But if such an oversolemnized trickster makes a laughable general and an even more undependable private in that war or any other, his irreducible ambiguity presents one clear problem for all his interpreters, namely, how to juggle the whirling mass of relationships which traditional societies view as their world and for which the trickster is somehow a symbol.

SOME METHODOLOGICAL ISSUES

In part, the modern intelligence tends to undermine at the outset the task of understanding how those who tell trickster

19. Ricketts, "North American Indian Trickster," p. 348. See Paul Radin's opinion that the trickster is the creation of "common man," while the creator-god is the invention of priests and shamans, in "Religion of the North American Indians," pp. 358–59. Ricketts notes that Joseph Campbell, in *Masks of God: Primitive Mythology* (New York: Viking Press, 1956), p. 231, also contrasts "priestly" and "titanic" religious attitudes, though Campbell associates shamanism with the latter.

20. For example, those tricksters which do not show Promethean features Ricketts assumes to have been tampered with by shamans or exhausted by "semantic depletion" (see Adolf E. Jensen, *Myth and Cult Among Primitive Peoples*, trans. Marianna Tax Choldin and Wolfgang Weissleder [Chicago: University of Chicago Press, 1963], pp. 4–5. Eliade's discussion of the "degradation and the infantilization" of symbols is a more useful way to deal with the exhaustion of symbolic meaning; see *Patterns*, pp. 440–46). However, such historical evidence as does exist, e.g., the cave paintings at Lascaux and the presence of shamanism among the Eskimos and the indigenous peoples of Siberia, suggests that hunting cultures have found in *both* the shaman and the trickster an apt expression of their inner lives at least since paleolithic times.

tales understand them. First, it often assumes that the tensions between the High God and the trickster, between shamanism and folklore, between "earlier" and "later" versions of the tales reflect our own recent Western experience of two unyielding visions warring in the bosom of a single culture. One need not be bedazzled by a romantic image of the total harmony of premodern societies to believe that such societies did indeed both enjoy and strive after a unity of experience. This unity—realized or hoped for—suggests that one can best approach the many aspects of premodern religious life by searching for the logic that knits diversity together, a logic through which Ricketts in particular seeks to understand the trickster. To assume that such a wholeness is not worth looking for is to posit an almost universal premodern schizophrenia and to breathe new life into outworn theories of foxy priests and sheeplike people.

An even greater difficulty lies in the essentially comic nature of the trickster. Recent studies of the role of comedy in the Christian tradition of the West have shown how greatly estranged the comic and the holy have become since the Renaissance and the Reformation.[21] Furthermore, this estrangement has reinforced the leveling tendencies of what I would call, with William Lynch, "the univocal mind," that great enemy of the muddiness of actual human life.

I call univocal that kind of mind which, having won through to all the legitimate unities and orderings of the logical and rational intelligence, insists, thereafter, on descending through the diversities, densities and maelstroms of reality in such a way as to give absolute shape to it. . . . This mentality wishes to reduce and flatten everything to the terms of its own sameness, since it cannot abide the intractable differences, zigzags and surprises of the actual.[22]

21. See, for example, M. Conrad Hyers, ed., *Holy Laughter: Essays on Religion in the Comic Perspective*; Enid Welsford, *The Fool, His Social and Literary History*; Hugo Rahner, *Man at Play*, trans. Brian Buttershaw and Edward Quinn (New York: Herder & Herder, 1965); Harvey Cox, *The Feast of Fools* (Cambridge: Harvard University Press, 1969); Sam Keen, *To a Dancing God* (New York: Harper & Row, 1970).

22. William A. Lynch, "The Humanity of Comedy," in *Holy Laughter*, p. 40.

Thus interpreters of the trickster are tempted to reduce his many meanings to only one—be it archaic Prometheanism, protognosticism, psychic growth, or symbolic exhaustion.

Certainly one must ask whether hunting-culture tricksters differ from those of agricultural societies, and how religious symbols are linked to social and psychological change, but as Eliade sees, a "mythology of the human condition" remains a mythology. The language used to describe the trickster's shaping of our inner and outer worlds has, on the whole, lacked the imaginative depth needed to grasp the sacredness of ordinary landscape, the ritual of daily time, the mysterious passages in normal social order, and the multiformity of the power to which the trickster gives man access. For example, Ricketts believes that the trickster has "gone away" and has even less "presence" than the High God, except in the order of the world which he has helped to shape and in his tales.[23] That is simply not the case with Legba, Eshu, and Ogo-Yurugu, as we shall see; they are very much present to their societies, and in several ways. Yet even Ananse, who is not worshiped, can hardly be said to be absent since he is remembered whenever his stories are told. Thus we need to find a way to speak about "remembering" so that we can understand how the trickster links the mythical past to the present, how that linkage discloses the meaning of his offhanded acceptance of death, and the real reason why he gives such delight.

The language of interpretation

Ricketts himself has raised this issue by insisting that the trickster symbolizes not only the mythology of human life, but the myth-making processes of the human mind itself. There are three theories of the trickster that base themselves, for widely differing reasons, on this insight; they are the psychological interpretation of Jung, the structural analysis of Lévi–Strauss, and the neo-Durkheimian hypothesis of Makarius. I

23. Ricketts, "North American Indian Trickster," pp. 343–44.

will discuss these theories later, but I mention them here because each wrestles with the problem of interpretive language and yields insights into the "logic" of the trickster's many guises. Each represents a way of handling religious discoveries and creations, and all—depth psychology, philosophical anthropology, and social anthropology—will help to probe the inner shape and order of the West African materials we will look at here. The questions they raise are useful, even where their answers are partial and even mistaken, but more importantly, each of these visions of religious behavior and symbolism places the trickster within the larger framework of religious hermeneutics.

However, I believe that these interpretive modes cannot alone provide the language needed to uncover the trickster's meaning. In a real sense, the history of religions is based on the intuition, or conviction, that the many modes of speech—historical, psychological, philosophical, anthropological, sociological, and even theological—our culture has devised to talk about religion are not fully suited to the task, no matter how much each may contribute to it.[24] Of course, simply to point to the subjectivist bent of Jung, which is subtly related to the denser rationalist determinism of Freud, to the Cartesian and Kantian presuppositions of Lévi-Strauss, and to the Durkheimian limitations of Makarius, neither refutes their arguments nor produces a more suitable way of speaking about the subject. Indeed, historians of religion have had as much trouble finding words able to bear the weight of religious experience as have others. Certainly Eliade's lifelong work, to take only one well-known instance, attests to the struggle that historians of religion share with all those who seek, in the intellectually secularized and fragmented world of the West, to know what it means to speak about the sacred.[25] It is enough to sug-

24. See Eliade, *The Quest*, pp. 68–75, and *Images and Symbols*, pp. 28–30.
25. See such important works as Langdon Gilkey, *Naming the Whirlwind: The Renewal of God-language* (Indianapolis: Bobbs-Merrill, 1969), and Bernard J. F. Lonergan, *Method in Theology* (New York: Herder & Herder, 1972).

gest here that language which the history of religions finds reductionistic and thin can still have its uses, and to undertake to meet the issue of finding less univocal speech squarely, if modestly, within the boundaries of this book.

The meaning of pattern

There are other methodological issues that need to be dealt with openly. The first of these involves a logical difficulty. Just what does it mean to study the trickster in a particular culture? Do we already know what he is so that every study is merely a search for a new embodiment of him? Or is it just the other way around, so that we understand the word "trickster" to be merely a *nomen*, purely a work of the mind that we apply to a vast array of more or less similar phenomena which remain nevertheless irreducibly particular? A failure to ask such questions makes it easier, for example, to assume, as Radin does, an unrelenting warfare between shamanic and "popular" religion. Such an assumption can lead to a foregone conclusion that the differences among tricksters spring from their victory or defeat in the battle with the High God for the religious allegiance of their respective societies.

We touch here one of the knottiest of philosophical problems, and my aim is not to resolve the quarrel between the followers of Plato and those of Occam or even the more contemporary dispute between Lévi-Strauss and Sartre. However, to find a way to proceed between the devil of idealism and the deep blue sea of nominalism (even if others must draw the metaphysical charts), it seems necessary to avoid, on the one hand, the trimming of the material at hand to fit a ready-made form and, on the other, the dilettantism of the encyclopedist, who buzzes from culture to culture collecting, arranging, and displaying the exotica he has gathered.[26] Whether Platonist or

26. J. Z. Smith's term referring to a method of comparison based on private or superficial categories so that materials are simply brought together for display, not ordered according to any inner logic. See his essay, "Adde Parvum Parvo Magnus Acervus Erit."

structuralist, the idealist will ignore the trickster in favor of the Pure Idea, while the nominalist will treat him as an intellectually impenetrable surface.

The Platonic temptation is probably the greater of the two, since man is everywhere confronted with particularity, yet his mind always moves to establish unity and essence. In this, man goes beyond both the tendency to explain the less by the better known and the contrary tendency to elucidate the familiar by the strange, for awareness itself seems to insist that the experience of continuity be accounted for by the linkage of moments and the discernment of patterns. The danger is that, once drawn out from experience by the mind, abstract forms will be used not as tools for further exploration and enlightenment, but as molds into which all reality must be poured.

Thus no one ever saw, or even heard tell of, a Trickster with a capital "T," but the process of abstraction that tends to capitalize the "T" is not a perverse function of the academic brain. Everywhere one looks among premodern peoples, there are tricky mythical beings alike enough to entice any human mind to create a category for them once it had met two or three. They are beings of the beginning, working in some complex relationship with the High God; transformers, helping to bring the present human world into being; performers of heroic acts on behalf of men, yet in their original form, or in some later form, foolish, obscene, laughable, yet indomitable. They tend to be animal figures, but are not always. Ogo is there in the beginning with Amma, the High God, yet Ananse is not. Ricketts gives several instances where the trickster defeats, and even replaces, the High God, yet Ogo's defeat by Amma creates the world of men. Is the trickster part of a protodualistic structure, as Bianchi says? Perhaps, yet Eshu does not in any way stand alone against the High God, but is in complicated relation to him and to other divine figures. All tricksters are foolers and fools, but their foolishness varies; sometimes it is destructive, sometimes creative, sometimes scatological, sometimes satiric, sometimes playful. In other words, the pattern itself is a shifting one, with now some, now others of the features present.

The temptation is to impose the trickster pattern on any likely candidate, when surely what we are interested in and best able to deal with is not the degree of deviation from some ideal type, but rather the specific creative discovery disclosed by any one instance of the trickster. For example, Radin relies so strongly on a preconceived pattern of psychological development and on the remarkable order of the Winnebago trickster cycle that Jung can create an archetype from Radin's analysis. On the other hand, from dozens of North American Indian societies, Ricketts tends to draw a least-common-denominator trickster, who is too abstractly characterized as "culture hero," "transformer," and "trickster-fixer." Far worse are the motif-analysts, who destroy every individual myth and myth figure in their distillation of myth and folklore into a colorless list of pure ideas,[27] or their opposite numbers in popular magazines and Sunday supplements who have only one category for all the creations of nontechnological peoples —quaint. It is fair enough to talk of the trickster abstractly, as one does of the High God, but even if he were an archetype, realized more or less perfectly by the different figures, an overly rigid use of the form makes for a purely descriptive analysis of a new figure and hinders one's seeing the life of the figure in relation to other social and religious features of its cultural context.

The hermeneutic usefulness of the trickster pattern, then, lies in its power to help us see how any single trickster functions and what he indeed "means." The important point is not how many trickster features Ananse, for example, may possess, but how his structure works in relation to the other structures of Ashanti society and how it exists as a peculiarly Ashanti discovery of significance. The pattern thus enables us

27. See Lévi-Strauss's critique of the morphological analysis of folklore, "L'analyse morphologique des contes russes," *International Journal of Slavic Linguistics and Poetics* 3 (1960): 122–49.

to approach Ananse with certain general questions in mind, but these questions stimulate others that are aimed more specifically at Ashanti life. In looking at the trickster, then, we must be ready to ask about animal characters and ritual transformations, the bipolarity of sacred reality, the function of jokes in shaping a culture, the mythicization of the human condition, and the power of divination to find doors in seemingly blank walls. Yet the trickster pattern raises these issues to probe a culture's inner workings, not to fill in its apparently empty spaces. If it seems that such a pattern is more suited to asking questions than to answering them, we have only to remember what happened when the Fisher-King was asked the right question at the right moment. And if it should seem that the pattern lays more emphasis on dissimilarity than on similarity, the reason is that it is not an archetype, but a kind of entelechy—a form shaping both ends and means, yet so embedded in a single earthly context that both ends and means arise from its interplay with just those elements and forces of which its very concreteness makes it subject, master, and neighbor.

Where to begin

But after choosing four trickster-figures and trying to unpack and lay out in full view all methodological baggage, where does one begin? More precisely, how can one avoid either imposing on the material the hypothesis taking shape in one's head or ordering the material, not by laying bare its own inner shape, but by squeezing it into non-African categories? Since the trickster especially can be understood only as a fundamental part of a cultural self-understanding, I believe that we must concentrate on his relationship with the societies which have imagined him so carefully and enjoyed him so hugely. I am thinking not only of his links to specific institutions and practices, but to the living core of these West African societies, that is, to their verbal and nonverbal expressions of their origins and their boundaries, to their sense of their own meaning and purpose, to their understanding of their involvement with all that is nonhuman.

At first, I thought that this placing of the trickster in the context of cultural hermeneutics could best be accomplished by treating the apparent elements of his pattern thematically, moving across cultural lines to grasp how the different societies deal differently with similar issues and thus develop these elements in diverse ways. It seemed possible to treat the trickster as transformer and mediator, as social creator and interpreter of the socialization process, as diviner and discoverer of freedom, and as revealer of the holiness of the ordinary —to treat him, in short, morphologically, so as to bring each of the four figures into play in suitable order and without undue repetition. I found this method too abstract. The historical material that might disclose reasons for the development of these themes is largely lacking, but even more to the point, the knotty logic of the trickster is best unraveled by keeping him firmly situated within the cultural context. In this way Ananse's primordial foolery, Legba's rampant sexuality and mastery of language, Ogo-Yurugu's rebellion and banishment to the wilderness, and Eshu's never-ending disturbance of social peace might best take on the ironic dimensions that I began to see as the deepest purpose of the trickster's ambiguity. At the same time, looking clearly at the trickster on his home ground would unveil the common, though analogical, imaginative process that shapes him in each culture, without obscuring the special African ability to gaze carefully at the ordinary and discover within it the transcendent.

But once I had decided, on these grounds, to study each of the four trickster figures in turn, allowing pattern, comparison, and symbolic process to emerge gradually, the question still remained: where to begin? It seemed wise to begin with Ananse, who, as an animal figure, dwells in what is often assumed to be the trickster's natural habitat, the forest that is folklore. True, such a beginning begs the question of why this assumption is made and the even more theoretical question of the nature of folklore itself. However, it possesses the great advantage—never to be scorned and indeed, in dealing with the trickster, speedily to be embraced—of handling what we know instead of supposing we know what we do not. Thus, whether the trickster is historically on the way up or the way down or holding his own, whether statistical and morphological surveys would prove that he is present more often in folklore than in mythology, or whether such a distinction has any final meaning, we know that the trickster's animal form ordinarily causes him to be placed in a lesser category of the oral literature of those who know him, a category customarily called folklore. Indeed, despite the different views of Lévi-Strauss and Ricketts, there is widespread agreement in this judgment not only among contemporary Western scholars,[28] but also between Western scholars and nonliterate peoples. In both theory and practice, the latter most frequently distinguish, as do the Fon and the other peoples to be dealt with here, between a form of "sacred history" and a "literature of the imagination." which is also true, but in a somewhat different sense.[29] It is this second sort of literature that the trickster is assumed to inhabit and even to exemplify.

Even if one suspects that the distinction between myth and folklore is not at all absolute, and even if one knows from the Fon, Yoruba, and Dogon trickster-figures that the trickster is also perfectly at home in mythology, it seems wise to respect his association with folklore and begin our investigation there. It is precisely the trickster's earthiness, his popular inelegance, and his delightful inconsequence that have made our intellectual equipment for dealing with him look as ponderously inept as a steam shovel grasping for a grasshopper. It is true that the trickster embodies a theory of man and his culture, but if we were to begin to study him in, say, the Dogon context,

28. See John Greenway, *Literature Among the Primitives*, p. 72.

29. Cf. Melville J. Herskovits and Frances S. Herskovits, *Dahomean Narrative: A Cross-cultural Analysis*, pp. 13–22.

where his theoretical possibilities have emerged into conscious mythical elegance, we would be tempted simply to substitute abstractions for myth without really looking at the funny, gross, vexing, messy creature who causes both his enemies and his analysts such trouble. Once again, we would tend to reduce him to a set of ideas, qualities, and themes and thus fail again to understand why his tales should be amusing or even interesting to so many human beings. The Ashanti identify Ananse, their trickster-figure, so strongly with their folklore that all of the stories, even those in which he does not appear, are called *anansesem*, or "spider-stories." It seems to me that if we begin by studying Ananse, we will not only come to understand the reason for this identification, but also further possibilities of the trickster which the other three peoples have exploited even more elaborately.

There are still other methodological difficulties. For the most part, the *anansesem* are apparently simple tales, at least in contrast to the complex workings of Fon, Yoruba, and Dogon mythology. Yet it seems highly difficult to find a simple method to deal with them. In part, this difficulty springs from the cultural gap between the Ashanti and us. They are a people of southern Ghana, and their stories are oral literature, told on soft tropical nights especially to entertain the children, in a communal setting, in which all the other social and religious apparatus of the society is present in the very bodies of the listeners, who know the stories as the quintessence of play. Here I sit, in the grip of a Canadian winter, looking out a window at pine trees and three feet of snow. I read the stories in English, not Akan, printed and collected, not heard individually, and I grapple with them in solitude, grasping them and the culture out of which they rise only with great intellectual difficulty, knowing them above all as extraordinarily hard work.

Yet cultural differences alone do not explain the hermeneutic problems. These also arise from the hermeneutic nature of the stories themselves. That is, the stories are already interpretations of reality, and consciously so. They mean to interpret human life, and to interpret interpretations puts one at a second remove from reality, and one's reader at a third remove. Those who listen to the stories, on the other hand, are not at a second remove, simply because the oral story exists just at the moment it is being told. This is the reason why Ruth Finnegan is right to insist on the creativity of the teller—not because the modifications he or she makes are so very important from our literary point of view, but because the teller is the story's medium, directly experienced by his audience.[30]

But all this means, then, that the Western academic interpreter begins with the unconscious conviction, flowing from the way his craft shapes his perceptions, that the stories must be demythologized. He cannot take them as they are; he must assume that there is an abstract language that explains their aims and meanings better than the symbolic, pictorial, humorous, "imprecise" language in which they have originally been told. At least he must search for such an abstract language, since he is convinced that his interpretive task demands it. Why else would he be writing about the bothersome things? If we all understood them as the Ashanti all do, why go to so much trouble?

This puts the best face on it. One could after all take the Bultmannian tack and say, as anthropologists and biblical scholars and historians of religion used to, that since we are so much more sophisticated than these representatives of mankind's infancy, who believe in a three-decked cosmos and fairies and gods and demons and sorcery, we must look for the existential message, the clear grain under the dusty chaff. This message will instruct us, the demythologizers insist, and enable us both to recognize these strangers' humanity and to understand what they are really trying to say despite their clumsiness.

30. See Ruth Finnegan, *Oral Literature in Africa*, pp. 1–25, especially pp. 5–12.

The Ashanti, however, are not *trying* to say something; they *are* saying something.[31] To find out what is the job of the interpreter. We recognize the value of the critic because we know that even our own art is not usually self-interpreting, but arguments about the value of the critic show that he too can so abstract the work of art that he stands between it and its audience. His words properly shed light on meanings and patterns so that the work can be enjoyed more deeply; or, since far fewer people read criticisms than read books, watch films, look at paintings, or attend plays, he provides food for those who want to reflect on their artistic experiences at greater depth. The critic, then, converses not just about a work of art, but with the vision of the artist embedded in that object which he both portrays and creates. At his best, the critic helps to map a new world.

If the interpreter is a critic, he is also in some sense a translator. Demythologization may be Cartesianism in its most angelic insistence that truth lies hidden beneath layers of useless matter in "clear ideas," but surely there is such a thing as foreignness—in words, concepts, symbols, patterns of meaning—that begs for translation if understanding is to take place. It is perhaps woefully ethnocentric to think that another way of looking at things is both outmoded and so essentially confused that it means whatever we take it to mean, but it is simply human to poke into the creations of another people to discover their inner sense.

It is still by no means obvious just how to begin to interpret Ananse, but it seems wise to confront him first in the densest story the Ashanti tell about him. In this way one can see at once

31. In highly technical language Paul Ricoeur expresses this understanding of language as disclosure and participation: "The sense of a text is not *behind* the text, but in front of it. It is not something hidden, but something disclosed. What has to be understood is not the initial situation of the discourse but what points toward a possible world, thanks to the author and his situation. . . . Beyond my situation as reader, beyond the author's situation, I offer myself, to the possible modes of being-in-the-world which the text opens up and discovers for me." Quoted by Joseph Sittler in "The Scope of Christological Reflection," *Interpretation* 26 (July 1972): 3.

that his "simplicity" is a simplicity of immediacy, not a simplicity of theme, symbolism, or purpose. Even if a single story
cannot reveal all there is to know about Ananse, it can open up
many of the winding paths that the interpreter needs to explore and suggest to him many of the questions that he must
ask. Furthermore, to be forced to face the subtlety of meaning
that Ananse's seeming triviality discloses is to begin with an
awareness of the interpreter's most needed trait—humility.
After all, "all civilizations are going to be more complex than
any of the people who study them," and indeed so-called
primitives are really more intelligent, as a people, than any
individual who investigates them.[32]

We lack so much knowledge that we would like to possess.
Even the best ethnography will necessarily be sketchy, as a few
men and women try to grasp what so many others have
created over such a long period of time. Often our documents
are inadequate because we lack the indigenous commentary
on the stories that multiple versions would supply, and even
when multiple versions exist, in the original languages, we
usually lack the ability to analyze them in depth linguistically.
Clifford Geertz frames the problem with special grace:

The culture of a people is an ensemble of texts, themselves ensembles,
which the anthropologist strains to read over the shoulders of those to
whom they properly belong. There are enormous difficulties in such
an enterprise, methodological pitfalls to make a Freudian quake. . . .
But to regard such forms as "saying something of something," and

32. Michael D. Coe, "On the Track of Ancient Cultures: An Interview with
Michael D. Coe," *Yale Alumni Magazine*, February, 1974, p. 21. Finnegan (*Oral
Literature in Africa*, p. 15) warns against mistaking "the shallowness of our *own*
understanding" for shallowness in the people we study. There is no truly suitable word to describe the kinds of peoples we are dealing with here. Primitive,
traditional, premodern, preliterate, nonindustrial, savage, archaic, and
non-Western have all been used, and all are inadequate—at best misleading,
at worst simply false. "Traditional" seems most useful to me, widest in scope
and least pejorative, and "primitive" by far the worst because of its overlapping meanings and its tone of cultural smugness. J. Z. Smith's "I Am a Parrot"
deals with the confused uses of the word "primitive," and a fine study of the
development of the word's meaning is contained in *The Concept of the Primitive*,
ed. Ashley Montagu.

saying it to somebody, is at least to open up the possibility of an analysis which attends to their substance rather than to reductive formulas professing to account for them.

As in more familiar exercises in close reading, one can start anywhere in a culture's repertoire of forms and end up anywhere else. . . . But whatever the level at which one operates, and however intricately, the guiding principle is the same: societies, like lives, contain their own interpretations. One has only to learn how to gain access to them.[33]

Thus the struggle to put the stories in their cultural context begins the task of "close reading," which, as Biblical research shows clearly, calls for both an intuitive sensitivity to symbolic patterns and the willingness to listen, test, then listen again, over and over, until the text begins to tell its own story.

Humility, then, is crucial. The trickster's fancy footwork teaches us care and patience in piecing together the evidence, and modesty in reaching conclusions. But modesty is not incompatible with sticking one's neck out, and humility is altogether compatible with boldness, simply because it does not confuse textual puzzles with the spiritual and intellectual condition of those from whom the texts have been gathered so imperfectly but so earnestly. Besides, there is something fitting about dealing with the trickster with modest boldness. He seems so small and light, yet the earth weeps and the people grieve at the thought of his death. So much disclosed by so little. He is the primordial braggart, yet his very braggadocio is humble—not so much because he speaks the truth, but because, in bringing him low, it reveals the transcendent in all that is commonplace. Humble braggadocio, gamy holiness, sacred profanity—these are the ironies that the trickster challenges us to understand so that his very inconsequence may open to us the large and intricate universes of these four societies and other traditional cultures.

33. "Deep Play: Notes on the Balinese Cockfight," p. 37.

CHAPTER TWO

Ananse:
Spinner of Ashanti Doubleness

This coincidence of opposite processes and notions in a single representation characterizes the peculiar unity of the liminal: that which is neither this nor that, and yet is both.

VICTOR TURNER, *The Forest of Symbols*

If you kill Ananse, the tribe will come to ruin! If you pardon Ananse, the tribe will shake with voices!

ASHANTI TALE

ANANSE AND HIS STORIES

ONCE, the Ashanti say,[1] there was a man named Hate-to-be-contradicted. Because of his peevishness, he built a small settlement and lived in it by himself. One day the duiker went to visit him, and the two of them sat down beneath a palm tree. Some palm nuts fell, and the duiker said, "Father Hate-to-be-contradicted, your palm nuts are ripe." Hate-to-be-contradicted said, "The nature of the palm nut is that three bunches ripen at once. Then I cut them down, and when I boil them to extract the oil, they make three water pots of oil. I take this oil to Akase to buy an old woman, who comes and gives birth to my grandmother, who bears my mother, who in turn bears me. When my mother gives birth to me, I am already

---

1. This story is taken from Rattray, *Akan-Ashanti Folk-tales*, pp. 106–9, the chief source of the stories analyzed in this chapter. The only other source that gives both an Akan and an English text is Charles van Dyck, "An Analytic Study of the Folktales of Selected People of West Africa." Van Dyck's tales are most useful, even if their rough edges seem more worn down by European influence than those in Rattray's collection, and wherever possible I have integrated his material with Rattray's. Other sources are Leo Frobenius, *The Childhood of Man*, pp. 349–72, and W. H. Barker and Cecilia Sinclair, *West African Folk-Tales*.

standing there." The duiker said, "You are lying." Then Hate-to-be-contradicted took a stick, hit the duiker on the head, and killed it. Next an antelope came along, and he too sat down with Hate-to-be-contradicted under the palm tree, and the same series of events took place. So it went with all the animals.

Then Ananse slung his bag across his shoulders and went off to Hate-to-be-contradicted's village. They greeted each other, and Hate-to-be-contradicted had a meal prepared for Ananse. When they sat down under the palm tree and palm nuts began to fall, Ananse stuffed them in his bag until it was full. After he had eaten, more nuts fell, and Ananse said, "Father Hate-to-be-contradicted, your palm nuts are ripe." Then his host told Ananse the same story he had told the others. When he had finished, Ananse said, "What you say is true. As for me, I have some okras on my farm, and when they are ripe, I join seventy-seven long hooked poles, but even then I cannot reach them, so I lie on my back, and am able to use my penis to pluck them." Hate-to-be-contradicted said, "I understand. Tomorrow I shall come and see."

As Ananse went home, he chewed the palm nuts he had gathered and spat them out on the path. Next morning, Hate-to-be-contradicted set out for Ananse's village. Now when Ananse had arrived the day before, he had told his children, "A certain man will come here, one who hates to be contradicted. When he arrives and asks for me, tell him that yesterday my penis broke in seven places, and I had to take it to a blacksmith to repair, and as he could not finish it at the time, I have gone to have the work finished." When Hate-to-be-contradicted arrived, he asked, "Where is your father?" The children repeated what Ananse had told them, and asked if Hate-to-be-contradicted had not seen the blood on the path. He said that he had, and then asked where their mother was. They replied, "Mother went yesterday to the stream, and her water pot would have fallen and broken had she not caught it just in time, but she did not quite finish catching it, and has returned today to do so." Hate-to-be-contradicted did not say anything.

Then Ananse arrived. He ordered his children to cook some food for their guest, but they used only a single small fish and a great quantity of peppers. When Hate-to-be-contradicted ate the stew, the peppers burned so much that he asked Ntikuma, Ananse's son, to draw him some water. The boy went to the water pot but brought no water. When Hate-to-be-contradicted asked again for the water, Ntikuma said, "Our water is of three different kinds. That belonging to my father is on top, that of my mother's cowife is in the middle, and that belonging to my own mother is at the bottom. I want to draw for you only the water belonging to my mother, and if I do not take great care, it will cause a dispute." Hate-to-be-contradicted said, "You little brat, you lie!" At once Ananse said, "Beat him until he dies." Hate-to-be-contradicted said, "Why should they beat me until I die?" Ananse said, "You hate to be contradicted, and yet you have contradicted someone else, and that is why I say they must beat you to death." When Hate-to-be-contradicted was dead, Ananse cut up his flesh in little pieces and scattered it about. That, the Ashanti say, is how contradiction came among the people.

This story touches many of the themes of all trickster tales. If the spider-trickster has things his own way here, the very pleasure he takes in leading the father of contradiction to contradict himself suggests that contradictoriness may sometimes get the best of Ananse himself. If Ananse's aim here is not what it is so often, the gratification of physical or sexual appetite, his phallic boasting and his manhandling of everyday reality hint at far greater breaches of physical and social boundaries. If Ananse here reveals his transforming power rather offhandedly, the ease of his victory makes clear its availability for larger tasks, its links with the present order of the human world, and its baffling ambiguity. Indeed, it is this very ambiguity of the trickster-figure that the Ashanti story stresses and that Ananse demonstrates in all the stories about him. He is both fooler and fool, maker and unmade, wily and stupid, subtle and gross, the High God's accomplice and his rival.

The *anansesem* show that this multiformity accounts for both Ananse's comic value and his mythic importance. He is a schemer and a thief, a lecher and an ingrate, yet he is, prototypically, "wonderful." He wins one wife by tricking her impotent husband and subdues another by convincing her that she has wet her bed. His bad temper and brashness constantly bring him to grief. His gluttony causes his hair to be scorched away and his head to be stuck to his anus. Yet his persistent self-assertion helps to bring the world into being. His etiological function can be trivial, as when his antics spot the leopard, point the rooster's beak, or shape the elephant's bottom. He can also remake the world more significantly—as when in a fit of pique he causes wisdom to spread, out of greed disobeys a witch's magic and fills the world with animals,[2] through ignorance introduces the hoe to men, or by lust brings jealousy into society. Ananse's rivalry with Nyame causes disease to spread over all the earth, but at other times his trickiness is put at Nyame's service. Yet whether outwitting the High God or mastered by his power, Ananse remains the agent of ambiguity.

Thus the story of Ananse and Hate-to-be-contradicted shows that neither motif-analysis nor a purely descriptive morphology will disclose the deepest meanings of Ananse and other tricksters. Certainly the contest between liars is a familiar theme in folklore, but the very range of the oppositions in this story gives it a depth that a listing of motifs and submotifs cannot exhaust. It is also true that Ananse acts in a manner "typical" of such figures, but the working out of the story warns us away from a trickster form that sacrifices the messiness of the trickster for the sake of simplicity. We have in this story a witty exploration of the relationship between truth and falsehood, an exploration that plays with common assumptions about possibility and impossibility to reveal the social character of

2. Barker and Sinclair, *West African Folk-tales*, pp. 89–94.

those assumptions. In turning on its head that most social of human realities, discourse itself, Ananse and Hate-to-be-contradicted are in fact struggling to define the fundamental shape of human life. Hate-to-be-contradicted lives in isolation and defeats overtures of friendship from the animal world by his rejection of biological and social necessity, while Ananse is at home with his family and the forces of "nature," and destroys Hate-to-be-contradicted, finally, by his insistence that even water is somehow capable of bearing the impress of social order. In his victory Ananse claims contradiction for the life of men, yet one must beware of a premature closure here, too neat to be faithful to the story. It is in fact contradiction—disorder and opposition—that Ananse brings into human life, and this singular ability of the trickster to be a medium of coherence and incoherence at the same moment calls for great care in dealing with him.

Yet it is as easy to shy away from the deeper levels of these stories as it is to balk at the notion of complex dream symbolism, and for many of the same reasons: the meanings seem too heavy to hang from such slender threads. It may be true that the stories have grown apart from a previous connection with the great myths of the Ashanti (or that such a connection was never consciously made),[3] but we cannot refuse to look at their complexities by protesting that they are "only" folklore or children's tales or *Just So* stories. Like the archaic, unconscious logic of dreams, the meanings of these stories and their links with the more conscious life of the Ashanti are *there*, embedded in the narratives, easily overlooked, but still open to investigation and understanding. One need not romanticize what the "folk" know, or play down the distances between a culture's "great" and "little" traditions, to suspect that what peo-

3. Cf. Laurens van der Post, *The Heart of a Hunter*. For the Bushmen, Mantis is a great mythic figure precisely as a grossly hilarious trickster. See Ira Progoff, *The Death and Rebirth of Psychology* (New York: McGraw-Hill, 1973), pp. 171–72, where he discusses Carl Jung's experience of a people's "forgetting" the meaning of their daily salute to the rising sun.

ple teach their children and why they say that things are "just so" disclose, when analyzed, far more than meets the casual eye. Nor does such an analysis aim at proving, either in the functionalist or the more sophisticated structuralist sense, that everything in a particular culture reflects everything else. The point, rather, is that the Ashanti are saying something through the many levels of their trickster tales that they do not choose to say in any other way.

The *anansesem*, then, are more than a field for Ananse's many games. The subtlety of Ananse's battle against Hate-to-be-contradicted suggests why merely listing and describing trickster qualities in detachment from the stories themselves fails to plumb their depths. To do so, we must deal with a collection of tales that is neither a unified whole, like that of the Dogon, nor a cycle, like that of the Winnebago, nor variations on a theme, like those of the Ge, but an aggregate, a compilation of stories whose inner principle of order is somehow Ananse himself. It is the Ashanti, after all, who call the stories *anansesem*. But to grasp Ananse's own inward shape and to delve more thoroughly into the meaning of his antic ambiguity, we need first to ask more questions about the themes and the symbolism of the stories; second, to look carefully at the stories themselves; and finally, to relate the stories to Ashanti life as a whole.

According to R. S. Rattray, the titles of the stories simply repeat or sum up the last sentence of each story. They give broad Ashanti descriptions of the stories, which we can use to probe their inner order. Of the seventy-five *anansesem* that Rattray has collected, Ananse appears in twenty-five, which fall into three thematic groupings.[4] The first concerns Ananse himself. In this category are tales telling how Ananse came to dwell on the ceiling, how he got a large bottom and a small head, how he became bald, poor, and foolish, why he travels on the surface of the water, why all stories are given his name, and why

---

4. Van Dyck's *anansesem* can be similarly categorized.

he is called wonderful. A second category deals with Ananse's role in shaping the physical world. Here we find the stories of his impact on other animals. A third category includes those stories which tell how Ananse has affected human society. In these we learn why children are whipped, why man relates to sun, moon, and night as he does, how marital confidentiality came into being, how speech originated, why one helps a friend. Here too we discover how Ananse helped to bring into human life certain forces—wisdom, disease, contradiction, and jealousy—which give life its real density. These categories treat, of course, surface phenomena, and we will need to analyze the symbolism, the juxtaposition of characters, and the cultural weight of each story. Still, these thematic groupings help to disclose more of Ananse's inward style and prepare us to ask further questions about him and his stories.

Animality and liminality

With his usual clear-sightedness, Rattray has asked two of these questions.[5] Why, he wonders, are these folktales so coarse, and why do they use animal names for figures so evidently human? True, the tales seem far less coarse now than they did when Rattray collected them fifty years ago, but if one remembers that they are told especially to children[6] and that they contrast sharply with the moral attitudes taught to these same children at other times, one must admit that the question is still pertinent. To say simply that the Ashanti attitudes toward what is or is not proper differ from our own begs the question. We are trying to discover what these attitudes are and how they mesh with a far keener sense of propriety than our own. Rattray's explanation is that the stories provide a time for social and psychological release when resentments can be aired and rascals satirized in a way that does not entail the rup-

5. Rattray, *Akan-Ashanti Folk-tales*, pp. vii-xiv.
6. See van Dyck, "An Analytic Study," p. 155. Cf. Joyce Cooper Arkhurst, *The Adventures of Spider* (Boston: Little, Brown & Co., 1964), pp. 1–4, and Evans-Pritchard, *The Zande Trickster*, pp. 23–31.

ture of communal ties, but instead corrects faults by ridicule and thus mends the social fabric. The same stories, however, are told night after night, and Rattray does not point out that it is above all in the stories about Ananse that the coarseness appears, thus failing to see the connection between the excess of Ananse's appetite and the boundaries of Ashanti society.

The second question Rattray raises is the real key to understanding the trickster's grossness. Rattray knows that the general assumption of his day, that the "primitive mind" is incapable of making a clear distinction between animals and humans, is false.[7] Yet the ability not only to make this distinction in the course of daily life with all the ease that any observer could wish for, but also to do the other mental work that "non-primitives" do is precisely what has baffled those who have tried to understand theriomorphism (the use of animals with human traits in myths and folklore). Rattray suggests that the Ashanti have produced a kind of African euhemerism, in which animals are substituted for historical figures who are being lampooned:

It is true there are certain stories which introduce us to animals, which may possibly be what the late Sir E. B. Tylor would call "animal myths pure and simple." . . . The majority of these "Beast fables," however, are apologues, and I am inclined to believe (and in this, to agree with my African informants) that . . . the names of animals, and even that of the Sky-god himself, were substituted for the names of real individuals whom it would have been very impolitic to mention. Later, no doubt, such a mild *exposé* in the guise of a story often came to be related *qua* story. The original practice is still resorted to, however, in order to expose some one whom the offended party fears to accuse more openly.[8]

The chief difficulty with Rattray's hypothesis is that he does not give a single case where such a fictional transformation has

---

7. See Smith, "I Am a Parrot," pp. 398–405. Finnegan, *Oral Literature in Africa*, pp. 344–54, summarizes the problem of the trickster's theriomorphism, but does not go beyond a literary-psychological interpretation.

8. Rattray, *Akan-Ashanti Folk-tales*, p. xii.

taken place. No doubt the stories can be used satirically, but to say that they originated as personal satire is to bind oneself, probably, to a theory of universal diffusion (as Rattray does)[9] to account for such absolute forgetfulness. Moreover, Rattray's hypothesis implies that the theriomorphism of the *anansesem* is merely accidental and that the stories themselves are little more than Ashanti vaudeville.

We can find the meaning of Ananse's animal form, I think, in the work that Mircea Eliade and Victor Turner have done in the area of shamanic and initiatory transformations. Eliade has spoken of these transformations as "metaphysical"—changes in the deepest orientations of the initiates' biological and social being.[10] In exploring the period of liminality in the ritual process, Turner has enlarged Arnold van Gennep's notion of it by concentrating on liminality as an "interstructural situation." As he says, rites of passage

are marked by three phases: separation, margin (or *limen*), and aggregation. The first phase of separation comprises symbolic behavior signifying the detachment of the individual or group either from an earlier fixed point in the social structure or a set of cultural conditions (a "state"); during the intervening liminal period, the state of the ritual subject (the "passenger") is ambiguous; he passes through a realm that has few or none of the attributes of the past or coming state; in the third phase the passage is consummated.[11]

However, Turner has discovered that liminality is a positional as well as a temporal phenomenon. This discovery has enabled him to explore its structure, or, more properly, its antistructure, a set of conditions and modes of behavior reversing normal social structure to make clear the true inwardness of the social transformation taking place. Thus Turner supplies social

9. *Ibid.*, pp. vii–viii.
10. Eliade, *The Quest*, pp. 112–16. Cf. Eliade's *Rites and Symbols of Initiation*, trans. Willard R. Trask (New York: Harper & Row, 1965), pp. 3, 106–8, and passim.
11. Victor W. Turner, *The Forest of Symbols: Aspects of Ndembu Ritual*, p. 94. See pp. 93–111; also Turner's *The Ritual Process: Structure and Anti-structure*, pp. 94–130, for an exploration of the social and religious meanings of liminality.

correlates for many of the symbolic patterns that Eliade has made so familiar.

As Eliade has vividly demonstrated, in the liminal state symbols of birth and death, of sexual reversal and social dissolution abound. Turner has shown that these symbols—by a marked "economy of symbolic reference" whereby nakedness represents both birth and death and the liminal hut both womb and tomb—focus on the creation of a society that, in its lack of status and hierarchy, in its intimacy and simplicity, appears to be the antithesis of normal social order. This *communitas*, however, is in some sense the great symbol of liminality itself, for even more than the formal instructions in the meaning of sacred realities that the initiands receive, it reveals the hidden depths of social order, its true center. Thus the movement outside, where life is lived "betwixt and between," is in fact a movement inside, a movement disclosing the inner cohesion of society even as it makes available to society those forces of contradiction and anomaly which ordinarily seem to lie outside its scope.

In an important passage, Turner says:

Since liminality represents what Erving Goffman would call "a leveling and stripping" of structural status, an important component of the liminal situation is . . . an enhanced stress on "nature" at the expense of culture. Not only does it represent a situation of instruction . . . but it is also replete with symbols quite explicitly relating to biological processes, human and non-human, and to other aspects of the natural order. In a sense, when man ceases to be the master and becomes the equal or fellow of man, he also ceases to be the master and becomes the equal or fellow of non-human beings.

It is culture that fabricates structural distinctions; it is culture too that eradicates these distinctions in liminality, but in so doing culture is forced . . . to use the idiom of "nature" to replace its fictions by natural facts, even if these "facts" themselves only possess what reality they have in a framework of cultural concepts. Thus it is in liminality, and also in those phases of ritual that abut on liminality, that one finds profuse symbolic reference to beasts, birds, and vegetation. Animal masks, bird plumage, grass fibers, garments of leaves swathe and enshroud the human neophytes and priests. Thus, symbolically, their structural life is snuffed out by animality and nature, even as it is being regenerated by these very same forces. One dies *into* nature to be reborn *from* it.[12]

This linkage of animal form and the renewing power of the liminal state shows the deeper implications of the trickster's animality and his coarseness, for in this view theriomorphism would be both essential to Ananse's structure and intrinsically bound to his transforming power.

Some years ago, Turner pointed out that the "antinomian, multiform, and ambiguous" character of the trickster was like that of man himself in certain liminal states,[13] but here his insight into the nature of liminality suggests that the trickster is more than a symbol of liminal man. It seems closer to the truth, rather, to say that the trickster is a symbol of the liminal state itself and of its permanent accessibility as a source of recreative power. Thus Ananse is free to modify his own bodily parts and those of others and to shift them around according to whim or need. He can break or invert social rules by maltreating guests, by having sexual relations with a daughter-in-law or a mother-in-law, and by giving his mother, not his daughter, in exchange—freely, not mandatorily—for Nyame's stories. He can disregard truth, or better still, the social requirement that words and deeds be in some sort of rough harmony, just as he can overlook the requirements of biology, economics, family loyalty, and even metaphysical possibility. He can show disrespect for sacred powers, sacred beings, and the center of sacredness itself, the High God, not so much in defiance as in a new ordering of their limits.

But Ananse's rejection of the distinctions of cultural exis-

12. Victor W. Turner, "Passages, Margins, and Poverty: Religious Symbols of Communitas," pp. 410–11.

13. Victor W. Turner, "Myth and Symbol," *International Encyclopedia of the Social Sciences*, ed. David Sills (New York: Macmillan Co. and The Free Press, 1958), 10: 578.

tence both in its loftiest and in its most casual terms leads neither to chaos nor to Promethean boundlessness. Nor is there some sort of arcane method in his madness that brings about good results at certain times (the spreading of wisdom, the availability of the hoe, the privacy of the marriage bed) and bad results at other times (the spreading of disease, contrariness, and jealousy). Rather, his rejection of culture and his loosing of the forces of nature release the power of both to produce, not another primordial world, but the world which is *now* in existence. Ananse, then, does not need to bedeck himself in birds' feathers to steal the secrets of Nyame, as Nyame knows. As a spider, Ananse breaks through the boundaries separating nature from culture in such a way that human life is seen to transform perpetually what is given from both above and below. He is far more truly a metamorph than he is a theriomorph; *because* he belongs to many worlds, he is a transformer.

THE SHAPING OF SOCIAL ORDER

We must proceed carefully here, for Ananse reveals the Ashanti understanding that there can be no pure centrifugality. That is, just as the turning of the center creates movement away from the center, so Ananse's movement away from order in the end creates order. Ananse operates in mythic time, yet the distinctions he overrides and the boundaries he breaks through are the distinctions and boundaries of the present world—the very world that comes into being through his transforming actions. Furthermore, although Ananse does not satirize the processes of priestly and initiatory transformation as sharply as the Winnebago trickster, his buffoonery still has a keen edge. He shows the power of liminality precisely by stressing its negation of ordinary structure. Thus there is a double doubleness about him: if he parodies sacred mysteries by disguising himself as a bird, by claiming the power to heal, or by fishing with the spirits, his parody brings about creation, not destruction; and if he makes a fool of himself in the process, still he reveals himself as wonderful in his power to draw forth the delicate balance of forces that is the human world. As in his contradiction of the contradictor, he negates negation and thereby gives birth to a dialectic whose aim is not synthesis, but a never-ending juggling of thesis and antithesis.

Order out of disorder

At this point we need to look more carefully at just what Ananse does when he rejects cultural norms and looses the forces of nature. What sort of disorder creates order? And what sort of order comes forth from the embrace of disorder?

First, let us consider the third thematic group, which includes the tales about Ananse's role in shaping society. In these stories Ananse seems to be far more the agent of social order than the embodiment of structurelessness, yet we ought to resist any temptation to see the work of the parental or the priestly hand here—tidying, refining, or editing. The stories remain bawdy and, to everyday sensibilities, outrageous. Ananse is still a liar and a lecher. The clue to the meaning of this apparent paradox, in which Ananse is at once creator of order and lawless fool, has already appeared in the story of Hate-to-be-contradicted. It is he, not Ananse, who seems to represent liminality; he lives apart, rejects social life, subverts even its physical and metaphysical bases, and kills his guests, who seek to bring him into the community both by their presence and by their denial of his denials. Ananse, on the other hand, is relentlessly social, yet it is he who brings contradiction into the human world by murdering his guest and by lying more extravagantly than his antagonist. This story suggests, then, that the true limen lies not on or outside the margins of society, but in its midst.

Again and again this type of story shows Ananse achieving some element of ordinary social structure by acting counter to ordinary rules of behavior. Ananse introduces the whipping of children into society because he discovers, during a famine, a magic dish that will provide him with food on command. [14] He uses the dish for himself, supplying his family only with what he can scrounge in the forest each day and lying to them about his reasons for forgoing his share in their meager rations. When his son discovers his deceit and destroys the dish's magic, Ananse finds a magic whip, whose secret a bird tells him and which he tricks his family into discovering. The whip punishes them, and when Ananse cuts it up into pieces so that the punishment of children spreads abroad, his own gluttony and deceit have resulted in the creation of that sanction of parental authority that helps to guarantee the transmission of social life. To say, "When you tell your child something and he will not listen, we whip him," is to say that there is a boundary between listening (or obedience) and not listening, the crossing of which must penalize the child even as it imperils society and indeed human life itself. Life is handed over only when parents have brought their children up from biological to social existence. This boundary Ananse creates by exploring the wild and the magical worlds beyond the world "starving" for the possibilities of transformation.

Two stories in which Ananse appears as a sort of archetypal gardener have a similar structure. In the first, [15] Nyame has planted a great garden, which has become overgrown with weeds and nettles. He offers to marry his ninth daughter to whoever can clear the garden without scratching himself when stung by the nettles. All who try cannot resist the desire to scratch, but Ananse outwits Nyame. He weeds the garden only on market days, so that as people pass by and ask him why he has undertaken such a hopeless task, he answers by praising the girl's beauty, accenting her desirability by slapping and rubbing the parts of his own body corresponding to

14. Rattray, *Akan-Ashanti Folk-tales*, pp. 62–67. Note that Ananse feeds his family with "wild" food, while he eats food that is cooked. For a different version, see van Dyck, "An Analytic Study," pp. 323–29.

15. Rattray, *Akan-Ashanti Folk-tales*, pp. 128–31.

the parts of hers that he is praising. Ananse weds her, but when he confesses his ruse to her, she threatens to reveal his dishonesty to Nyame. Ananse claims that she must treat what he has told her as a sleeping-mat confidence, but she responds by moving her own mat to the other side of the room. When she has fallen asleep, Ananse pours water over her and wakes her, accusing her of wetting herself and promising to make her shame public. She asks him to let the matter drop, but he swears to press his case because she has sworn to press hers. At last, out of shame, she agrees to drop both cases, and thus it is that "sleeping-mat confidences are not repeated."

In the story explaining why the Ashanti say, "When anyone at all is engaged on any work and he asks you, help him," [16] Ananse also appears as a gardener. In this case he is married to Aso (whose name means "hoe"), who most often appears as his wife in these tales. She will not help Ananse clear the ground, burn the weeds, or plant the seed, claiming that a woman "taboos" these things. As harvest time nears, however, she is eager to help bring in the crops. In response, Ananse digs a huge hole into which he puts the whole harvest. Then he tells Aso it has been foretold that he will die in eight days and that he has dug his own grave. He pretends to die, and is buried with the harvest. After the eight days of mourning, Aso goes to the garden only to find the crops gone. As she curses those whom she believes to have robbed her, Ananse sings from his grave, telling her to cease complaining since he has only "eaten" what is his own. Aso asks the Hare to interpret Ananse's song. He tells her that Ananse has merely taken what is his own, for ever since the Creator created, never was there a woman who did not help her husband.

Now in these stories Ananse shapes human society in several ways. He socializes the earth through farming; he establishes both the inner intimacy and the outer socioeconomic working of marriage; he links the sharing of work to the crea-

16. *Ibid.*, pp. 140–45.

tion of life; and he domesticates the force that males persist in seeing as the vastest, most threatening, most essential irruption of nature into culture—woman herself. On the one hand, he joins together the institutions of the market, agriculture, and marriage, and on the other, he separates the marriage bed from the claims of lineage and jurisprudence. Similarly, he restores the harmony that Nyame intended to exist between a husband and a wife in their daily work, and indeed he becomes a model for social cooperation. Yet in all these things the force that moves him is not obedience, but self-interest. The source of his transforming power is his capacity for deceit. He joins the market to the garden by a clever ruse, and draws a line of privacy around the marriage bed by falsely accusing his wife of having crossed the boundary culture draws between the body and its wastes.[17] Ananse shatters the false disjunction between Aso and farming by establishing an even more deceitful connection between himself and death, and he reveals the necessity of sharing by causing the earth to consume what it has produced. To create the lines of force binding society together, Ananse breaks the connections assumed to exist between what is said, what is done, and what is meant.

The stories are not always so thick with symbolic detail, yet their meanings follow the same pattern. For example, Ananse kills a monster bird, which strips the people of their jaws and thus their speech each day at noon.[18] He enrages the bird by abusing its ancestors, hides in a calabash dish, and cuts off the bird's head as it searches for him. He wins speech for men chiefly by abusing it, and they can hardly credit his victory because he is such a renowned liar. However, even though Ananse makes speech possible, enables time to move beyond noon, and demystifies birds, his action also creates the dysfunction of toothache, for not everyone manages to retrieve his own jaw.

17. The ordinary practice, of course, is to defecate and urinate outside the family compound or outside the village itself.

18. Rattray, *Akan-Ashanti Folk-tales*, pp. 178–83.

This same doubleness is present in the story about the spread of wisdom.[19] Seeking to put wisdom out of men's reach in a gourd at the top of a tree, Ananse realizes that all knowledge is not contained in the gourd because his son knows better than he how he should climb the tree. Furious, Ananse breaks the gourd and hurls it to the earth. Van Dyck reports that a common Ashanti euphemism for defecation is "going to the top of a tree,"[20] and if the story is playing with that expression, then it mockingly equates wisdom and feces while laughing at the fool who must be taught by his child how to relieve himself. Yet the story hints that Ananse succeeded after all; anyone who did not get to that place to gather wisdom is a fool. Ananse is master of wisdom because he yokes together the mysterious ambivalences of ordinary life—speech and pain, emptiness and fullness, wisdom and waste.

The spread of jealousy

Two other stories treat Ananse's complex role in the spread of cultural forces; both of them, like contradiction, are seemingly negative. Akwasi-the-jealous one, like Hate-to-be-contradicted, is radically antisocial, and, in contending with him, Ananse seizes for human society the negative force that he symbolizes.[21] Akwasi lives wholly apart with his wife, Aso, for he wants no one to see her or talk to her. Since he is sterile, he fears that if they live with others, someone will take her from him. Nyame gives permission to the young men to woo Aso, but they all fail. Ananse claims that he can succeed, provided that Nyame give him gunpowder and bullets. These Ananse takes to various villages and distributes to the villagers, with the understanding that they will give him the meat from whatever animals they are able to kill.[22] He fills a huge basket with

19. *Ibid.*, pp. 4–7.
20. See "An Analytic Study," p. 155.
21. Rattray, *Akan-Ashanti Folk-tales*, pp. 132–38.
22. The bullets are "transformed" into food through the medium of trade, a symbol of the transforming power of all economic activities.

this meat, goes to the house of Akwasi and Aso, announces that he comes from Nyame, and gives them the meat to prepare for dinner, pretending that it is only a small portion of all that he has.

As he and Akwasi are eating, Ananse asks for salt, and while Akwasi is away from the table, Ananse puts a purgative into his food. After the meal, Ananse tells his host that his name is "Rise-up-and-make-love-to-Aso," and when they prepare for sleep, Ananse insists that the only place he can sleep without dishonoring his master, Nyame, is at the threshold of the bedroom of Akwasi and Aso. (He refuses to sleep in a closed room or in the open veranda room.) Ananse bars the door of the bedroom, and in the middle of the night, as the purgative does its work, Akwasi must call out to Ananse, "Rise-up-and-make-love-to-Aso!" Ananse unbars the door, and, while Akwasi is defecating outside, does as he has been bidden. The scene is repeated nine times during the night. Ananse leaves the next morning, and two months later, when Aso's pregnancy begins to show, Akwasi is puzzled and wonders if she is sick. She reminds him that he told their guest to rise and make love to her. He insists that he will give her to Ananse, and they leave for Nyame's "village." On the way Aso gives birth, and when they reach the village and tell Nyame their story, he asks them to point out the culprit. Ananse is roofing huts, and when Aso points to him twice, he falls off the ridgepole. He accuses Aso of sorcery, and Akwasi is made to sacrifice a sheep in payment. Aso becomes Ananse's wife, but the baby born of the adulterous union is killed, cut into pieces, scattered about, and becomes the source of jealousy.

Here Ananse is the enemy of a jealousy whose core is sterility and a consequent rejection of human community. In Ananse and Akwasi two excesses meet, for Ananse embodies the drive toward human intercourse, while Akwasi (whose sterility implies impotence) represents a withdrawal from intercourse, which symbolizes a repudiation of human life. The humor of the story seems as significant as the story itself, which is widely known in one form or another. It is not simply that laughter masks an instinctive hostility toward both impotence and cuckoldry as threats to life, but that Ananse transforms aggression into a lifegiving force. As the agent of human community, he is the guest who brings his own food, a superabundance of the very food, obtainable only through the combined efforts of many people, whose transformation symbolizes culture. While Akwasi, who is so sexually retentive, literally cannot stomach such food and must go out of the space of cohabitation to eliminate it, Ananse, with unflagging exuberance, penetrates that space again and again to create life. The one can only go from inside out to empty himself; the other goes from outside in to fill another.

It seems a paradox that the fruit of the union of Ananse and Aso should be the spread of jealousy. Yet once again, it seems to me, Ananse is claiming for society a force that threatens it. It is not adultery that is being condoned or glorified here, but human intercourse and its consequences. Even though Ananse has overstepped the normal boundaries of society in such a way that Aso gains a certain power over him (when she points her hand at him, he falls), still it is Akwasi, not Ananse, who must make reparation, because he has denied the structure these boundaries are meant to create and protect. Ananse, on the other hand, has passed beyond that structure only to recreate it. In doing so he brings jealousy into the center of life, where it has a procreative function at the service of potency, not of impotency. Ananse is both "he who defeats jealousy" and "he who fathers jealousy" because he represents the imperious demands of intercourse. Insofar as jealousy atomizes, indeed prevents, society because it is the enemy of sexual potency itself, Ananse opposes and vanquishes it. But insofar as jealousy is the inevitable result of giving sexuality its rightful and necessary place in society, Ananse is its father.[23]

23. For a brilliant analysis of jealousy, see Leslie H. Farber, *Lying, Despair, Envy, Sex, Suicide, Drugs, and the Good Life* (New York: Basic Books, 1976), pp. 180–202.

It is important, however, to see that Ananse fathers jealousy in its procreative dimension not grudgingly, but exuberantly. We do not have here a separation of jealousy into two aspects, one purely destructive and the other functional and therefore perfectly acceptable. We have instead an earthy story hinging on the use of humor as a mode of transcendence. Jealousy as sheer retentiveness and possessiveness is inherently sterile and antisocial, but its emptiness, for the Ashanti, reaches beyond danger to absurdity and finds its imaginative conclusion in uncontrollable diarrhea. He who would hold everything can hold in nothing; he whose impotence is such a threat reveals the depth of that impotence and the hollowness of that threat by inviting his own cuckolding. Impotence is transformed into possibility with a dexterity whose other face is laughter, a laughter that is not a sigh of relief but a shout of delight at the discovery that danger is merely opportunity in scary clothes.

Moreover, Ananse's cocksureness must not be confused with some somber, Teutonic exaltation of the sexual principle. To be cocksure means to be carefree, but Ananse's insouciance springs from a relentless desire to experience human intercourse, not from an ignorance of its consequences. Like Akwasi, he too is absurd, but the laughter he provokes signifies delight that he has broken through unnecessarily rigid boundaries to seize for society the forces of incoherence. No one who has ever lived in a small community could sentimentalize the pains of jealousy, but Ananse discloses that they can become labor pains heralding—instead of avoiding—new life. Jealousy becomes a cause for laughter the instant Ananse reveals it to be the hidden face of desire (which can possess only by squandering) and of fidelity (which can hold life only by constantly yielding to it).

Thus Ananse's unmasking of disorder never shows disorder as mere illusion, a mask over the face of a univocal state of being. On the contrary, Ananse's in-betweenness manifests the many layers of human life. He may disclose that what helps also hurts and that what hurts also helps, but in every instance he is an agent of the many-sidedness of what is.

Disease and centripetality

Even as Ananse brings jealousy and contradiction into human society, so he is also the cause of disease.[24] He tells Nyame that he will bring him a beautiful maiden if Nyame will give him, to kill and eat, the sheep that Nyame sacrifices to himself on Saturday. After eating it, Ananse discovers a village filled with women, all of whom he marries. A hunter reports that Ananse has fed the sheep to the women and married them, and Nyame claims them all except one who is sick. She asks Ananse to bathe her, collects the water in a gourd, and becomes beautiful. Again the hunter reports to Nyame that Ananse has made a fool of him by keeping the most beautiful woman for himself, and Nyame takes her too. Ananse then invents an insulting song about her, and in vexation begins to dance with his sons. The crow reports this to the High God, who wants the dance as well, but Ananse will only perform the dance in Nyame's harem. Nyame and his wives dance with Ananse, but the one who had been sick will not dance until Nyame forces her. Ananse strikes her with the gourd, and the diseases are scattered everywhere.

The thread of this story is not easy to follow. It is not clear who is the cause of disease, Ananse or Nyame, and indeed the story ends by blaming them both: "Once there was no sickness among mankind, but Nyame was the cause of Ananse bringing diseases among the tribe." Furthermore, what is the link between the episodes? Why does Ananse collect physical disorder only to release it? What is the relationship between disease and society?

The story seems to hinge on the power ("virtue," in the old sense) within the sacrificial sheep and on Ananse's inability to

24. Rattray, *Akan-Ashanti Folk-tales*, pp. 76–81.

make that power work permanently for himself. The High God surrenders what is his own in exchange for future considerations (as traders will), and in effect Ananse makes a sacrifice to himself. This sacrifice empowers him. He does not need to feed it to the women to gain them for himself, for its power has become his. Once again, there is a conjunction between Ananse's insatiable desire and antisocial sterility or disorder. A village of women is an ontological as well as a social impossibility, and Ananse's power works to bring these women into human society. His power also claims the sick woman for human life, and even when she is taken away, enough "virtue" remains with Ananse for him to create a splendid dance, a symbol of ritual order.

What has happened is that Ananse has received a share in the power of Nyame, the center that brings everything into order by drawing all things into relationship with it. Yet because the center is Nyame, not Ananse, as soon as Ananse transforms disorder into order by socializing, curing, and ritualizing experience, Nyame must claim his work. Ananse is left only with disorder, now symbolically concentrated in one small cup, but more truly embodied in the incessant centrifugality of his will. He collects disease (disorder) while serving his own desire, and the more his power diminishes, the more concentrated the disorder becomes. He releases it, not really for the psychological satisfaction of revenge, but for metaphysical reasons. The disorder lies within him, in his desire. It is the other side of his creativity, which is so potent that it can transform concentrated disorder into ritualized play; the disease gourd even becomes a drum. Nyame must demand both dance and drum, for the dance humanizes forces that are the most "natural" of all. Yet to demand for human life those forces which threaten to dissolve the body is also to introduce them into that life.

There is, therefore, a double movement here. There is a movement out from the center, bearing the power of the center and literally refining disorder, and there is a movement back into the center, bringing into human, social existence all those forces of nature—women, beauty, play—that, when refined, are necessary to culture. This second movement brings physical disorder into human life because Ananse creates the dance, or cultivates play, out of the very elements—desire, anger, envy, and disease—used, but never used up, in the refining process. To embrace the dance (a higher ordering of the body) is to accept also the possibility of the body's disordering.

Furthermore, Ananse's collection of disease in a single gourd mirrors his collection of wisdom. When Ananse puts all wisdom in a gourd, he cannot bring it successfully to the periphery, that place "outside" where waste belongs. He flees the center, but cannot keep it from exerting centrifugal force. When he collects disease and dances with it, he has captured disorder, but he cannot overcome centripetality. As irresistibly as he moved out from the center, he moves into the center. As surely as he brings the power of the center into play, he brings the potency—the rawness, the structurelessness—of the limen into the workings of the center. The wholly active tends to be the merely inert, as the High God's otiosity shows, and the merely possible tends to become pure potency and thus chaos. Ananse moves between the two, linking their forces, overcoming the inertia of the one and the chaos of the other, and in this process he becomes the agent of the creation of human existence.[25]

Ananse's socialization of nature

The Ashanti understand very well that Ananse is an agent of creation—in fact, the agent of Nyame himself—but they never think of him as a folkloric demiurge. We cannot shy away from the deeper meanings of these stories, but neither can we lose sight of the comic quality of Ananse's agency. Of course

25. Ananse never replaces the "center." See van Dyck, "An Analytic Study," pp. 193–97, where Ananse shames Nyame into leaving the earth by making it appear as if the Creator has defecated indoors. Ananse uses waste and laughter to give himself more room.

Ananse makes laughter work for him, but his funniness has nothing earnest or one-dimensional about it. He is no sweaty metaphysical pioneer hacking the actual out of the jungle of the possible, nor is he a good-natured cosmic mechanic, revving up the motor of social order by injecting a richer mixture of chaos into its fuel. He does these things, but his style is radically oxymoronic. He yokes together elegance and coarseness so that what is appears as a dazzling display of improbability, resulting from a perfect inward fidelity—not to mere selfishness or exaggeration or buffoonery, but to the demands of every mode of intercourse. He makes a dance which so links order and disorder that it cannot help being drawn into the center of life, where it both explodes into its component parts and continues to exist as an image of potential wholeness.

Ananse's peculiar style lies at the heart of another story that treats of the creation of the human world and of the socialization of natural forces. Nyame has three children, Night, Moon, and Sun, and when they grow up, each builds his own village.[26] One day Nyame prepares a royal stool, and asks if anyone knows what he is planning. Ananse claims to know, but is boasting falsely. To discover Nyame's secret, he plucks feathers from every bird, adorns himself with them, and flies back to Nyame's village. The people marvel at this extraordinary bird, and Nyame says that Ananse would surely know its name, since he had been able to divine Nyame's intention to make Sun the chief by means of a contest to give the correct name (*Kintinkyi*) to a certain yam. With that, the "bird" flies away, and, after removing his feathers, Ananse travels to the village of each of Nyame's children. Night gives him a meal of roasted corn, and Moon prepares mashed yam for him; but when Ananse reaches Sun's village, Sun declares that he would have wished his father to examine and judge his life, but that Ananse's coming is equivalent to Nyame's coming. Sun then kills a sheep to feed Ananse. Ananse tells Sun his fa-

26. Rattray, *Akan-Ashanti Folk-tales*, pp. 72–77.

ther's secret, and to make sure that Sun will remember the yam's name, Ananse promises that he will make a drum that will play with the sound "*kintinkyi bomo*." When the contest begins, Night and Moon fail, but as the drum sounds and Ananse "turns cartwheels," Sun gives the correct name, insisting that he remembers it from his childhood, when he learned it from his father as they walked together. Nyame punishes Night and Moon for their forgetfulness by decreeing that wicked things will be done during the former's time and that only children will play when the latter reigns. Nyame makes Sun chief and declares that all disputes, except household cases, will be settled during his reign. Finally, he rewards Ananse, who has been able to read his thoughts, by changing the name of those "words" formerly known as *nyankonsem* to *anansesem*.

Ananse seems so thoroughly the agent of Nyame here that at first it is difficult to see why his duplicity should be necessary at all. Why must he pretend to be a bird? Why must he invent such an elaborate method of helping Sun to "remember" his father's secret word? Of course Ananse's wiliness makes the story, and that is just the point. The story, which works to establish probable, commensensical equivalences through improbable linkages, is really about that very same process understood as the process creative of man's world. That is, an innate symbolism links the High God, the Sun, and the resolution of human conflict without which society could not live, as there is a kind of symbolic link between darkness and evil, between moonlight and that representation of adult life which is children's play. But, the story suggests, this symbolism is not so self-evident that it immediately ties Nyame to the Sun and the Sun to the world of man. It must be "remembered" by a discovery of the hidden potencies of light and by a disclosure of memory itself. To establish the connection between Nyame, Sun, and human order, mediation is needed. Ananse, then, by discovering Nyame's secret and "reminding" Sun of it, is the mediator of the creative process and of the resolution of conflict. Nevertheless, he does not act from noble motives or by a rational, straightforward method, but by following faithfully his own way of making connections—by shattering the accepted boundaries of language, action, and even modes of being.

Thus he makes himself such a bird as no one, not even Nyame, ever saw, and in this bizarre parody does indeed penetrate the High God's mind. Thus too, the anamnesis of the Sun is an elaborate deceit, which Ananse literally plays out with drum, dance, and cartwheels, except that in some sense it is not a deceit at all. Both Nyame, who expects that Ananse will convey his desires to Sun, and Sun, who greets Ananse as if he were Nyame (in word and by offering him a sheep), accept Ananse's mediatorial role, and this acceptance implies that the "light" needed to fashion order out of the tangle of human wills can be focused only through a duplicity that restarts the processes of speech. There is a danger here of settling for an easy sort of coincidence of opposites and a consequent trivialization of both harmony and disorder, when it seems far more likely that Nyame's obtuseness and Sun's forgetfulness are metaphors for the High God's inertness, which Ananse overcomes by his persistent itch for intercourse.[27] This theme, however, is only lightly implied here; it will become much clearer when we examine Legba's and Eshu's connection with divination. For now it is enough to say that, even in a story where Ananse appears as a relatively well-behaved agent of creative order, he makes the necessary connections only by disrupting the given structure.

The aim of the story is to show that Ananse creates social intercourse by disclosing, plunging into, heightening, or even embodying the raw forces out of which human life is made. He renews by the power of antistructure. His relentless willfulness is not some archaic version of laissez-faire, but a pas-

27. See *ibid.*, pp. 236–41, for a witty explanation of how "Odds" and "Evens" push Nyame away from Asase Yaa, yet ironically limit the distance between them by making it equivalent to a darkened room.

sionate entry into the rawness of precultural relationships to reclaim and restore their potencies, to make them available for new patterns of order. It is not culture or structure that Ananse rejects, but those distillations of nature which tend to become mere stagnations, sources of pollution instead of life. Ananse is, after all, the enemy of Hate-to-be-contradicted and Akwasi-the-jealous-one. He loves to contradict because he loves to relate; he makes jealousy because his name is "rise-up-and-make-love." Thus Ananse rejects truth in favor of lying, but only for the sake of speech; temperance in favor of gluttony for the sake of eating; chastity in favor of lasciviousness for the sake of sex; honesty in favor of trickiness for the sake of human interchange, the deeper aim of productive work. Because Ananse goes out and up into birdness, Nyame's creative word is freed to make Sun's light sovereign in human dealing. Furthermore, the social order molded by that dealing has an abiding potential for renewal, for in rejecting pure stasis as the ideal social order and in embracing both the raw sources of social life and the apparent enemies of that life, Ananse transforms disruption from a destructive into a creative force.

Spear-grass and boundaries

The question that arises here is what, if anything, prevents Ananse from being a primitive symbol of *nostalgie de la boue*, a hankering for (more or less metaphysical) muck? But Ananse's genius for seizing the raw and the negative has little in common with the sentimental optimism of those who like to think that *The Story of O* and *Saint Genet* are manuals of spiritual rejuvenation,[28] for Ananse draws new boundaries even as he opens new spaces.

The story "How spear-grass came into the tribe" contains a fine example of this side of Ananse's symbolic work.[29] In a

28. It is "optimism" inasmuch as they believe that good infallibly flows from a rejection of the sociosexual order. It is a grim, Hegelian optimism, of course, not the sunny American variety.

29. Rattray, *Akan-Ashanti Folk-tales*, pp. 212–19. Cf. van Dyck, "An Analytic Study," pp. 335–41.

great famine Ananse's son goes off into the forest to look for food. He meets Nana Aberewa ("Old grandmother"), who tells him not to pluck from her field the yams that ask to be plucked, but the ones that ask not to. Next she tells him to throw away the yam itself and cook the skins, which turn into good food. When he asks for meat, she tells him to insult the monkeys grossly. They start to beat him, and she orders her knife to cut off their heads. Ntikuma takes the food home, and Ananse takes out one yam, which he says he will eat during his monthly period. He and his family eat the rest of the food, and the next morning Ananse claims to have his "period," retires to a secluded place, and eats the remaining yam.

Then Ananse and Ntikuma return to the forest. They come back with the knife as well as with more food. Ananse orders his son to insult some pigs, and the knife kills them, but it begins to cut down trees as well, because Ananse does not know how to make it stop. Ntikuma has learned the right words, however, and stops it. Ananse, however, decides to visit Nyame, refusing to heed Ntikuma's advice not to show off the knife. He offers to slay Nyame's enemies, and orders the knife into action against a hostile army. When it disposes of the enemy, the knife turns against Nyame's army and finally lops off Ananse's head. It cuts on and on, until at last it turns into spear-grass, whose edge is "very, very, very sharp."

This story tells how contradicting contradiction brings both death and life. In a sense, it is the mirror image of the story of Hate-to-be-contradicted. The three significant elements of the story are the disclosure of the woman's nature as "Love-to-contradict," Ananse's utter fidelity to his own contrariness, and the location of the end of the story—outside instead of inside human society. Like Hate-to-be-contradicted, the old woman lives outside of society, but her apartness gives life, while his produced only death. Where his hatred of the contradictions inherent in human life threatened life in its social dimension, her love for contradiction, symbolized by her knife, can renew society when it can no longer make the transformations necessary to feed itself. She is a transformer whose contradictoriness makes "nature" available for "culture."

The conflict between her and Ananse arises because he too is "Love-to-contradict." His own inner being drives him first to contradict her and then to try to use the instrument of contradiction in the wrong way and in the wrong place. It is both significant and amusing that even before Ananse meets the old woman, he begins to parody her by pretending to have a female nature (but that of a young woman) and by separating himself from his family. His parody, however, reverses her situation. She is outside society and he is within it, so that his activity is from the start antisocial. His love to contradict enticed Hate-to-be-contradicted into human society and cut him up for the benefit of social order, but here it brings into society the instrument of contradiction, the transforming power of which produces death within the social order.

The full power of the knife is released only when Ananse takes it to Nyame and attempts to use it in his service. At the center of life contradiction can only tend to total death. However, in terms of the story it is far more important that the knife kills Ananse and, finally, is transformed into spear-grass. Ananse is not invulnerable. He can claim disorder for society and transform it into a lifegiving force; he can renew the constituent elements of social life by breaking through to their raw nature; but when his love to contradict gets turned against life itself, then it is he who dies. It seems likely that the story is more than a warning not to go too far, or an assertion that the collective is superior to the individual, or a parable about careful handling of the powers of magic, for the knife is transformed into vegetation symbolizing the limits of human life. Where spear-grass is, society is not. Thus even as Ananse makes society possible by claiming for it the power to relate and renew, he also establishes a limit for it. If human life requires contradiction, then it is necessarily limited; as culture must have constant recourse to nature, so life must be fed by death.

Ananse and the animals

It is, therefore, as boundary drawer as well as passage opener that Ananse shapes the physical world. Although W. H.
Barker relates a story in which Ananse causes the animals to
spread, Rattray gives only five stories in which he transforms
animals. When Ananse slew the monster bird, he established a
boundary between birds and men and a potential relationship
between them by making the birds both ubiquitous and harm-
less.[30] Two of the other stories are short and slight, while the
two treating the transformation of the elephants are far more
elaborate. Each of these latter tales involves a trick that Ananse
plays on the elephant to obtain food. In one story, Ananse
slices off most of the elephant's rump to help him make his way
through the forest. He then keeps the meat for himself and his
family by playing such a compelling song that the elephant allows Ananse to keep the meat in exchange for the dance.[31] In
the other story, Ananse supplies his family with meat by accepting a head-butting contest with the elephant.[32] By using a
yam to wipe himself after defecating, thus leading them to
think that he wastes food so grossly because he has a secret
supply, Ananse tricks various animals into taking his place in
the contest. After each night's encounter, the dead animal becomes Ananse's food. Finally Ananse drives an iron wedge
into the elephant's head, but he cannot immediately claim the
body. The elephant's relatives insist that he must be buried inside a rock, but Ananse carves a wooden hunter to convince
the elephants that they are in danger of being shot. They flee to
the tall-grass country, and Ananse takes the dead elephant for
food.

On one level, these stories acclaim the triumph of cleverness
over brute strength. But they also rest on a central point of

30. A spider, Ananse is at home in the air, yet out of his element just the
same.
31. Rattray, *Akan-Ashanti Folk-tales*, pp. 182–87.
32. *Ibid.*, pp. 146–51.

mythology, the contrast between the raw and the cooked, the wild and the human, and also on Ananse's own metamorphic powers, which are rooted in his ability to cross, break, and re-create the ontological margins that both join and separate these parallel worlds. Laughter is somehow the key to Ananse's power. The cock's mouth becomes pointed because he laughs at Ananse's children, and the cricket's teeth are burned because he laughs disbelievingly when Ananse claims to have spoken to inanimate objects. So too the elephant is pushed out of the human world through a dance and a game, two modes of ritualized glee. Within the stories, then, laughter is not the means by which Ananse transforms, but the sign of his power to transform. Ananse so links transcendence and absurdity that his presence simultaneously dissolves old boundaries, evokes laughter and foolishness, and establishes new shapes.

It is noteworthy that each of these stories concerns a quest for food (and the fifth, that of Ananse and the monster bird, the restoration of man's jaws), for Ananse's animal form discloses the doubleness of man's relationship to the animals. There is intimacy and dependence, but there is also distance and domination. Other *anansesem* explore this relationship with even greater clarity than do those in which Ananse appears. For example, one story tells how, when certain Bush-pigs became men, their origin had to be kept secret lest it disrupt the village,[33] while the animal origins of the Python and Buffalo *ntoros* (clans) seem both near and remote because of the complex exchanges made as the animals became men.

The most moving of these stories tells how the relationship between Kofi the leopard's child and Kofi the human child brings the interplay of friendship into the world.[34] When the leopard kills the boy's (hunter) father and pregnant mother, the leopard's child delivers the boy, nurtures the child and

33. *Ibid.*, pp. 124–29.
34. *Ibid.*, pp. 206–11.

hides him from the leopard, and, in effect, names him at puberty. Together they kill the leopard and "become as equals." Later, the leopard Kofi discovers the boy's village, outfits him with clothes and gun, and returns him to human life, promising to bring him meat each night. The human Kofi marries, but lies apart from his wife so that the leopard Kofi can bring him the meat undetected. One night the wife reaches for her husband and touches the leopard. The next evening the townsfolk shoot the leopard, who dies exclaiming that humans have no gratitude. The human Kofi shoots himself, and the two friends are buried together.

This story bears striking similarities in both structure and detail to an Opaye-Shavante myth reported by Lévi-Strauss.[35] In the Ashanti tale the intermediary is humanized, while in the Opaye tale the intermediary becomes an animal; consequently the order of death or expulsion of the intermediary and the wild counterpart is reversed in the former. Nevertheless, in both there is an intimate relationship created, yet it is one in which all the advantages belong to the human partner. Thus the human Kofi takes everything from the leopard Kofi, even his father and his name, with the result that instead of their becoming equals the leopard Kofi becomes superfluous. Only in death do they find the equality of friendship, which is the final gift of the wild to the world of men.

Although this seems a long way from Ananse's playful dealings with the animals, there is, I think, a real parallel. The Ashanti stories, both humorous and somber, tell how the animal world has a primordial intimacy with the human world. The animals serve as the source of the human world's life—of its food and even of its people. Yet as the animals are transformed into food or humans, the intimacy is lessened, and the worlds draw apart. Still, what was once the source is now a resource; not only do the animals exist even now as game, but

35. See *The Raw and the Cooked: Introduction to a Science of Mythology*, pp. 82–83.

their transforming potency is present among men. Clans, friendship, marriage, food, and other social realities must be treated carefully because of their power to renew or destroy human life, a power derived from an inherent "wildness" never altogether domesticated. In just this sense, Ananse is a metamorph, an embodiment of liminality, because of his animal form. He is a living connection between the wild and the social, between the potentially and the actually human. Moreover, the absurdity of Ananse, as well as the laughter he evokes, is a kind of respect accorded to and flowing from his power to harness the energy of the wild. Ananse faces two ways—out into the bush and in toward the depth of human life. As he masters the animals and claims what is theirs for men, he also reveals the hidden roots of man's life. We cannot quite see yet what it is that makes this revelation so funny, but even here, as Ananse plays and plays, and the elephant dances and dances, we can see something of what the Dinka know about the ambiguity of man's relationship to the animals, about the difficulty of saying who is master and who is mastered.[36]

Multiformity and exchange

Here the ambiguity, the multiformity, of Ananse opens itself before us. In every story the Ashanti tell about the physical shape of Ananse they show their consciousness of his ambiguity. For example, in the story telling how he became bald,[37] they relate that, since he ordinarily tries to feast while others starve, on the occasion of his mother-in-law's funeral, when the mourners feast for eight days, Ananse resolves to fast. In the end he cannot bear the hunger, steals some beans, hides them in his hat, and burns his head. Ananse is not antisocial,

36. Godfrey Lienhardt, *Divinity and Experience: The Religion of the Dinka*, pp. 24 ff.

37. Rattray, *Akan-Ashanti Folk-Tales*, pp. 118–23. Cf. van Dyck's "An Analytic Study," pp. 280–83.

for he goes to the funeral and even contributes to it lavishly. He is burned, rather, by his love to contradict, but his attempt to reverse the mourning rite, which insists that death itself holds a potential for life, results in a seizure of that potential in the merriment his foolishness evokes.

Ananse's love to contradict is a structural characteristic; his inner form is that of a personified limen. When Ananse encounters the spirits (*nsamanfuo*) during a famine, they teach him a song that enables him to detach his head and to use it to bail a stream dry to catch fish.[38] Ananse, however, cannot cease singing the song, and ends by clapping his detached head to his anus. As the story makes sport of Ananse's gluttony, it also plays imaginatively with the spider's anatomy to symbolize Ananse's power to juggle reality, a power so "empty-headed," so open to reversal, that it transforms even the transforming power of magic.

Similarly, stories telling how Ananse came to live on the ceiling use a "just so" explanation of the spider's natural habitat to comment on Ananse's inner form.[39] One story given by Rattray is a different version of the funeral of Ananse's mother-in-law, who in this instance is Nyame's mother. Ananse travels to the funeral carrying in a bag his "relatives," king jay, monkey, and sheep, who make a spectacular lamentation when they arrive. Nyame rewards Ananse with fine food, but Ananse does not share it with his relatives. Thus, when the eight-day celebration comes round, they refuse to lament, and split away from the clan. Humiliated, Ananse leaps to the rafters. In another story, Ananse jumps to the ceiling to escape those who are dunning him to pay compensation for nipping at their palm-wine. In two stories given by van Dyck, Ananse flees to the ceiling in shame because he is caught by a tar baby set out

38. Rattray, *Akan-Ashanti Folk-tales*, pp. 66–71.
39. *Ibid.*, pp. 4–5, 248–49. These stories do not refer to the spider's web, even though it seems a fitting symbol of Ananse's power to spin linkages out of his own substance. Cf. Evans-Pritchard, *The Zande Trickster*, p. 23. Frobenius, in *The Childhood of Man*, pp. 371–72, sees in the web evidence of solar symbolism, but his reasoning is not persuasive.

by his family and in desperation because the tricks he has played on the animals have endangered his life.[40]

In these stories Ananse moves to the fringes of life at the expense of all obligatory ties—familial, economic, and "natural." Hunger thrusts Ananse into conflict, and hunger satisfied or thwarted pushes him away once again. This hunger is a constant metaphor for Ananse's emptiness, which differs from both sterility and stasis because he yearns for fullness; thus it becomes a passageway into life. Ananse lives on the ceiling but inside the house; the spatial image insists on both his social presence and his distance from the center, a distance that fosters his spinning of links between the center and the edges, between life's order and its sources.[41]

The ceiling, then, is not an image of isolation, but that symbolic place from which Ananse's emptiness can move him most readily to become a medium of exchange. The tales showing Ananse as a trader make this same point even more clearly.[42] Ananse always begins with a tiny, almost valueless item given him by Nyame. Then, after a series of outlandishly deceitful barters, he ends with something of great size or value, which he either loses or turns over to Nyame. In one case his trades benefit both him and his trading partners. For a piece of lime he receives a gourd of water, which he gives to some thirsty workers for a yam, which he trades to a man eating charcoal. So it goes, as Ananse then gives a hoe to a man cutting palm-nuts with his penis, palm-oil to a woman washing her children with her spit, one of the children to a woman without any, a spoon to a woman grinding corn with her elbow, and cornflour to elephants with only muddy water to drink, until at last Ananse loses his elephant while chasing a beautiful bird. In other stories he cheats his partners so successfully that he ends with a whole village obtained by convincing the people that

40. Van Dyck, "An Analytic Study," pp. 241–54, 314–18.

41. Rattray, *Akan-Ashanti Folk-tales*, pp. 138–41.

42. *Ibid.*, pp. 256–61, 268–71. Cf. van Dyck, "An Analytic Study," pp. 212–18.

they had killed a rotting corpse, which they thought was sleeping and were beating to stop its flatulence. In both versions of this story Ananse hands over to Nyame the people he has won, in one case accepting the reward of rulership, in the other asking only for a place on the rafters.

But whether Ananse trades up or down, whether he leaves his partners poorer or richer, whether he ends as chief, rafter-dweller, or fool, it is all the same to him. He has shown that trade is a mode of transformation, of which he is both agent and medium. He enters the human world to make things happen, to recreate boundaries, to break and reestablish relationships, to reawaken consciousness of the presence and the creative power of both the sacred Center and the formless Outside. Then he returns to that hidden threshold which he embodies and makes available as a passage "to save the people from ruin."

ANANSE AND OTHER ASHANTI INSTITUTIONS

Since we have been dealing with Ananse's active role in the Ashanti consciousness, it is not at once apparent just how hidden that threshold really is. When one looks, however, at the complex patterns of Ashanti society, one cannot help but be struck by Ananse's absence. Rattray himself wrote his four great books on the Ashanti with hardly a reference to Ananse.[43] Even if his decision to publish the Akan-Ashanti folktales only after he had said everything else reflects more

---

43. R. S. Rattray, *Ashanti Proverbs*, *Ashanti*, *Ashanti Law and Constitution*, and *Religion and Art in Ashanti*. Rattray's work, which began with his attempt to discover for the British the significance of the Golden Stool (see *Ashanti*, pp. 5–11, 287–93), has still not been superseded. See, for example, K. A. Busia, "The Ashanti of the Gold Coast," p. 190. Although more recent books and articles scarcely mention Ananse, several help to reveal further his Ashanti context. See especially: J. B. Danquah, *The Akan Doctrine of God*; Noel Q. King, *Religions of Africa*; and Benjamin Ray, "African High Gods: A Study of the Concept of Supreme Being in Six African Societies," pp. 333–462, which has a superb treatment of Nyame. For other sources see the historical and bibliographical material contained in Nehemia Levtzion, *Ancient Ghana and Mali*; and Basil Davidson and F. K. Bush, *A History of West Africa*.

closely the priorities of the West than those of the Ashanti, still the Ashanti lead their lives in a rich order of familial, political, religious, and economic traditions that seems to give very little place to Ananse. No matter how deep may be the vision of human life which the *anansesem* display, none of the major institutions and beliefs of the Ashanti—the mode of rulership, the network of gods and spirits, the sacred geography, the complex of laws, rituals, and clans—seems linked directly to Ananse either in daily practice or in theoretical reflection.

Rattray did not, of course, ask the kinds of questions that someone interested in tricksters might ask, but then the *anansesem* themselves make clear that Ananse has little to do with the origins and explanations of most of these institutions and beliefs. There are stories about the *ntoro*, the *abosom*, and marriage, and undoubtedly others that we do not have; but Ananse does not appear in these stories, or even in many of the animal tales. On the other hand, the collection bearing his name witnesses unmistakably to his significance, for the stories give word, eloquently and delightfully, to an Ashanti understanding of human life. The question, then, is this: how is Ananse, who is as Ashanti as the Golden Stool, linked to other ways of expressing that understanding?

It will not do to say that Ananse represents "popular" as opposed to "official" culture, not merely because such a distinction is largely foreign to the Ashanti, but because it solves nothing.[44] It labels but fails to explain the relationship among various aspects of Ashanti life. If the *anansesem* are humorous yet profound commentaries on that life, and intimately linked to its institutions and beliefs, what and where is the link? One can see that the stories reveal incidental features of Ashanti society. The food, the dependence on farming and trading, the presence of certain animals, the casual references to the sacred stools, and especially the constant awareness of Nyame—all

44. However, see Rattray, *Akan-Ashanti Folk-tales*, p. xiii; *Ashanti Proverbs*, pp. 20–21; and *Ashanti*, pp. 145–46.

these form a background that puts the whole collection within a definite social setting. Yet that setting only confirms that Ananse is an Ashanti creation. It does not explain his place in the totality that is Ashanti life.

The answer to the question—once one accepts that the Ashanti themselves have not been asked or that they take the answer for granted—lies within the elaborate social order described so vividly by Rattray. It is, after all, an intellectual and religious as well as a political and economic order, and it stands in its own right as an interpretation of human life. If we can read the outlines and guiding principles of this interpretation, we will know something, if not everything, of the way in which the presumably complementary interpretation given by the *anansesem* relates to it. It is true that such a reading would be simpler if the Ashanti "sacred history," the myths that tell their origins and reasons for being, had a greater narrative consistency. Yet the notion that the social order is itself a kind of mythic text is reinforced by the legends surrounding Komfo Anokye, the eighteenth-century priest who "brought from the sky" the Golden Stool for the Ashanti kings.[45] First, by attributing the modern founding of their kingdom to the magical powers of Anokye, the Ashanti insist on its mythic shape. But second, the nature of these powers shows that the Ashanti know, in a context other than that of the *anansesem*, the socially transforming potency of one who can move up or down or out in a way in which most humans cannot. Thus it is said that Anokye could stand on a flower, change the shapes of teeth and lips, leave his footprints on the top of palm trees, knot an elephant's trunk, turn a chewing-stick into a tree, battle spirits, transform himself into a woman and have a baby, and duel with death itself—all in the process of recreating the Ashanti world. Whatever the relationship between Anokye's magic and Ananse's liminality, Anokye's power shaped a world

45. See van Dyck, "An Analytic Study," pp. 31–39.

charged with a sacredness whose patterns seem likely to tell us much about Ananse's analogous power.

Ashanti doubleness

The most striking features of Ashanti life are its matrilinearity, its combination of a sacral kingship and a sacral queen-mothership, its reliance on both agriculture and a female-dominated system of trade, its sense that bodies of water are hierophanies of Nyame's children (the *abosom*), its linkage of social and inner being through the system of clans and ancestors, and its emphasis on the centrality of both Nyame and Asase Yaa. Each of these is a complex reality, but with Rattray[46] one can briefly say that Ashanti society is rooted in an awareness of a doubleness of life disclosed by maleness and femaleness, not as biological principles, but as ontological poles between which the world comes into being. All Ashanti beliefs and institutions embody this doubleness so that the everyday flow of life reveals an ultimate order.

The Ashanti share this understanding of the world with other preindustrial peoples and, in an even more precise way, with other peoples of West Africa. Yet even should it be true that all such peoples build their societies on a symbolic system of binary oppositions, the life of the Ashanti has a definiteness to it that cannot be abstracted away. Their world has come into being through a primordial hierophany of Nyame, in which he sent his "children" down to earth. They bear the names of the great lake and the rivers of Ashantiland so that the world's outer shape encloses a sacred geography revealing the inner boundaries of Ashanti and the channels of its sacredness.[47] Asase Yaa shares Nyame's primordiality. Many prayers begin by calling on them both; great oaths are sworn invoking both

46. Rattray, *Ashanti*, pp. 81–85. See Busia, "The Ashanti," pp. 196, 200; and Ray, "African High Gods," pp. 343–48.
47. See Rattray, *Ashanti*, pp. 146–48; and Ray, "African High Gods," p. 334.

their names; and from the earth (*asase*) sprang the ancestors of royal and other aristocratic clans.[48] Asase Yaa is neither Nyame's wife nor his creation. Moreover, their relationship cannot be termed that of pure act to pure potency, for both are equally "given," always there, just as both have their own forms of hiddenness. It might be possible to describe their interaction as that of source and resource, but one must pay attention to the likelihood that each has a hidden aspect somehow reflecting the chief characteristics of the other.[49]

In any event, the Ashanti have been more interested in elaborating the meanings of these two divinities in their social order than in speculating about them. Although Nyame is, like most High Gods, the god-who-went-away so that "no one shows a child Nyame";[50] and although Asase Yaa does not even have shrines dedicated to her,[51] the preoccupation of the people with lesser gods and ancestral spirits by no means drives Nyame and Asase Yaa from their consciousness. Both have days of the week consecrated to them and offerings made to them, but more important, for both hiddenness is a mode of presence. *Nyame*, after all, also means "sky," and like the sky both Nyame and Asase Yaa are so massively *there* that one cannot take them in. As we say of those who are able to be present to us fully, they are transparent.[52]

This massive presence is revealed in two very significant ways in the social system itself. In the first place, the extraordinary working of political power in Ashanti is equated with the presence of and the relationship between Nyame and

48. See Rattray, *Ashanti*, pp. 122 ff., 165, and 228.

49. See King, *Religions of Africa*, p. 10; and Ray, "African High Gods," p. 457.

50. Ray, "African High Gods," pp. 412–14; and King, *Religions of Africa*, p. 8.

51. Rattray, *Ashanti*, p. 214. See Ray's excellent discussion of the relationship between Nyame and Asase Yaa, "African High Gods," pp. 361–68.

52. The cosmonaut Gagarin's announcement that he did not find God in space prompted the ironic question in Ashanti, "Why did he expect to see God more (or less) up there than down here?" King, *Religions of Africa*, p. 8.

Asase Yaa. All power, an Ashanti proverb runs, is in the land (*asase*).[53] Yet the Golden Stool, the sacred symbol of the soul of the people, has descended from the sky through the power of Anokye, a gift from Nyame to make the people great.[54] Furthermore, this stool must never touch the ground, nor may he who sits on it ever sit on the ground or even allow his naked feet to touch the earth.[55] This double source of power, linking but never merging the two poles of the cosmos, finds its expression in a double rulership, for as Rattray discovered to his amazement, the Queen Mother shares the King's power, and each chief and subchief also shares power with a Queen Mother.[56] The relationship is, of course, not marital, but neither is it that of biological mother to son. Though the King must be a member of the Queen Mother's clan, her power is not limited to playing a major role in his selection. She has her own courts and other privileges, but essentially she is the power behind the Golden Stool in a nation where power is understood as a true hierophany, a manifestation of that creative power which establishes and sustains the people. The Queen Mother is to the King as Asase Yaa is to Nyame: the resource out of which the source of life draws life and renews life.

This same double presence of male and female power is revealed most intimately in the Ashanti interpretation of the matrilineal system of descent. "A woman gives birth to a man," they say.[57] This saying means more than that children belong to the mother's clan. The Ashanti believe that this is so because *abusua* ("clan") is synonymous with *bogya* ("blood"), which only a woman can transmit. On the other hand, the man passes on to his child his *ntoro* ("spirit"), that aspect of the person's being which is his and his alone and "upon which

---

53. Rattray, *Ashanti*, p. 233: "*tumi nyina wo asase so.*"
54. *Ibid.*, pp. 288–89.
55. *Ibid.*, p. 123.
56. *Ibid.*, pp. 81–85.
57. *Ibid.*, p. 78.

depend health, wealth, worldly power, success in any venture." [58] Yet the *ntoro* is not a purely individual characteristic, for each person is related to others through his father as well as through his mother, and thus there are varieties of *ntoro* just as there are varieties of *abosom*. Here, however, the female element has primacy, and the male is the more hidden element. Nevertheless, both are necessary. Each human being, each individual life, like the life of the people as a whole, comes into existence as the fruit of a complex meshing of male and female. At the sixth or seventh month of pregnancy, the time of "quickening," a man and woman take part in an elaborate ceremony, which ends when they "cast out on the ground and on the roof of the hut, for the spirits of the Earth and for the Sky God," [59] some of the sacred food they have shared. The child to be born will show forth the power of both Nyame and Asase Yaa.

Ananse: mediation and remembrance

Ananse's connection with the ceiling and with Nyame we have seen again and again, but his relationship to Asase Yaa is less visible. However, it is revealed when Nyame spares Ananse at the apparent request of Asase Yaa. Ananse gains his reprieve by a trick, but the trick expresses a structural reality. While Ananse often works in Nyame's stead in shaping the social order, his love for contradiction has another source. The "old woman" whom he meets in the forest, as he searches for the sources of the food his son has brought home, is unquestionably Asase Yaa. [60] Her love for contradiction provides the other half of the transforming power that makes life possible, that destroys it and recreates it.

Still, it is not Ananse's formal association with the two great gods of the Ashanti that ties him so closely to the whole of

58. *Ibid.*, p. 46.
59. *Ibid.*, p. 52.
60. Rattray, *Akan-Ashanti Folk-tales*, pp. 212–19. "Aberewa" is one of Asase Yaa's names. See *Ashanti*, p. 215.

Ashanti life. He is the image of the openness of the passageway to transformation—an openness that again and again
brings into relationship center and boundary, source and resource, and one sort of potency with another, and thus enables
human life to be made and remade. Particularly as the agent of
this sort of doubleness, Ananse is an Ashanti creation. He is
"wonderful" because, even as he focuses the clarity of Nyame,
he draws forth from Asase her hidden powers. In another and
related sense, he is wonderful because without him life would
be boring—not only devoid of verve and gaiety, but empty of
meaning itself. Meaning for the Ashanti, after all, is the story
of the creative interchange between Nyame and Asase Yaa,
whose embodiment is the Ashanti people. There are many in-
termediaries in this interchange who widen and deepen the
process, such as Tano and the ancestors, but Ananse is the one
whose special function it is to show that the passage to new life
is also an ongoing story, a story that is, moreover, delightful at
its very core.

For reasons reaching to the roots of Ashanti life, therefore,
the *anansesem* are stories told to children. Since premodern
societies do not teach their children to despise social order, the
hearers are not being trained to renew society by disrupting it.
On the contrary, the stories are so important to the orderly up-
bringing of children that an unruly child might well be given
over to someone known as a good storyteller.[61] No doubt the
stories teach indirect moral and even more subtle structural
lessons, but what precisely are these lessons?

The setting of the stories begins the instruction.[62] It is night,
and the day's work has been put away. The people are sitting in
a circle or a rough horseshoe. The storyteller is at the focal
point of the group, with the children sitting closest to him,
while some adults are sitting or standing behind them. It is all
most natural, for the stories are meant for the children, and

---

61. See van Dyck, "An Analytic Study," pp. 165–66; and Rattray, *Ashanti
Law*, p. 12.
62. See van Dyck, "An Analytic Study," pp. 57–67.

how else could they see and hear? Yet the scene is an image of social life, in which babies are born in the center of a people, but as they grow, they move outward toward adulthood, old age, and death. At the heart of the circle is the storyteller, often a woman, who is for the moment both the chief elder and the Prime Infant, the witness to what the people know and can become. In this old man or woman, the edge of the circle is brought back into its heart, and the movement outward and the movement inward are shown to be movements of metamorphosis, ontological passages.

This image of renewal has another dimension. In the first line of nearly all the *anansesem* given by Rattray there appears the word *ho*, which he usually translates as "once" or "once upon a time." In other contexts the word ordinarily means "there."[63] An English-speaking reader, of course, identifies the time of this "once" and the place of this "there" as the "once upon a time" of fairy tales. It is a conventional way of expressing a time outside of linear history. But what, after all, does this "outside" mean? Is it the mythic time of life's beginnings, or is it some other form of sacred time?

In the first place, the story itself, reinforced by its setting, announces a dislocation in ordinary life so that the listener can expect to suspend his everyday knowledge of physical causality and appearance, of social relationships, and of the hiddenness of magical and divine beings. The very telling of tales thus proclaims that both teller and listener are now in a different place, another world, whose relationship to the daily world is strange, ambiguous, and mysterious. This relationship is ambiguous and not simply discontinuous because the story, with or without its introductory "once" or "there," speaks of the past. Often this pastness is obvious, for many of the stories tell of events that have shaped the present. They say that things have not always been as they are and explain how what is now

63. J. G. Christaller, *Dictionary of the Asante and Fante Language*, 2d ed. (Basel: Basel Evangelical Missionary Society, 1933), p. 176.

has come into being. In this sense the stories are a form of that sort of "sacred history" which most interpreters recognize as characteristic of mythology. Furthermore, insofar as the stories explain the causes of the present, they depict a time that is nonrepeatable, especially when it involves the actions of Ananse, who is not a figure to be imitated.

Yet the *anansesem* are meant to transcend history in our secular sense. Each begins with the disclaimer, "We do not really mean, we do not really mean what we say." On one level, this phrase simply witnesses to the Ashanti distinction between either the empirical or the traditional "real" and the folkloric "real."[64] The former is denied, and the latter affirmed. Still, the stories are told to children as a way of imparting tradition and renewing the present world. But in these stories the Ashanti are concerned, not so much with the physical shape of the world or with the solemn mythic acts that created it, but with its inner shape—its doubleness, its closeness to and distance from the "wild," its absurdity and delightfulness, its renewability. As the children learn this inner shape, they become the source of that renewal. As Ananse reminds the Sun of Nyame's word and so bestows clarity on the social order, so he is the agent of social anamnesis for the children and, through them, the whole society.

Yet Ananse is more than sugar-coated civics or philosophy in animal metaphor. Here social anamnesis and renewal, as in very different myths of eternal return or forms of sacramental re-presentation, do not happen only or even chiefly through the active intellect. The story itself is a part of the Ashanti process of renewal, as is Ananse in all his ambiguity, funniness, and unyielding urge for intercourse. Moreover, like the foolery of Apo, the great Ashanti feast of reversal and cleansing, Ananse's very twisting of words—those magical building blocks of the universe—unplugs the clogged arteries of the

64. See, for example, Eliade, *Patterns*, pp. 388–97, 429–31; and Lévi-Strauss, *Structural Anthropology*, pp. 203–8.

body social.[65] Thus the Ashanti tell the meaning of their lives in stories and name those stories *anansesem* for reasons having little or nothing to do with their aptitude for abstraction or for adult forms of psychosocial differentiation. They are conveying to their children, and reminding themselves, that life itself is a twisted story, a process in which the human mind and human words are always drawing forth from the rawness of the earth and the body a surprising pattern, which, however partial and dimly known, is charged with permanent value and meaning. They are saying that Ananse, whose actions are so outrageous and nonimitable, nevertheless reveals, especially when this pattern seems most darkened and dead, both the rawness and the order hidden in all of Ashanti life. His stories are a passage enabling structure to enfold chaos and become again *communitas*.

The mythic time, then, which *ho* signifies is more truly understood as a mythic space. The "there" where Ananse lives and acts as the agent of Nyame and Asase Yaa is, simply, Ashanti. It is an Ashanti that never existed, but that always exists and always keeps coming into being as the people who are Ashanti remember and celebrate who they are. It may be difficult for us to know how large is the role Ananse plays in this remembrance and celebration, but it is certain that he reminds the Ashanti that, perhaps in the deepest sense of all, their existence itself is celebration because he is always there to fill their nights with laughter.

65. See van Dyck, "An Analytic Study," pp. 12–13, 86–87; and Rattray's chapter on the Apo ceremony, *Ashanti*, pp. 152–71.

CHAPTER THREE

Legba:
Master of the Fon Dialectic

The man who wishes to wrest something from destiny must
venture into that perilous margin-country where the
norms of society count for nothing and the demands and
guarantees of the group are no longer valid. He must travel
to where the police have no sway. . . . Once in this
unpredictable borderland a man may . . . acquire for himself,
from among the immense repertory of unexploited forces
which surrounds any well-regulated society, some personal
provision of power.

CLAUDE LÉVI-STRAUSS, *Tristes Tropiques*

Legba everywhere dances in the manner of a man copulating.
FON SAYING

LEGBA, the trickster-god of the Fon,[1] raises at once a
question directly contrary to the one asked by Rattray about
the *anansesem*: if animal forms speak so fittingly of a trickster's
metamorphic powers and meanings, why do the Fon not picture Legba as an animal either in their myths or in their iconography? Despite the wealth of historical data concerning the
Fon, who live for the most part in what is now Benin and who
have been influenced greatly over the centuries by their

1. Among the works that deal with Fon religion the following were the
most useful sources for this study: W. J. Argyle, *The Fon of Dahomey: A His-
tory and Ethnography of the Old Kingdom*; Melville J. Herskovits, *Dahomey: An
Ancient West African Kingdom*; Herskovits and Herskovits, *Dahomean Narrative*;
Bernard Maupoil, *La Géomancie à l'ancienne Côte des Esclaves*; and Paul Mercier,
"The Fon of Dahomey." Among older studies, of most interest are A. Le
Hérissé, *L'Ancien Royaume du Dahomey*; and R. F. Burton, *A Mission to
Gelele, King of Dahomey*. Herskovits (*Dahomey*) and Argyle supply fine bibli-
ographies, as does Robert Cornevin, *Histoire du Dahomey*.

I have not tried to reproduce the scientific orthography of Fon words. For a
note on Fon phonetics, see Herskovits, *Dahomey*, vol. 1: facing p. 1.

Yoruba neighbors,[2] we lack the documents, written or archeological, that would give us a historical answer to that question. Thus we do not know whether Legba is an "exalted" theriomorph, or if the animal tricksters that the Fon do have are trivialized gods—or if there exists any historical link between these tricksters and Legba.

What we do know is that the metamorphic possibilities of the trickster are expressed well, but not exhaustively, by animal forms. Ananse realizes some of these possibilities, but as a god and, above all, as a divine mediator, Legba discloses others. The Fon know him as a powerful and many-faced agent of transformation, who mediates among the gods, between the gods and mankind, among humans, and even among the many forces that bring humans into being. Legba's nickname, *Aflakete*, or "I have tricked you," clearly suggests that he shares Ananse's randy, lawless, comic sacredness. Yet the Fon stress Legba's role as mediator, and by studying this role in all its dimensions we can best grasp the way he shapes the inner workings of their lives.

LEGBA AS MEDIATOR

The myth describing the origins of the Fon pantheon portrays Legba as divine linguist. Mawu-Lisa, the High God of the Fon, is androgynous, but Mawu, the female "element," predominates. She has seven children, and to each she gives a specific dominion—rule over earth, sky, sea, animals, etc.— and a unique language belonging to that dominion and replacing the language of Mawu-Lisa. But Mawu tells Legba that she will not give his brothers authority over him because he is her youngest child and is so spoiled that he has never known punishment. Instead she decides to keep him with her, and appoints him to visit his brothers' kingdoms and to report back to her.

2. See Herskovits, *Dahomey*, vol. 2, p. 223.

So Legba knows all the languages known to his brothers, and he knows the language Mawu speaks, too. Legba is Mawu's linguist. If one of the brothers wishes to speak, he must give the message to Legba, for none knows any longer how to address himself to Mawu-Lisa. That is why Legba is everywhere.

You will find Legba even before the houses of the *vodun* [gods], because all beings, humans and gods, must address themselves to him before they can approach God.[3]

The world issues from Mawu's power to bear divine children, but it is Legba who has the "words" needed to foster and sustain the unseen cosmic relationships on which the visible universe rests. He alone knows and links the speech of primordial intimacy and the many tongues of less numinous realms. The myth, then, uses the imagery of family relationships to affirm, first, that the force at the heart of the process shaping the cosmos is not purely physical energy, but a dynamic of intelligence, choice, and chance; and second, that Legba's mediation discloses the underlying connection between the transcendent center of reality and the human matrix of life, the family.

We are not accustomed to taking such imagery seriously. Centuries of rationalism have taught us to explain it as animism, personification, and projection, but a far more subtle way of thinking is at work here. The Fon, first of all, believe that the story, not the mathematical formula, expresses more truly the origins and the meanings of the universe. Their story does not emphasize the immutabilities of blindly interacting elements, but the possibilities of persons relating by choice and chance, the best image of which is the human family, with its unique power to transform biological force into cultural structure. This way of understanding the world's beginning, moreover, intends to focus on the human world. Thus the Fon creation myth speaks of divine and cosmic origins in deliberately familial language. This myth is not "primitive science,"

3. Herskovits and Herskovits, *Dahomean Narrative*, pp. 125–26.

which will wither away before what "real science" says about the origins of the world, any more than Genesis is made meaningless by the knowledge that creation did not take place in seven days of twenty-four hours. Just as one might speak of the first chapter of Genesis as the projection of sacred time (already known as a kind of sacred space) onto the whole cosmos to disclose its specific, *created* sacredness, so the Fon speak of the creation of a sacred physical cosmos in images drawn from their vision of the holiness of the "space" of the human family. This is not to claim that the Fon must have thought of the family as a sacred space before they knew the sacredness of the cosmos, but simply to point out that the Fon, like the Hebrews, use anthropomorphic language deliberately and sophisticatedly, not unconsciously and naively.

The Fon pantheon, therefore, does not represent either the actual or the ideal Fon family. Rather, the myth draws symbolic parallels both between the divine and human familial relationships and between the creative workings of those relationships. These parallels reveal why Legba appears to be the most human of the gods and how his work is the shaping of a human cosmos. He is charged with the maintenance of the divine relationships between Mawu and her children and among the various children in their management of the world. Legba simultaneously ensures the continuation of the familial links of the pantheon and the human character of a cosmos that is holy precisely because its human relationships are an icon of divinity itself.

The separation of heaven and earth

This interpretation of one aspect of Legba's mediatorial role is supported by the myth telling how earth and heaven are separate yet still related. There are three variants of this myth.[4] All three tell of the quarrel between Mawu's eldest sons, Sagbata and Hevioso, the gods of the earth and the sky.

4. *Ibid.*, pp. 126–34. See also, Herskovits, *Dahomey*, vol. 2, pp. 132–34.

All agree that Hevioso gains preeminence over his elder brother through his power to withhold the rain which the earth needs to become fruitful. Mawu wants the brothers to "be together like a closed calabash,"[5] but she cannot resolve the quarrel. The first two versions describe a more or less ignominious surrender by Sagbata, but in the third Legba acts as mediator between his brothers at Mawu's behest. Although Legba promises to help Sagbata, he has previously stimulated the quarrel by telling Mawu that no water was left in the sky, giving Hevioso a reason to stop the rain. However, Legba encourages Sagbata to kindle a fire so great that Mawu fears for the safety of heaven as well as earth. She commands Hevioso to let the rain fall, and Legba is credited with reconciling the two brothers "so that today man lives without fear of another such severe drought."[6]

Certainly the different Fon cults use the myth on behalf of the gods they serve, but the underlying "story" tells that the harmony between earth and sky was produced for the well-being of mankind. This harmony resulted from the mythic work of several gods so that the first variant can stress the endurance and the humility of Sagbata, the second Hevioso's cleverness and power, and the third Legba's role both in sparking and in extinguishing the quarrel. The devotees of the gods doubtless urge their own version of the myth, but the very coexistence of the variants is a vivid symbol of the successful reconciliation of the gods and their mutual creation of a world fit for humans.

To understand Legba's role, therefore, one need not discover whether he represents an earlier or later strand in the development of the myth, or prove that his mediation is accepted in the same way by all the Fon. The mythic message is simply that Legba is at once an agent of disruption and an agent of reconciliation. Legba, of course, "enjoys" causing trouble, but

5. Herskovits and Herskovits, *Dahomean Narrative*, pp. 129–30.
6. *Ibid.*, pp. 133–34.

behind such enjoyment lies an unspoken structural assumption: that the quarrel itself disclosed a primordial rift between the two great life-creating powers. The healing of that rift makes human life possible because it yokes together these two forces to bring forth a world less simple than the divine realm but stable because it has synthesized absolutely opposed potencies.

Legba helps Mawu to bring about this resolution, but so subtly that her work is unacknowledged. As Mawu's agent, Legba is far more than a divine youngest child whose wiliness fits him for the special role of reconciling his siblings to parental purposes. Rather, the familial imagery points to Legba's possession of just that aspect of the High God's power which achieves the particular wholeness that is human society. Although Mawu seems otiose because she cannot impose her will, does not know of the quarrel between her sons, and must accept Legba's duplicity, in reality her sons act out the roles she has bestowed on them. Thus Legba's very deception of her shows how she has willed the humanity of the cosmos, for his actions reveal that the features of divine power that seem most inimical to man—its acceptance of, permission for, or creation of divine and human conflict—are those which make human life possible. Legba is the agent of heaven, but also the friend of earth, because he, like Ananse, domesticates conflict, which the Fon know to have a life-creating purpose. He helps Mawu to bring the human world into being by focusing and refining the divine power. He fosters the primordial quarrel, which is inevitable in any event, to prevent a premature victory of one side or the other and to ensure the interplay of all the forces embodying Mawu's ultimate aims. He thus makes possible a reconciliation that neither stifles the earth nor ignores its needs. The place where men live is far enough from the divine center so that men are free, yet close enough, above all in the very intimacy of the social structure, to guarantee that this structure will not spin down into nothingness, but in its spinning be renewed. Legba moves from divine center to human periphery and back to enable each always to find its full manifestation in the other.

Legba's trickery of Mawu

A delightful story about Mawu's going away is built on these same ideas.[7] In the beginning, Legba did good deeds for everyone, but the recipients of his favors always thanked Mawu, not Legba. He obeyed her completely, and no one praised him, but when something evil happened, and the people complained to Mawu, she blamed Legba. When he asked her why praise and blame were shared so unfairly, she told him that masters must always be known as good and their servants as evil.

In response, Legba began to scheme. He told Mawu that thieves were planning to steal the yams from her garden, and so she warned the people that whoever stole from the garden would be killed. Then Legba stole her sandals on a rainy night, entered the garden, stole the yams, and left sandal prints in the earth. In the morning, Legba gathered the people together to find out whose feet matched the prints. When no match was found, Legba suggested that Mawu herself might have come and had forgotten. Mawu was annoyed at this suggestion. She told Legba that it was because of such insolence that she did not like him, but when she compared her foot with the print, the two matched.

The people shouted, "There is an owner who is herself the thief." Mawu was humiliated and told everyone that it was Legba who had played this trick on her. As a result, she swore to leave the earth for the sky. Since the sky in those days was only about six or seven feet above the earth, Mawu received a report each night from Legba, and when he committed a fault, she saw and scolded him. Irritated at this surveillance, Legba

7. *Ibid.*, pp. 149–50.

encouraged an old woman to throw her dirty wash water at Mawu's resting place. In anger Mawu moved farther away, but she left Legba here on earth.

Many peoples, including the Ashanti, know similar stories, in which the trickster shames the High God into withdrawing from the earth. The Fon use the dynamics of the mother-son relationship to account for both Mawu's and Legba's actions. As the youngest son, Legba finds his lack of independence and differentiation from his mother oppressive. Thus he maneuvers her first into withdrawing her direct control over him and then into abandoning any real supervision of his activities. The human world develops through tricks, not tragedy, and thus the myth is not a veiled cosmic matricide, despite its oedipal overtones. Legba succeeds by using the very wiliness Mawu has given him. True, to become a mediator Legba must create a distance that only he can span, but in doing so he is carrying out Mawu's creative intent. If he pushes her away from the earth, he is using the force that she shared with him to do so. If he establishes a lasting role for himself on an earth truly separated from heaven, he is only doing what he has been born to do, and if he helps to make Mawu, like other High Gods, the god-who-went-away, at the same time he himself embodies her presence in the new space created by her withdrawal.

The Fon believe, then, that family relationships are neither too ordinary nor too untidy to symbolize matters as exalted as the creation of the world. We who live in largely desacralized worlds are tempted to think that the symbolic use of such familiar facts cannot say anything serious about the world's origins. But the Fon insist that the process of psychosexual differentiation means so much more than a struggle over possession of either self or mother that this process reflects the maturation of the world itself. Once again, we need to see that Legba does not kill his mother, but wins the role she has given him. His achievement is to join by separating Mawu and the world, center and periphery, originator and originated. Thus

Legba's mediation is authentic, a dynamic maintaining of true mutuality.

Perhaps the deepest meaning of this little story, however, lies in its disclosure of the peculiar mode of Legba's mediation. He achieves his role by double-dealing, yet there is a double meaning to this double-dealing that shows both his aptness for mediation and its inner quality. That is, Legba becomes a mediator by means of a lie that is really a truth, a deception that is in fact a revelation, and a conspiracy that should have been no secret. He tells Mawu that a thief is planning to steal her yams; indeed one was. He fakes Mawu's footprint and throws the blame for the theft on her, but she has been treating him as if he had no identity of his own and existed merely as her surrogate. If that were so, then his apparent fakery simply reveals what she has consistently claimed: that his acts are hers so that his footsteps are, in fact, but *vestigia dei*. Finally, his conspiracy with the old woman can only succeed because Mawu has already withdrawn from the earth and because the spiritual distance this withdrawal has created has already caused mankind in some sense to forget her and to rely on Legba to reveal who and where she is. Thus the truth in Legba's trickery and the trickery in his truth not only bring into play his mediatorial power; they are the twin halves of its essence. He becomes what he is—a kind of reconciliation of the opposites of discourse and, therefore, the apt "linguist" of Mawu.

Yet Mawu remains the source of Legba's power, just as the maintenance of the human world remains its rationale. It is she who sentences the prospective thief to death; it is she who accepts responsibility for Legba's thievery by a symbolic death; and it is she who yields to the kind of autonomy proper to both Legba and the world by submitting to the implications of her own will. This is a crucial point, for if we forget it, we have no way of dealing with the humor of these stories except to treat it as masked and transposed aggression. In fact, as we shall see in looking at Fon divination, this humor is intimately related to the trickster's greatest metamorphic feat: that of transforming Mawu-Lisa's absence into transparent presence and of unveiling her/his creative purposes in all that mankind regards as most destructive and opaque.

COMMERCE: MAGICAL AND SEXUAL

The Fon speak of and experience Legba's mediation as metamorphic power made known chiefly in the day-to-day happenings of their life. He is the linguist of the gods, but it is above all among men and on their behalf that he exercises his role. In the two lengthiest and most complex myths dealing with him, the Fon tell how Legba gave magic to the world, became mediator between gods and men, was recognized as the agent and spokesman of Fa (the god of divination), was named the guardian of humans and their houses, became the embodiment of male sexual potency, and received the name *Aflakete*. The first of these myths begins with a vivid dramatization of Legba's promotion from the least to the chief of the gods.[8] Mawu told the gods that whoever could simultaneously play a gong, a bell, a drum, and a flute while dancing to their music would be their chief. One after another the strongest of the gods—Hevioso, Age (the god of the hunt), Gu (the god of iron)—tried and failed. When Legba tried, he succeeded, and Mawu gave him a wife and made him first among the gods.

The creation of magic

After proclaiming in song his beneficence ("If the house is peaceful/ If the field is fertile,/ I will be very happy"), Legba began to make magic charms (*gbo*, which denotes both charms and their antidotes), in this case, serpents that bit those on their way to or from market. For a price he then cured those who were bitten. One day a man named Awè asked about the serpents, and Legba showed him how to make such a charm.

8. *Ibid*., pp. 139–42.

Legba also gave Awè the medicine to cure those bitten by the serpents.

Legba gave Awè other charms and even began to make them with him in Awè's house. However, Mawu was displeased by Legba's actions and made him invisible so that he would not continue to spread magic. Awè, therefore, took Legba's place, giving charms to those who asked for them and often working mischief so that those whom he troubled would have to come to him for the appropriate "medicine." Then Awè decided that he possessed enough magic for him "to see the world." He rolled cotton and silk thread into great balls, and threw them toward the sky. Mawu caught them, and Awè climbed (or was pulled) up to her, announcing that he wanted to measure his knowledge with hers. He tried to make a man, but the figure he produced could not talk, breathe, or move. Mawu, on the other hand, took a grain of corn, and in the same day planted, harvested, milled, cooked, and ate it. When Awè left, Mawu sent Death to follow him, giving him instructions to kill whoever was evil. Then Awè attacked Death with a charm. In those days there was no fire, and cooking was impossible, but when Mawu said to Awè, "If you attack Death, whoever tries to prepare his food will find that it is raw again," she made an implicit gift of fire to mankind to complement the presence of Death. Awè let Death go, and Mawu told him that he was to care for the sick, but that she reserved the right to send Death to kill them. That, the Fon say, is how "Awè mastered Legba's knowledge, and became a practitioner of magic. Awè and Death are the two friends of the world." [9]

In the first place, it is Legba's versatility that puts him before all the other gods at the center of human life. This versatility symbolizes his multiformity and his independence of ordinary structure, social as well as physical, human as well as divine. Like the *jongleur* whose acrobatic feats established a bond with

9. *Ibid.*, pp. 141–42.

the Mother of God, in whose body the barriers between earth and heaven were overcome, Legba wins preeminence because his skillful playing discloses his power to shatter the limits of normal movement and to create a new harmony out of the seemingly disparate actions that his efforts bring into relationship. The dexterity of his hands and feet reveals his far greater ability to move across various planes of existence. This "rupture of plane," according to Paul Mus, lies at the heart of that power to transform which we call magic.[10] Through such a rupture the invisible spiritual world not only lies open to the visible world, but acts upon it, acts in concert with it, or is acted upon by it. Legba, then, as an ontological master of sleight-of-form, is a prime agent of Fon magic.

The planes that Legba ruptures, however, are chiefly social. Although his activity has a truly cosmic or metaphysical basis and shows itself in his power over physical reality, Legba normally shatters, reinforces, or rearranges the human planes and relationships that, taken all together, make up the elaborate network that is society. By now the social character of magic has become an anthropological commonplace. Yet even though the functionalism of A. R. Radcliffe-Brown and his followers has helped to overcome the antiritual prejudices of nineteenth-century British anthropology,[11] Legba's mediatorial role is not adequately understood by making it a rather large gear in a smooth-running social machine. In part this inadequacy is the result of functionalism's tendency to shrink Emile Durkheim's already rather one-sided view of the relation between religion and society. Mus—with his sense of the symbolic mutuality of the Brahmanic and Buddhist religious and

10. See Paul Mus, *Barabudur: Esquisse d'une histoire du Bouddhisme fondée sur la critique archéologique des textes* (Hanoi: Imprimérie d'Extrême Orient, 1935), vol. 1, pp. 51–52.

11. Unfortunately, many have believed that functionalism explains religion; in fact, it interprets social order. See Hans Penner, "The Poverty of Functionalism," p. 94; A. R. Radcliffe-Brown, "The Comparative Method in Anthropology"; and Mary Douglas, *Purity and Danger: An Analysis of Concepts of Pollution and Taboo*, pp. 81–82.

social enterprises—enlarged the view of this relation, while Evans-Pritchard linked specific social institutions and systems of magic to each other, [12] thus opening the way toward a deeper understanding of how magic and indeed all rituals "create and control experience." [13] In this sense, the Fon believe Legba to be present in potentially dangerous social situations—the market, pregnancy, child-rearing, and royal administration are the four directly referred to in the myth—to stir up as well as to allay, to rechannel far more than to neutralize, the various forces present in such situations.

But it would be a mistake to lay all the blame for our difficulty in understanding the nature of this magical activity at the feet of the antiritualists of the nineteenth century or the functionalists of the twentieth. Fon magic is a reality neither univocal nor metaphorical, but many-faceted, even sacramental. For her purposes Mary Douglas is certainly justified in placing magic into the larger category of "ritual," yet the differences among rituals are more than nominal. In his chapter on Fon magic, [14] Melville Herskovits shows that besides Legba, Da, and Sagbata, there are lesser gods, twins, and especially the *aziza* and the *abiku* (types of forest-dwelling spirits), who are also sources of magic. The Fon like to compare the leaves of the forest to the gods of Dahomey, [15] yet even if this comparison depends on the significance of the forest as a liminal source of healing and renewal, we do not know enough to link specific gods and spirits with the mending of specific boundaries. But Herskovits also shows that the *gbo* do function as a device for social healing. Some of their uses (the protection of houses, fields and possession, the assistance of litigants, the support of traders) are directly communal, while others (the defense of pregnant women, hunters, river travelers, the dying, and

---

12. See *Witchcraft, Oracles, and Magic among the Azande*. Cf. Douglas, *Purity and Danger*, pp. 17–40, 73–93.
13. Douglas, *Purity and Danger*, p. 82.
14. Herskovits, *Dahomey*, vol. 2, pp. 256–88.
15. *Ibid.*, vol. 2, p. 195.

those attacked by the spirits of the dead) help those whose situation makes them most vulnerable to nonhuman life. Nevertheless, neither Herskovits nor any other analyst has found the relationship between the disorders in need of remedy and the various plants and animals used to confect the types of *gbo*.

One short account, however, does insist that the *gbo* of Legba and those of the forest spirits differ and that Legba's help is especially powerful for the dying, warriors, and travelers.[16] Together with the myth of Awè, this account enables us at least to outline Legba's role as breaker and mender of social planes. By himself or in league with Awè, Legba charges with power society's internal lines of structure (economic, administrative, sociophysical) or protects those passing outside or into that structure. By inventing magic, he draws into the open the power of all boundaries, opens passageways to new life, and makes transformation possible even as he stimulates conflict. Thus Legba works for his own ends, but serves society's; his manipulativeness is part of what is "given" to enable society to find its way back to its true shape.

In short, the Fon look at Legba as one of the ultimate sources of culture in Lévi-Strauss's sense. His magic does not create the world or challenge Mawu for its dominion. Awè, his human agent, cannot make man breathe, while Mawu holds the essential cultural powers of cereal growth, human technique, and cooking, as well as the power of ending life. Through Awè, however, Legba can frustrate death, and if Mawu can prevent the establishment of social order by keeping food raw, it is still Awè's "unbinding" of death that also unbinds this order and makes death its servant and not its solvent. Legba, then, is a creative agent, not the creator—a shaper, not a maker. Although his mediation suggests comparisons to other mediators, he cannot be mistaken for an insufficiently abstracted demiurge. The mystery of being that concerns the

16. *Ibid.*, vol. 2, p. 259. He also helps those suffering from headache, colic, dysentery, leprosy, eye trouble, and rheumatism, but without a full Fon taxonomy of disease one cannot reliably establish a symbolic pattern.

Fon is the mystery of their own being together in the world. It is this mode of being, in its inner structure as well as in its daily forms, which Legba shapes.

Legba's sacred phallus

The most complex of the myths telling of Legba's mediation illustrates this two-fold shaping with great clarity.[17] In this myth Legba's origins are considered functionally. He is the "son" of Agbanukwe (the divining house) and Kpoli (the embodiment of the destiny that divination reveals). Legba, his elder sister Minona, and his elder brother Aovi had all been married, and each had killed his or her mate. The three decided to form a band to play and sing at funerals. At a certain funeral they met Fa, the god of divination, who was Legba's master, though he needed to speak through Legba. The son of the king of Adja had come to consult Fa, for he was married to the daughter of King Metonofi and sought a powder to insure his potency. He feared that he would fail with the woman as his father, who had married her first, had failed. Fa promised to help him, but Legba gave him the red powder of impotency rather than the white powder of potency.

On the way home from the funeral Legba, his sister, and his brother sat down at a crossroads to divide the gifts they had received. There was an extra cowry, and each claimed it. As they argued, a woman on her way to sell wood in the marketplace came along. They asked her to divide the cowries for them, but when she gave the extra one to the eldest, Aovi cut off her head, Legba struck her with his stick, and they threw her body into the bush, where Legba had intercourse with it. A second woman, who was going to draw water from the well,[18]

17. Herskovits and Herskovits, *Dahomean Narrative*, pp. 142–48.
18. Both "going to the market" and "journeying to the well" are phrases associated with significant Fon rituals—the "installation of the newly deified spirits of the ancestors" (Herskovits, *Dahomey*, vol. 1, p. 207) and the initiation of new members into the cult of Mawu-Lisa (*ibid.*, vol. 2, p. 119). It seems that Legba is not only linked to the experience of liminal "death-rebirth," but also to the reentrance of the dead into the living clan.

also failed to divide the cowries evenly. She was killed by Minona and Legba, who treated her as he had the other dead woman. A third woman, on her way home from the market, met the same fate after assigning the extra cowry to Legba. This time the two eldest killed her, and again Legba violated the dead body.

While in the bush Legba took from Fa's sack, which he was carrying, the carved figure of a dog. He transformed it into a living dog, gave it instructions, and rejoined Minona and Aovi. When the dog approached and was asked to divide the cowries, he dug a hole for the one left over and buried it, telling them that in his country such a leftover was given to the ancestors. The three blessed the dog, promised that it would always guide humans, and then, back in the bush, Legba turned it into a figurine once again.

Meanwhile, the son of the King of Adja had discovered his impotence, and King Metonofi had offered half his kingdom to any man who succeeded in having intercourse with his daughter. Men came to Fa for the powder of potency, but Legba gave them all the red powder. They complained to Metonofi that Legba had made them impotent, and Legba fled to the house of Ayo, his mother-in-law. His father-in-law was away, and during the night Legba slept with her.

When he returned to his village the next day, he was arrested and brought before Metonofi. He was accused of murder by the families of the three dead women, of sleeping with Ayo by his father-in-law, and of giving the wrong powder to all the men of the kingdom. In the first case Legba claimed that it was Aovi who had killed the women and that he had intervened to prevent further deaths. He supported his testimony by transforming the figurine into a living dog. Then Metonofi ordered Minona to live in the houses of women and Aovi to live among the gods. Legba he made the guardian of men and women and of all the gods and gave him the right to live anywhere. Thus Legba came into people's houses.

To the second charge Legba pleaded guilty, but excused

himself because his mother-in-law had been sleeping in his wife's place. Metonofi did not accept this excuse, but could not revoke Legba's guardianship. He limited it, however, so that Legba would not be allowed to live within houses, but only in front of them.

Legba denied the third charge. When told to show the powder he had given to the men, he changed the colors of the powders and ate some of the "red" powder himself. Two days later the men of the kingdom were still unable to have intercourse with Metonofi's daughter, and they claimed that they were inhibited by the crowd waiting outside her house. Legba scoffed at them and offered to have intercourse with her in public. Strengthened by the powder of potency and accompanied by the beating of drums he had made, Legba entered and deflowered her with ease. Then he emerged from the house to pantomime intercourse with all the onlookers. Metonofi gave him his daughter (whom Legba gave to Fa) and ordered that the drum should henceforth be played in her honor. He commanded that Legba be allowed to sleep with any women he chose and "named him intermediary between this world and the next. And that is why Legba everywhere dances in the manner of a man copulating."[19] Thus it is that one must go through Legba to approach a god or to use Fa and that all men and women have their own Legba as a guardian. It was on that day that Legba was given the name meaning "I have tricked you."[20]

Here we have a wonderfully complex linking of liminality, magic, commerce, judicial process, sexuality, and ritual dance under the rubric of transforming mediation. This linkage is not so much a matter of interwoven causalities as it is a disclosure of the logic of symbols. In exploring the implications of social transformation, the Fon discover a cluster of meanings that Legba embodies. When Christian missionaries first arrived in Dahomey, they thought that Legba was Satan in native guise

19. *Ibid.*, vol. 2, p. 229.
20. Herskovits and Herskovits, *Dahomean Narrative*, p. 147.

because of his seeming lawlessness and unbridled sexuality. The Fon, however, while not monotheists, were neither lawless nor sexually profligate, and they have insisted, rather, that Legba is the divine linguist—the master of their unique dialectic, the copula in each sentence, and thus the embodiment of every limen.[21] If the threshold has become his special place, and if he is intimately associated with the crossroads and the market, it is because he is preeminently a being of the boundaries. He has sexual relations with any woman he chooses because these boundaries—physical, social, religious, and even metaphysical—dissolve and reform in his presence. Yet even as the Fon know that Legba is not the prince of darkness, they are aware of his daimonic explosiveness. They realize, that is, that he cannot live inside their houses or reign over their kingdom; his power to open passages and to shut them will serve human life, and not debauch it, provided that he not be allowed to assume control over its center.

Society as the meeting of worlds

Thus the Fon never sentimentalize Legba's power. He lives where separate worlds meet and can move back and forth between them, yet he cannot substitute one for the other. Legba's sexuality is the great symbol of his transforming power, not because it is capable of bringing the dead to life, of changing the givenness of kinship ties, or of legitimizing promiscuity, but because it forces responses that reveal possibilities hidden within the existent world. Indeed, it reveals that the limits of this world can become horizons. To put it another way, the confrontation of boundless sex with wholly bounded sex brings forth neither chaos nor a new absolute. Instead it joins center and periphery, centripetality and centrifugality. It discloses that for each Fon a threshold is always present—a "way in," an entrance into a truly human place, and a "way out," an opening into the larger world of the human community.

21. See *ibid.*, pp. 150–51.

This larger world is human, the Fon are saying, because Legba's grossness, like Ananse's, insists on the necessity and the possibility of human intercourse. "When Worlds Collide" might well describe the perils of human encounter, in which those who meet seek to dissolve boundaries in such a way that the meeting brings harmony, not conflict. Social structures are an attempt to create a network of symbolic harmonies, enabling people to pass through the process of dissolution and reintegration again and again—not only without harm, but with continued growth, not merely in individual meetings, but especially in communal encounters. The structures themselves, however, can calcify and block real passage. Even where they are supple, they so emphasize moments of transition and intersection that they will always be charged with dangerous tension whenever those moments create special instability.

For example, commerce is always a chancy structure. Because humans do not have equal gifts, and because goods have neither equal nor fixed value, trade will always benefit some more than others. Furthermore, the desirability of trade and its indispensability to "culture" as a life-enhancing series of transformations make the market a fertile source of conflict. As the myth shows, the failure to make a transaction can be as destructive as a bad transaction; if that extra cowrie is not disposed of properly, the whole system freezes. Yet the ordinary skills of marketing, gained through experience or custom or even ritual (e.g., the advice of the woman on her way to the well), are not enough to overcome the conflicts of commerce, which can make it a deadly business indeed. Only Legba, moving beyond the boundaries of the actual into the realm of the potential, the prestructure of the bush and the poststructure of death, wrests intercourse from the destructiveness of unresolved opposition. That intercourse too is an inadequate solution. Thus he dissolves the boundaries between artifact and nature, between animal and man, and between the living and the dead until commerce has a field large enough to play itself through satisfactorily. This transforming power, working especially through divination for the enlargement and the clarification of the familial and social fields, gives Legba his unique place of honor in Fon society. The Fon set him squarely at all the joints and crossings of the social order to make sure that transactions become transformations as they are meant to.

Some transactions, however, are so loaded with danger that they must be forbidden altogether lest structure give way wholly to chaos. Some such intuition seems to be at work in all incest taboos, which reflect the nearly universal human belief that, if some female spaces are not seen as too sacred to enter, the sacred space of society itself cannot hold together. Freud's myth of the earliest human society, no matter how unrelated to any actual situation, at least takes into account the murderous energies let loose where unbounded potency is allowed to be translated into limitless rivalry.[22] Legba does not embody such potency, but he has access to it. This access is the source of his mediatorial power, but if that power were used indiscriminately, chaos would result. Women would remain forever human irruptions of nature, unclaimable for culture because they could only turn male desire into the disorder of pure rivalry.

The domestication of sex

The rest of the myth, then, works out the conflicting claims of potency and order in terms of the domestication of Legba. He cannot be driven away from the threshold because Metonofi has already given him the position of guardian.[23] What is really "given" is the certainty of conflict and paralysis in

22. Eliade has often exposed the nonscientific character of the theory of the origin of religion that Freud espoused in *Totem and Tabu*. See *Images and Symbols*, p. 23, and *The Quest*, pp. 19–21. Cf. Claude Lévi-Strauss, *Totemism*, trans. Rodney Needham (Boston: Beacon Press, 1963), pp. 69–70.

23. Metonofi is the king of the primordial world, the "purity" of which needs to be transformed so that human order can emerge. See Herskovits, *Dahomey*, vol. 2, pp. 181–83, and *Dahomean Narrative*, pp. 391–95.

human life, and Legba is needed to provide ways out of isolation and into lifegiving intercourse. However, he cannot be allowed to live inside, lest the most intimate order of all be destroyed by the scandals he causes. Still, the conflict is not resolved. Legba has penetrated his father-in-law's house and wife because Metonofi has sought to punish him for giving the wrong powder to the King of Adja's son and the other men of the kingdom. But who was actually responsible for their impotence? Before Legba came onto the scene the King of Adja had already proved impotent with Metonofi's daughter, and his son and the other men were so unsure of themselves that they were forced to seek the help of Fa. The question, of course, is what will happen when intercourse with this girl is successfully completed. Will it be a blessing or a curse to receive half of Metonofi's kingdom? Is the dissolution of personal boundaries in sexual intercourse creative or destructive? Is the release of male potency and the access to female potency productive of renewed and deepened order, or does it lead to the chaos of utter exhaustion and the return to pure potentiality—in short, to death?

No wonder, then, that Metonofi builds a little hut for his daughter so that the renewed attempt by the men to have sex with her is equivalent to an initiation ritual. Success promises what initiation always promises—reintegration on a higher, more social, more human level of existence—while failure threatens total disintegration. In this context, Legba's deceit discloses the ambiguity of the situation and reserves for himself, empowered by all the resources of his own being as well as by those of Fa, the role of deflowering Metonofi's daughter and of claiming for human order the recreative potencies of sexuality. It is important to see that he does not act as a hero, but as a liar, a buffoon, and a lecher, for Legba's actions show that the situation is finally comic, not tragic. The very heart of his mediatory work is an initiatory demystification that enhances the creative power of sex because, as in all initiations, the deeper understanding of the symbol gives access to the transcendent power embodied in the symbol.[24]

As both initiate and initiator, Legba puts the power of sex at the disposal of the human community. With drums and phallic dance, he ritualizes sex. That is, he takes it out of the arcane and dreadful realm of the potential and fixes it firmly in the center of social life by the use of symbolic gestures, actions, and music. By making sex ritually public, he makes it socially creative. Thus Legba's dance is repeated each time that novices are initiated into the cult of Mawu.[25] The ritual domesticates the power of female sexuality even as it sets free the power of male sexuality. Sex no longer threatens to introduce chaos into human order because it has become true intercourse. When Fa marries Metonofi's daughter through the mediation of Legba, the seemingly chartless mysteries of both death and sex are forever linked to divination, which, the Fon believe, can trace the lines of structure and order past the boundaries of the visible. Having claimed for society these forces of nature, Legba is permitted to exercise his sexuality as he chooses. He cannot go back inside the house lest chaos be let loose, but he is allowed to penetrate every woman so that order can be continually enlarged. Furthermore, as we shall see, in becoming the personal guardian of each man and woman, Legba penetrates human consciousness itself. He reveals that most hidden and dangerous limen of all—the one inside each person. His ubiquity is synonymous with human life because he is identified with the inmost processes of that life.

Raiding the inarticulate

It is no accident, then, that this myth has for its setting a series of trials—trial as experiment, trial as test, and trial as judicial process. Wherever Legba's liminal powers can be ap-

24. See Alfonso M. di Nola, "Demythicization in Certain Primitive Cultures: Cultural Fact and Socioreligious Integration."
25. Herskovits, *Dahomey*, vol. 2, pp. 124 ff.

plied, he emerges victorious. Only when he fails to transform the second accusation by magic or by language is he convicted. Here alone he is unable to conjure or deceive, but simply tells the truth. I have suggested that his failure lies in the danger that a successful violation of the incest taboo would bring. If boundaries become horizons inside the house, life becomes all periphery—or, more exactly, a jungle. Here the myth's significance depends on Legba's inability to lie. His power to shape reality to his language exonerates him from the first and third charges, and when he can only mirror reality in his words, he is unable to transform it. If the Fon appear to give more weight to that aspect of justice which must be seen to be done than to that which is simply done, the reason is, once again, a preference for the concrete, rooted in a sophisticated sense of the power of human language to mold the human world. The Fon are not primitive juridical existentialists, living in a world without essences, hewing a rough order out of each event and calling it law. Rather, they sense that judicial order, like other deep social structures, grows and develops in and through particular cases. But not just any process of growth will do. The process must be "due," encompassing the worlds of all involved, for judicial truth depends on a language supple enough to bring "seems" and "is" into a new relationship. Legba cannot change appearance into reality or falsehood into truth, yet his lies display the inherent doubleness of things, a doubleness that his power to penetrate the hidden converts from threat to blessing. Thus Legba's boldness discloses how language can guarantee that judicial process is truly a due process creating a universe large and subtle enough to resolve the clashes of its parts. Aovi and Minona are not defeated, but replaced, situated properly. The powder that the men first receive may make them impotent, but it also allows Legba to claim the potency of sex from the impotence of dread on behalf of human society.

The various trials of Legba, therefore, show that he mediates the use of language for humans as well as for the gods. He is a creator of discourse, for his every movement is, in T. S. Eliot's phrase, a "raid on the inarticulate," a foray into the formless, which simultaneously gives human shape to the dark and fearsome and new life to a structure always in danger of becoming a skeleton. It is a huge joke that justice and society itself are built on the depredations of Legba, but it is stasis that he destroys, not seriousness. The myths of Legba's mediatory work reveal that a deeply ironic vision, which yokes together what is and what may be, has molded Fon life. That this vision has remained celebratory, neither freezing into stoicism nor dissolving into hedonism, gives it an unmistakably African stamp, and that Legba embodies such an important aspect of this specifically Fon irony underscores his contribution to the process that calls forth and maintains the social order. However, the social vision of the Fon does not hover, ghostlike, above their lives, and thus to understand fully what he means we must look at him in relation to the daily workings of Fon life.

LEGBA AND THE HISTORICAL IMAGINATION OF THE FON

The Fon know themselves to be a people of history. Shortly after Dahomey was conquered by the French in 1894, Foà claimed that it was "the only government of the Slave Coast to give its people an idea of the nation's past.[26] The significance of this claim does not lie in the accuracy of its judgment regarding other West African peoples, but in its insistence on the Fon awareness of the processive character of their society. Herskovits has pointed out that the Fon distinguish between *hwenoho*, which can mean history, tradition, or ancient lore, and *heho*, or tale.[27] Interpreters told Herskovits that the *hwenoho* tells the "true story," while the *heho* is a human invention from which "one learns . . . what one can."[28] Such a distinction is com-

---

26. E. Foà, *Le Dahomey*; quoted by Argyle, *The Fon of Dahomey*, p. 1.
27. Herskovits and Herskovits, *Dahomean Narrative*, p. 15.
28. *Ibid.*, p. 16.

mon in traditional and even in Western societies, but observers have always been struck with the special Fon fascination with the historic deeds of clans, lineages, heroes, and kings.

Before the French conquest, those whose task it was to preserve the royal history played a special part in court ceremonial, and had to recite their stories often in public: "Their bards, on solemn occasions, rehearse over the whole history of their country, sitting at the King's gate. This recital takes up several days." [29] According to Le Hérissé, some of the chroniclers were entrusted with the details of the reign of one king. . . . Others . . . preserved the general history of Dahomey. Hazoumé describes the activities of one chronicler who had to recite the whole history of Dahomey at dawn every morning whilst making an itinerary round the palace walls. [30]

The symbolism inherent in such recitals tells us that the Fon believe them to be a force which holds together their world. Each day the kingdom is recreated by an act of remembering that encloses and also discloses the present.

Similar bards were well known in the great kingdoms to the north and west. Ancient Ghana, Mali, and Songhay were all aware of the historical acts which had built their empires, and that awareness was kept alive by the performances of specially trained men. [31] Like Dahomey, these greater empires knew of the changes which they had experienced and caused, a knowledge shared to some degree by other societies much simpler in structure and smaller in extent. However, they also created, in contrast to simpler societies, a category of narrative that prevented their history from being wholly drawn into their myths. Still, that history contained mythic elements which gave it the character of saga, epic, or even legend in comparison to modern, rationalized history, nor was it disconnected from a framework of myth which gave ultimate meaning to the story of the kingdoms. Thus the importance of Fon history for us lies in its sensitivity to the historical processes of change

29. A. Dalzel, *The History of Dahomey* (London, 1793), p. xxii.
30. Argyle, *The Fon of Dahomey*, pp. 1–2. See Le Hérissé, *L'Ancien Royaume*, p. 27; and P. Hazoumé, *Doguicimi*.
31. See Basil Davidson, *A History of West Africa*, pp. 39–69.

rather than in its witness to the secularity of those processes.[32] That is, the Fon have a vivid sense of the adaptations that they have made in their society. In their history they keep the memory of their adaptiveness alive, and in their mythology they give expression to the underlying meaning of that adaptiveness. They understand their life to be built on a series of transformations, reaching outward to the details of daily routine and inward to the patterns of feeling, thought, and identity. Legba has, therefore, become a central figure in Fon reflection and action because he represents the constant possibility of transformation and thus of life itself.

Paul Mercier has recognized this feature of Fon society very clearly:

On the one hand, these people who today seem to be so conservative—at all events in the religious sphere—have always displayed an innovating spirit, even in that very sphere. Their religion and their cosmology undoubtedly have composite origins; up to quite a recent date they have borrowed, and more or less completely assimilated, a number of very diverse elements.[33]

It is simple enough to move logically from historical assimilation and diversity of cult to the need for an active symbol of mediation. However, it is not logic as such that has given the Fon the power to create a kingdom and a vision of that king-

---

32. Many have argued that awareness of causal complexity is equivalent to secularity. Yet because the Western experience may not be normative, one can see secularity as one response to a sharper discernment of the many strands of causality out of which life is woven, not the necessary consequence of that discernment. The indigenous histories of the West African kingdoms have interest as history, while remaining sacred narrative. As Mercier puts it ("The Fon," p. 312), "The dynasty which built up Dahomey . . . played such an important part that its history has provided the temporal framework into which all important events are fitted. This mainly secular time scale, which may be called 'royal time,' involves a certain secularization of thought. For the concept of a mythical time in which the present is immersed has certainly been modified. . . . Nevertheless, it is not entirely obliterated: this mythical time continues to provide the framework within which the relationships and the actions of the gods in the world are displayed." For a thorough analysis of historical rhetoric, see J. H. Hexter, *The History Primer* (New York: Basic Books, 1971).

33. Mercier, "The Fon," p. 212.

dom's meaning. Mercier points to that power even if he does not quite define it:

Among the notable characteristics of ancient Dahomey are to be found military and aggressive qualities closely bound up with a power of assimilation. Whether in the sphere of economics, of art, or of religious thought, it was able to gather a harvest everywhere. The ruling dynasty itself came from outside. . . ; imposed by force, it displayed on a number of occasions a remarkable power of innovation. . . . The Fon themselves are the first to admit the composite character of their religious ideas. Their traditions recount the introduction of a certain god or group of gods in a certain reign historically established. These cannot always be literally accepted, but this awareness that their religious and cosmological system has been gradually built up by borrowings is something which should be borne in mind. . . . The successive entries of gods at Abomey . . . [have] the character of revelations designed to complete a system into which, according to the people, the gods must needs be more or less systematically incorporated.[34]

This "power of assimilation," this ability "to gather a harvest everywhere," this "power of innovation," these "borrowings"—what are these but that power of the religious imagination which Eliade has so aptly called "discovery"? Mercier is right to see in the various entrances of the gods into Dahomean life a "revelation." What we have is an instance of transhistorical analysis, a small but brilliant example of a "maieutics" of history,[35] in which the political and religious leaders of Dahomey have served as midwives to the unceasing birth of new religious patterns that were accepted as further expressions of the old.

"Reevaluation" may sound too dry to name a process that prepared the way for a new irruption of sacredness into the world of the Fon, but one ought to remember that modern Western civilization springs out of the twin "reevaluations" of Christian culture that we call the Renaissance and the Ref-

34. *Ibid.*, pp. 212–13.
35. Cf. Eliade, *Images and Symbols*, p. 35.

ormation. Without making a theological judgment, one can stress the "givenness" of such a reordering, that side of it which makes it seem a breaking-in of divinity, and speak of it as "revelation." Yet it is precisely the two-sidedness of the Fon achievement, the sense of human adaptation as the channel for revelation, which shows how Legba's mediatorial work suits the whole Fon cultural process.

Moreover, it is in this environment of fluidity and diversity of thought that the Fon lived in the past and still, to some extent, live today. . . . In the remarkably vigorous thought of the Fon nothing is rigid . . . ; imported notions have been able to move from the circumference to the central core of myths already fully developed and generally accepted in their main outlines. This elaboration of composite data strikes the inquirer as one of the most original characteristics of Fon thought. In this meeting-place of influences . . . thought is always open, but not, on that account, unsystematic. A number of elements, the assimilation of which is not essential, remain on the fringe; fundamental data are adopted and used to enrich the already developed system.[36]

Legba's unflagging movement from center to periphery and back again is, therefore, symbolic of the deepest movements of Fon life itself. He provides not merely a justification of adaptation, but a disclosure of its meaning. In him reevaluation and revelation are linked inseparably so that the Fon are able to assert that the chief business—active as well as passive—of their society is the manifestation of the sacred center of the cosmos itself.

Legba, then, serves as one of the central institutions of Fon society. The line that our popular speech draws between symbol and institution, denying the former any concreteness and the latter any inwardness, betrays the iron grasp that a Cartesian-cum-Calvinist division between idea and object, individual and society has on our ordinary thought patterns. Such a division makes it difficult to imagine at first the reality of Legba's presence to the Fon, yet the notion is, in fact, not so

36. Mercier, "The Fon," p. 216.

foreign to us. We have only to reflect on the deepest aims of the institution of the Eucharist or of Passover to begin to understand how a religious reality can be simultaneously customary and mysterious, charged with sacred power and experienced in sequence with ordinary events, structured firmly by habit and embodying divinely free creativity. Legba embraces these same oppositions, as an examination of the processes of Fon initiation and kingship will show.

Fon initiation

When Herskovits describes the arrangement of sacred images and objects in the compound of an average family and in the pathways of an ordinary Dahomean village, he emphasizes the presence of Legba:

> In a clearing before the entrance, the most prominent of the complex of shrines is that for Legba, the seated figure modelled of clay with large phallus, at whose feet stands an earthen dish to receive the offerings given the god. . . . Nearby are other shrines to this god, low unroofed mounds of earth, on which dishes have been placed. The smallest of these are for the young children of the compound, the larger ones for the women and for the boys who have acquired their partial Fa.[37]

Of course there are many other shrines and sacred objects, with a special prominence given to the family *aiza*, the mound embodying its sacred ancestor or its link to the earth itself, yet Legba is granted a significant place in the village as well and "before each of the compounds where a pantheon of the Great Gods or a *tohwiyo* (clan founder) is worshiped."[38] We have already seen Legba's role as the mythic mediator of human sexuality, and at the center of family and village life too we find that same sexual imagery, which discloses how Legba works daily to bring Fon life into being.

Herskovits gives two reports that show how concretely Legba is involved in the creation of the Fon personality. One,

---

37. Herskovits, *Dahomey*, vol. 2, p. 298.
38. *Ibid.*, vol. 2, p. 300.

which describes the climax of the initiation of new members into the cult of Mawu-Lisa, explicitly joins mythic and ritual action. The other, in which Herskovits relates the series of events marking the passage of the adolescent from childhood to adulthood, only implicitly suggests the relationship between Legba's mediation and human sexuality, yet, as we shall see, it gives universal application to what only a small number of the Fon experience in the Mawu-Lisa initiation.

The Mawu-Lisa cult

Because of Mawu's status in the Fon pantheon, initiation into the Mawu-Lisa cult has a unique importance. Although each Dahomean family includes a member of this cult, the length and cost of the initiation help to keep the cult's membership smaller than those of the cults of the earth and the thunder deities.[39] Divination usually reveals to a family, sometimes even before a child's birth, that Mawu-Lisa desires that child for her/his cult. Usually before puberty the candidate undergoes a period of seclusion in a cult-house, where he or she prepares for an elaborate ritual experience of death and resurrection called *voduw'asi*, that is, "deity-kill-wife." After this ritual the candidate returns to the cult-house for a second period of seclusion, which lasts seven months. During this time the novices are taught the dances appropriate to the cult, learn the cult language,[40] are incised with the proper cicatrizations, and undergo generally the entire liminal phase of the ritual process.

The rite of emergence, or aggregation, for the Mawu-Lisa novices lasts ten days. It is a complex ceremony of dance, sacrifice, headshaving, and ritual reclamation, in which a double assimilation takes place. The whole society is assimilated to the novice group by the sprinkling of sacrificial blood, and later, after various rites of "possession," the novice group is united

39. *Ibid.*, pp. 123–27 and 178–87.
40. "Nago": not the present language of the Yoruba, but "the language of the ancient Nago who inhabited the region near Abomey." *Ibid.*, vol. 2, p. 188.

to the deity by the "transformation" of one of the group into Age, a child of Mawu-Lisa and the god of the bush and the hunt. On the fifth day, the novices, both men and women, appear wearing the folded cloth about their waists which is the mark of a married woman even though they are not yet *vodunsi*, "wives of the deity." On the next day "Legba" makes his first appearance. He is represented by a young girl dressed in a purple raffia skirt and a purple straw hat, and on the final days of the emergence ritual this "Legba" leads the dancing of the novices.

On the final day each of the novices receives his or her cult-name. Then the drummers begin to sound "Legba's" rhythm. When Herskovits observed the ceremony, the girl dressed as Legba came forward,

dancing toward the drums. When she reached the drummer, she put her hand under the fringe of raffia about her waist . . . , and brought out a wooden phallus. . . . This was apparently attached in such a way that it would remain in the horizontal position of the erect male organ, and as she danced . . . toward a large tree where many women were sitting watching the ceremony, . . . they ran from her, shrieking with laughter, and they were made the butt of many jokes by the spectators.[41]

Herskovits says that Legba continued to dance in "exaggerated mimicry of sexual connection," and then seized one of the younger girls, with whom he mimed intercourse.[42] When Legba moved back to the initiates, who had stood by quietly during the general merriment, he led them in a dance honoring Hevioso, after which they circled around the various temples several times and returned to their cult-house.[43]

During this ten-day rite the public ceremonies are a final preparation for and an epiphany of the deeper assimilation to the deity that takes place in the cult-house. There the initiates

41. *Ibid.*, vol. 2, pp. 125–26.
42. *Ibid.*
43. For another month they continue to speak "Nago" and beg in the marketplace, and it is a year before they "fully reenter their homes, 'relearn' Fon, and once again become normal members of society." *Ibid.*, vol. 2, p. 127.

have learned the most intimate secrets of Mawu, have received their *dokpele*, or bond, which unites them to her, have taken part in esoteric sacrifices, and have been "captured" by the god, who enters the initiate's head after a night of struggle and a priest's solemn invocation of the god's name. These secret events set the scene for the appearance of Legba on the sixth day and for his dance on the last day. Significantly, on the fifth day the novices, already captured by the deity, begin to wear the cloth of a married woman, even though only after the ten days have ended are they considered "wives of the chameleon" (the creature associated with Lisa).

In the light of the myth that we have already examined, we can see that Legba appears after the god has "taken" his devotees in the cult-house. Only when this taking is completed and the initiates have become the god's wives, does Legba come forth to take whatever women he wants in ritual intercourse. The capturing of the initiates by Mawu-Lisa is equivalent to a sexual possession, yet that possession is not complete until Legba possesses the whole people on behalf of the deity. Thus the two-fold assimilation of reaggregation, in which the emergence of the novices renews the entire society while their new being is confirmed by the ritual extension of their liminal state, culminates in Legba's dance. His penis becomes a moving limen through which Mawu-Lisa passes into both initiates and society, the initiates pass from outside to inside, and "outside" itself comes "inside."

The relationship between myth and ritual is subtle. Clearly, they are not script and drama, for the myth symbolizes the ritual as much as the ritual enacts the myth. The myth discloses both the sexual character of all cult initiation (even where Legba is not present) and thus the dynamic of social renewal. On the other hand, the ritual gives us the human richness of the myth, as the meeting of bawdiness and sacrality, holiness and humor, brings together in human life potency and order. Legba's dance becomes a prototype of all Fon ritual not only because it draws the High God and, implicitly, all the other gods into the center of human society, but also because it makes the vessel of that passage a sexuality that can be fully sacred inasmuch as it has been fully humanized.

Mawu-Lisa and Fon social order

Yet the larger meanings of the Mawu-Lisa cult reveal further depths of Legba's dance. For centuries the cult was intimately joined to the royal family of Dahomey. "Tradition holds that the mother of King Tegbesu [reigned c. 1728–1775] brought the cult of Mawu-Lisa from Adja, where she had been inducted into it as an initiate and priestess."[44] Although the use of "Mawu" to designate God by Catholic missionaries before that time certainly establishes the greater antiquity of the cult, this tradition witnesses to the way in which kingship and godhead have upheld each other in Fon life.

On the surface it all seems simple enough. Mawu-Lisa is an androgynous god or, more accurately perhaps, a male-female High God.

Mawu, the female, is the moon; Lisa, the male, is the sun. . . . Mawu is more beloved than her twin and spouse. Mawu, the elder, the woman and mother, is gentle and forgiving. Lisa, the male, the younger one, is robust and ruthless. During the day when he reigns, men are condemned to toil and strife. . . . But during the night when Mawu reigns, it is cool, and men sleep and refresh themselves after the day's work. It is then that the pleasures of life are enjoyed by mankind—dancing and story-telling and love-making. So it is said that "when Lisa punishes, Mawu pardons." The figure is carried even further, for . . . coolness symbolizes wisdom, and wisdom comes of age, and thus it is that in Mawu is concentrated the wisdom of the world, and in Lisa its strength.[45]

Mawu and Lisa, then, govern the twin forces ordering the world and ensuring its continued being. Herskovits shows

---

44. *Ibid.*, vol. 2, p. 103.
45. *Ibid.* Some Fon believe that Mawu-Lisa is the offspring of an even more primordial and remote deity, Nana-Buluku. Both Herskovits (*ibid.*, vol. 2, pp. 289–91) and Mercier ("The Fon," pp. 217–18) think that this belief suggests a succession of creators and creations.

that the Fon experience their parents in an analogous way. A child is likely to share his father with the children of other wives, yet it is his father, this more remote parent, who directs his life, gives him his past through the paternal lineage, and provides for his future through inheritance. His mother, on the other hand, not only shapes his early affective life, but represents a kind of antistructure within the social order. The child finds her more tender and compliant, and her family extends to him a gentler environment, where he may receive a portion of the ancestral sacrifices or find the money needed to pay a fine.[46]

Thus the female environment, though hidden or "dark" in this patrilineal society, keeps an inner priority and continues to uphold the child even after he or she has taken adult responsibilities in a largely masculine world. The two environments do not compete, any more than do the two lineages out of which each new family springs, yet they are not simply set side by side. They are complementary in the deeper sense of reciprocal doubleness known by the Ashanti and most other West African peoples. The relationship between night and day, moon and sun, symbolizes this doubleness clearly and naturally. Its meaning is not so much rooted in the coincidence of opposites or in the mere passage between structure and antistructure as it is in a perception of life as a rounded wholeness whose faces both mask and disclose each other. These faces are simultaneously present, but this is a simultaneity of process, a turning by which one face not only succeeds but is transformed into the other. The hard, bright day fades to reveal the gentle night; the night slides by and shows forth the face of day. It is as if the sky, the upper half of a single calabash in Fon imagery, were the mirror of the earth, revealing each twenty-four hours how its tangible stability is really the crystallization of a unique movement, a never-ending dialectic of manifest and hidden.

46. Herskovits, *Dahomey*, vol. 1, pp. 153–55.

The dialectic of Fon life

Thus far it is apparent that the Fon believe that both natural and familial patterns image the duality of Mawu-Lisa. The traditional structure of Fon kingship also shows a two-fold doubleness.

At the head is the king, and he is two in one. R. F. Burton was the first to point this out: "One of the Dahomean monarch's peculiarities is that he is double; not merely binonymous, nor dual . . . , but two in one." . . . There is only one royal personage, but there are two courts, two bodies of exactly similar officials, two series of rituals in honour of the royal ancestors. . . . Every title and every administrative office is conferred simultaneously on a woman within the palace and a man outside it.[47]

Mercier recognizes that the Fon stressed the metaphysical above the practical reasons for this arrangement, and indeed it would be hard to do otherwise when there were more than eight thousand people living in the palace in the mid-nineteenth century, most of them women.[48] These women were divided into several categories: the actual or symbolic mother of the king and the women representing the mothers of past kings; the actual wives of the king; and the female servants of the king and the high-ranking women. Some of these women where chosen to be *nayé*, female counterparts to all the important officials of the kingdom, and they were regarded as the "mothers" of these officials. Each time that an official reported to the king, his "mother" was there as well. It was her duty to remember how the topic had been dealt with previously.

Moreover, these women had their own functions within the palace which were parallel to those of the ministers outside. The "mother" of the *migan* had authority over the women of commoner origin and the "mother" of the *meu* over the princesses; in the same way as the *migan* was the great chief over the people and *meu* the great chief of the princes.[49]

47. Mercier, "The Fon," p. 232.
48. Argyle, *The Fon of Dahomey*, pp. 62 ff. Cf. Herskovits, *Dahomey*, vol. 1, pp. 110–11, and vol. 2, pp. 46–48; and Le Hérissé, *L'Ancien Royaume*, pp. 25–31.
49. Argyle, *The Fon of Dahomey*, p. 64.

Furthermore, all those who came before the king were given "mothers," so that "the 'English mother' figures prominently in the accounts of Burton and Skertchly."[50]

W. J. Argyle is certainly right to insist that the metaphysical meaning of this institution is bound up with the division between the "inside" and the "outside" of the kingship itself. "The institution of the 'mother' served as a means by which the 'inside' and the 'outside' could be brought together before the king, who ruled over both realms."[51] The "mothers" were mediators between the male world outside the palace and the female world inside it. That the "inside" of the kingship had a female valence is evident from the way in which the king appeared in public only in the company of his women, "separated from the men by a line of the midribs of bamboo palm laid end to end on the ground."[52] These markers were laid out, moreover, by palace eunuchs, who, as neuters, were able to link the two spheres outside the palace. Even the doubleness of such offices as *migan* and *meu* and their ministries of "right" and "left"[53] were traced to "the twins who reigned in the earliest days of the kingdom: Akaba and his sister Xagbe."[54]

As Mercier says, the dual monarchy, even if it had once been the custom, did not last. Yet as mythic entelechy it continued to shape Fon life. The crystallized movement which is the Fon earth is understood as a ceaseless exchange between male and female, outside and inside, manifest and hidden, actual and potential. Among the Ashanti the meshing of male and female, periphery and center, was symbolized by the analogy between the King/Queen Mother and Nyame/Asase Yaa. Here that meshing shows itself in the movement between female "inside" and male "outside" in both the kingship and the High God. With the Fon, however, the symbolisms of god and king

50. Herskovits, *Dahomey*, vol. 1, p. 111. Cf. Burton, *Mission to Gelele*, vol. 1, p. 322.
51. Argyle, *The Fon of Dahomey*, p. 65.
52. *Ibid.*, p. 67.
53. Cf. *ibid.*, p. 78.
54. Mercier, "The Fon," p. 232.

are even more tightly intertwined than are those of the Ashanti. The king embodies both the male and the female elements of rulership just as Mawu-Lisa is a double deity. In each the masculine face is brighter, more public, while the feminine aspect is darker, more inward.

However, the two institutions do not simply mirror each other, but rest in a reciprocal relationship of their own so that each shows the hidden face of the other. Thus the "inwardness" of rulership, and indeed of the whole patrilineal system, is female, yet the living embodiment of that rulership is necessarily a man. On the other hand, it is the day which gives Fon life its ordinary form, while it is Mawu, not Lisa, whose name is synonymous with divinity. The Fon earth continually comes into being as a synthesis that is neither a melding nor a juxtaposition of forces. Rather, that synthesis, manifested in the reciprocal symbolism of both kingship and deity, is an ongoing exchange in which light and darkness, nearness and remoteness, center and boundary are always in movement toward the opposite pole. The king in the depths of his palace is always both inside and outside; Mawu in the depths of the sky is always both near and far, vital center and dark margin.

The dialectic of Fon order requires mediators to draw forth the movement toward the opposite pole and to disclose the face that is momentarily hidden. The king's "wives" bring the outside world into relationship with the inside; the king's eunuchs help bring the inside world, in the person of the king himself, out into active contact with the outside. Similarly, Gu, the divine blacksmith and the god of iron, is the force through which Lisa reestablishes the world by ordering the world of men.[55] Da, or Da Ayido Hwedo, imaged as both rainbow and serpent, carries Mawu through the universe as she creates it, coiling about it to bind it together, moving in all its waters, those above and those below. He embodies that motion which draws forth the creative power of Mawu, and thus he sustains life and all its relationships.

55. See Herskovits, *Dahomey*, vol. 2, pp. 105 ff.

Rather than a person, he is a force which the *vodu* are constrained to make use of. He ensures the perpetuation of species and in particular of humanity. *Da* is man's penis, the sperm is the "water of Da," Da is the umbilical cord, the object of a special cult. It is in this sense that an informant could say: "It is Da who created man." In the task of preserving the world Da is the universal servant: of himself he does nothing, but without him nothing can be done.[56]

Although Da also has a dual nature, his masculine valence is foremost as he bears Mawu's power everywhere—through the arches of the rainbow and the spirals of the serpent, through the coilings and uncoilings of penis and umbilicus, through the movements of all things "flexible, sinuous and moist"[57]— out of the realm of primal darkness into the common daylight of human life.

The passage into sexuality

The Fon, however, think of Legba as a friendlier mediator than Da:

Da is powerful. We have no love for him. He gives and takes away. He is a thief. One is never done with being anxious about placating him, for he does not forgive readily, as Legba does.[58]

In one sense, Legba's greater popularity springs from the contrast between the cosmic dialectic, which Da represents, and the human process, which Legba serves and embodies. Da is a servant, but uncreated, most intimately wound into human life, yet impersonal. Legba is a deceiver, self-serving and capricious, but his caprice relentlessly enlarges the scope of the human. Thus in spite of the symbolic link between Da and the penis, it is Legba, not Da, who gives the deepest meaning to sex. It is Legba's penis which symbolizes, both ordinarily and most ceremoniously, the bond between the divine and the human worlds. He is a living copula, and his phallus symbolizes his being, the limen marking the real distinction be-

56. Mercier, "The Fon," p. 224.
57. Herskovits, *Dahomey*, vol. 2, p. 248. See Mercier, "The Fon," pp. 220 ff.
58. Herskovits, *Dahomey*, vol. 2, p. 255.

tween outside and inside, the wild and the ordered, even as it ensures safe passage between them.[59]

Furthermore, as the mythic humanizer of sex, Legba joins together the cosmic dialectic and the social process so that the implacability of the former loses its terror, while the latter gains stability without becoming rigid. Legba enables the Fon to laugh at sex, but in the deep structure of Fon society this laughter signifies that the male/female symbolism in which the cosmic and social dialectic is framed has been, literally, acculturated, even domesticated. One would like to know the Fon word used to describe Legba's readiness to forgive, but its meaning is clear enough: he understands the human condition because he has helped to shape it by his lechery, wiles, and disobedience. Moreover, both understanding and trickiness are reflections of that multiformity which gives him his place at the door of every house and in the center of every village. By his tricks he snatches absolute potency for ordinary life; in demystifying sexuality he further reveals the human possibility hidden in the divine dualism and the life-serving patterns implicit in the royal institutions.

Legba's involvement in the deep symbolism of Fon sexuality meshes with his larger role as transformer and living limen. Although Herskovits was told that the dancing of Legba during the Mawu-Lisa initiation imparts no sexual knowledge to the young, "sexual knowledge" for the Fon means more than the acquisition of a few biological facts.[60] At every stage in the process of sexual education, knowledge is elusive, charged with mystery. Thus Fon men claim that, although boys at the age of nine or ten begin to live together in their own small house, watch animals copulate, and engage in sexual play with girls their own age, it is the girls who teach the boys the proper human sexual position, as later wives teach their husbands the various positions for intercourse they have learned in the girls'

59. Cf. Kerényi, "The Trickster," pp. 182–83.
60. Herskovits, *Dahomey*, vol. 1, p. 280. See pp. 277–90.

"school." The women insist, on the contrary, that, although the girls are grouped together for instruction before menstruation begins, it is husbands who teach their wives how to perform the sexual act even if most brides know much more than they pretend on their wedding nights. Moreover, even if children are told to learn from the copulation of animals, they are reminded that human intercourse is a different matter.

Fon sexual education, then, aims to teach that sex is above all a fact of *human* life whose mysterious meanings are disclosed gradually and ritually until they are fully manifested in marriage. The shyness of the adolescent boys whom Herskovits questioned, therefore, the apparent ignorance of young girls about menstruation, and their seeming inability to relate the actions of animals; their own sexual play, and the dance of Legba to the performance of human intercourse do not display ignorance so much as the awkwardness of the uninitiated. What they lack is not biological information, but ritual insight into an event so completely human that it is to animal sexuality what cooked food is to raw.

The importance of all this for understanding Legba lies in the Fon way of speaking about and symbolizing the complex process of entering adulthood. Like most peoples, the Fon look on adolescence as a liminal period during which the young are instructed and prepared for full participation in the social order. Much of this preparation has a sexual orientation because the sexual changes of puberty are, simply in the order of nature, a liminal experience, outer signs of an inner passage from childhood to manhood and womanhood. Yet as Eliade has shown clearly, the peoples of traditional cultures never merely observe this natural process, but celebrate and insist on its deeper meanings.

In philosophical terms, initiation is equivalent to an ontological mutation of the existential condition. The novice emerges from his ordeal a totally different being: he has become another. . . .

In short, through initiation, the candidate passes beyond the "natural" mode of being—that of the child—and gains access to the cultural mode.[61]

Adolescent instruction and initiation, then, have an ontological character because sexual change must become human transformation. The power to beget and bear life must be drawn into the larger life-giving process that is human society —itself both fruit and image of an even greater movement.

Now among the Fon the revelation and consecration of sexuality that take place in age-group instruction—especially in the ceremonies surrounding the girls' first menstruation and their cicatrization and in the ritual circumcision of adolescent boys—depend on the reception of the "partial *fa*" and the first disclosures of the "personal Legba." At the very heart of the transforming process by which a Fon boy or girl emerges into the center of the culture, there is a revelation of his or her "destiny" and unique identification with Legba, who both mediates that destiny and expands it. In every society the growth of each child into adulthood renews the social order, not merely adding to its economic strength or diversifying its gene pool, but revealing that the powers which shaped the society in the beginnings are still working to give life its properly human shape. In this way the grand design of the cosmos, made visible in the social order, is disclosed once again in the passage of children from pure potency to full cultural actuality. We shall see with special clarity in the inner workings of Dogon life how Ogo-Yurugu provides the image of this process, its model and its antitype. Here, however, Legba speaks and "writes" the pattern of each adolescent's life through divination, as he has spoken Mawu's word from the beginning to establish both cosmic and human order. He is the master of a uniquely Fon dialectic, by which the great cosmic dualisms are brought into balance with each other, given a fully human dimension in social structure, and established as perpetually available and re-

61. Eliade, *The Quest*, pp. 112–13.

newable in human sexuality. Thus to understand fully how Legba is woven into Fon self-understanding, we must explore the special language that is their divination, and to grasp the full meaning of the trickster's involvement with divination, we must consider also Eshu's role in Ifa divination, the Yoruba system that the Fon have borrowed and made their own.

CHAPTER FOUR

Legba and Eshu:
Writers of Destiny

Then there is the spectacle of a quarterback and his receiver
together finding and splitting "the seam of the zone"—
actually the seam between zones, the place where defenders'
responsibilities in space and time do not quite mesh. The very
idea of a seam between individually patrolled zones implies
a highly refined formal arrangement of persons. . . .
Originality in anything is primarily a matter of finding a seam
between zones.

ROY BLOUNT, JR., "A Strange Kind of Love"

Eshu threw a stone yesterday; he killed a bird today.

YORUBA PROVERB

AFTER she gives birth to the gods, Mawu makes Legba
her linguist. From the beginning he is the master of languages,
the bearer of messages among his brothers, and the translator
of Mawu's purposes for all. We have already seen how firmly
Legba's mediating actions are grounded in the human world,
indeed, how these actions maintain the rhythms of passage
among the various modes and planes of being in the Fon cosmos and how these rhythms themselves are literally the
grounding of the world. Now we must look at Legba's mastery
over the inner language of the human self as the first step in
exploring the West African trickster's relationship to divination.[1] So closely do the Fon, like the Yoruba, whose divinatory

---

1. In addition to the works of Maupoil and Herskovits (*Dahomey*, especially
vol. 2, pp. 201–30), the chief source of information about the history, the practice, and the interpretation of divination among the Yoruba and the Fon is
William Bascom, *Ifa Divination: Communication between Gods and Men in West Africa*. The following were also especially useful: Bascom, "The Relationship of
Yoruba Folklore to Divining"; J. D. Clarke, "Ifa Divination"; Victor W. Turner,
Ndembu Divination: Its Symbolism and Techniques; Carl Jung's Introduction to *The*

system they have borrowed and whose understanding of the trickster they have learned from, tie Legba to divination that only in this relationship is it apparent how his knowledge of heavenly languages discloses the inner shapes of individual and community, the ways out of social strife, the patterns of times to come, and the true form of the world itself. Divination shows the full range of Legba's trickiness and the deepest meaning of his transforming power, for in divination Legba spells out the innermost structure of Fon life by translating its cosmic complexities into the ordinary workings of daily existence.

DIVINATION IN FON LIFE

Fa (Yoruba, Ifa) is the name given to the system of divination practiced by the Fon as well as to the god who personifies that system. However, *fa* also refers to that destiny or fate which is peculiar to each individual. It is this individual destiny which is partially revealed to a youth through divination at the onset of adolescence, when the consecration of his or her sexuality will enable him or her to enter fully into human, or cultural, life. At the time of this revelation, though, the Fon believe that the personality or, more accurately, the personhood, is already well established. This personhood consists in a complex, multi-faceted "soul."

The human soul (*se*) has many forms, although its essential unity is insisted on: there is the *joto*, the soul handed on from the ancestor of whom each living man is the representative, and who is his guardian; the *se*, which strictly speaking is a portion of Mawu, the great Se of the world; the *selido*, which is life, feeling, personality, the individual's peculiar qualities with which *kpoli*, the destiny revealed by Fa, is identified; finally, there is the *ye*; this . . . denotes the shadow, the indestructible portion of the individual, which, at the time of burial, becomes invisible and leaves the body.[2]

I Ching; and Richard P. Werbner, "The Superabundance of Understanding: Kalanga Rhetoric and Domestic Divination."

2. Mercier, "The Fon," p. 227. Cf. Maupoil, *La Géomancie*, pp. 378 ff., and Herskovits, *Dahomey*, vol. 2, pp. 230–44.

Finally, *da*—"the mobile, sentient quality in all things that have life" and in the individual that "power which brings riches or poverty"—is also included in this complex.[3]

No amount of juggling will enable us to harmonize completely this vision of the human person with one more familiar to us—Greek, biblical, medieval scholastic, Cartesian, or Freudian. Yet Freud has restored to us, after centuries of Cartesian mechanicalism, a sense of the person as a bundle of interpersonal forces. Thus once we pass beyond the surface strangeness of the Fon vision, it can help us understand the importance of the entrance of a "partial *fa*" and a "personal Legba" into the dynamic network that is a human being. It is clear that the Fon recognize several relationships as essential to each person. The most fundamental of these is the relationship to Mawu. Each person's *se* is his own Mawu, the "animating principle . . . brought to earth by Da."[4] Each possesses his *se* in his own way, and this uniqueness of self-possession, the *selido*, is related in a special way, as inner to outer pattern, to his *kpoli*, or destiny, and at death is neither returned to Mawu with his *se* nor passed on to an ancestor as a *joto*. One's *joto* represents his living relationship with his ancestry. He is the issue, not solely of Mawu's work, but of those humans to whose clan he belongs, of the clan's *tohwiyo* (its primordial founder), and, most specifically, of some one ancestor whose *ye*, or shadow, returns to help animate his body. His own *ye*, in turn, will live again as the *joto* of a future member of the clan. A person, then, is a gathering together into a single life of the forces that create all life, a microcosm or, more exactly, an epiphany of the human and divine familial relationships of which the universe itself consists. Nevertheless, one's individuality is real; and it is this individual self which one's own *fa* and Legba disclose as a unique, inward dynamism as well as an element in the cosmic system.

3. Herskovits, Dahomey, vol. 2, p. 201.
4. Mercier, "The Fon," p. 227.

Legba and Fa

Divination, the Fon say, is the "alphabet" of Mawu,[5] an aspect of that primordial language which only Legba remembers fully.

It is an abstract, indirect, and deductive mode of interpreting or revealing the past or the future, whereby an enquirer receives, through the medium of a specialist, an answer to the problem . . . exercising his mind. Above all, it offers to everyone the possibility of learning the fate which Mawu had appointed for his soul before giving it its earthly incarnation, and enables him to practise the cult of that soul.[6]

Divination rests on the belief that causality can never be divided into discrete physical, moral, and spiritual lines of force, but that the unceasing intersection of these lines brings the world into being. At moments of disruption, conflict, and doubt, intersection has become collision. Then divination seeks to uncover the forces at work and to reconcile them so that a safe passage can be made to whatever order lies hidden in the momentary tangle.[7] Thus the Fon consult diviners throughout their lives to plot the course along which they must move to overcome obstacles and live peacefully with their ancestors, their neighbors, and their own deepest selves.

Yet at two moments in life the Fon seek not merely the disclosure of a single element in life's pattern, but a revelation of the pattern itself. Adolescents receive only a "partial *fa*" (*fasise*). With this revelation, a young boy learns from the diviner "what he may eat and what he must refrain from eating, the places he may visit and the places he must not visit, and what special things he may and may not wear."[8] In short, a boy or girl at this moment moves out of "nature" into "culture." Where there has been patternlessness in eating, move-

---

5. Herskovits, *Dahomean Narrative*, p. 174.

6. Maupoil, *La Géomancie*, p. 17; quoted by Mercier, "The Fon," p. 228.

7. See appendix for further remarks on the theory and practice of divination.

8. Herskovits, *Dahomey*, vol. 2, p. 218.

ment, and clothing, now there is order, a specifically social order. Where mere biological order has held sway, now the adolescent enters a truly human, or communal, order. Where sexuality has been scarcely admitted, because its full human dimensions were lacking, now Legba, by means of divination, bestows maleness and femaleness, assimilates them to human generation, and makes them passageways to further life.

Later, after a man has established his family and entered more fully into the life of the community, he receives his complete *fa*, his *sekpoli*.[9] In the forest the diviner makes a cast for him, which is seen as the image of his life's true shape. He sews the sand on which this cast has been made in a square of cloth, which then becomes the chief embodiment of his *kpoli*, the earthly figure of his heavenly destiny. This figure governs from that time on all his experiences of divination. Every subsequent appeal that he makes to the diviner will be related to his *kpoli*, "who opens the door of the sky to Fa so that he may see the truth."[10]

In some sense, *fa* is a correlative of negative experience. Where all is well, destiny remains hidden, but when life goes awry, the need for change draws one to the discovery of one's *fa*. Although this need for redirection usually determines the actual moment when a man seeks his complete *fa*, its discovery transcends the particular difficulty he is experiencing and brings him into full consciousness of his own personal relation to the gods and to the unfolding order of the generations. Because this relationship is his own and because it is, first and last, the image of an order molded by choice and chance, a man's *fa* also reveals his freedom. It is Legba who manifests this aspect of personhood.

Man is not a slave. Though his fate binds him strictly to the structure of the world, it is no more than the guiding line of his life. He is not

9. See *ibid.*, vol. 2, p. 219. A woman "inherits" her complete *fa*, usually from her father, and thus her inner pattern remains independent from her husband's.

10. *Ibid.*, vol. 2, p. 212.

debarred from all freedom, and Legba insures this in the world of the gods. Legba has stratagems . . . to evade the rigid government of the world. It is clear that the mythology of Legba is connected with that of Fa, of which it is in some sort the reverse.[11]

As Mercier suggests, Legba discloses life's openness, but he is more than the "reverse" of the boundedness revealed by Fa. The Fon say that he is "before" Fa because he makes known the gods' wishes and must be approached before the gods or Fa. Moreover, his wiles have modified the plans of Mawu herself, and he is everywhere worshiped as the one whose intervention can modify destiny as well. So it is, then, that only after a man receives his complete *fa* is he entitled to erect a "great Legba," or wholly completed shrine, in front of his dwelling.[12]

Yet Legba is "before" Fa in a still more structural sense. One amusing story tells how, when Legba was absent from home one day, Fa came and deflowered his wife, who was still a virgin.[13] When Legba asked his wife why she had behaved so badly, she answered, "Your penis is not enough for me." Then Legba ate a great deal and told his wife that this very day she would "get plenty." He brought all the people together, and made his wife lie down in front of them. He then told her, "Today I will have intercourse with you until you are tired." As the people began to play the drums, Legba sang, "Gudufu, the path of my destiny, is large—large, large like a large penis. O Gudufu, you are large."

He told the people that he and Fa were friends and "gods of the same quarter." He said, "Fa is the first, and I, Legba, am second. In my absence, see what my wife has done! It is because of this that I shame her!" Then Legba ordered Fa to remain in the house. He promised that if those permitted to move about freely found anything good, they would share it with Fa. From that time on, when Legba went out, he took his wife with him, but he boasted, "If I find any woman, I will lie

11. Mercier, "The Fon," p. 228.
12. Herskovits and Herskovits, *Dahomean Narrative*, p. 178.
13. *Ibid.*, pp. 148–49.

with her, no matter whose she may be." Thus whenever any-one beats the drum for Legba he comes and dances joyously. He does as he pleases, and he always comes first, before Fa.

This story is built on a humorous equation of the sexual act and divination. At first, Fa supplants Legba and opens up "the path of destiny" so that Fa has priority over Legba and even ousts him from his dominion over that inner space (his house, his wife) which is destiny. Yet Legba's defeat leads to his victory. His capacity for "food" enlarges his penetrating power and enables him to outdo Fa. This great appetite refers to Leg-ba's role as divine intermediary, which entitles him to be "fed" before every sacrifice,[14] but Fa's initial victory spurs Legba on to extend his power over every human passageway. Fa keeps a certain dominion over destiny, or inner space, but Legba's elas-ticity gives him mastery over destiny's paths. Fa must remain stationary, while Legba can roam as he chooses, going in and out to bring men to their destiny, but never ceasing to widen the path for them. When he is summoned, he comes and dances joyously, always ready for intercourse. He is the master of sexuality, the juggler of language and experience, for he finds in all biological, social, and metaphysical walls doorways into a larger universe. He neither destroys the structures of life nor stoically accepts them, but inwardly enlarges them by the gleeful disclosure of their further possibilities.

The patterns Legba traces through Fa and the paths he opens up have a cosmic dimension. As one diviner put it:

We *bokono* take three things for our Mawu. We take Mawu, or Fa, as the author of man and his destiny. We take Legba as the son, the brother, and the power of Mawu and as Mawu herself. . . . Fa is the writing of Mawu, which was turned over to Legba to make man. Therefore, we say Fa is Mawu, and Mawu is Fa.[15]

The issue here is not the literalness of these statements, but their emphatically Fon character. In fact, even the objection

14. Herskovits, *Dahomey*, vol. 2, p. 179; see vol. 1, p. 377.
15. *Ibid.*, vol. 2, p. 203.

that another Fon informant raised, that "your arm is not you, and you are not your arm,"[16] only suggests further the complex intertwining of Fon divination and mythology. To see, therefore, how divination works in practice and how that working enables us to understand Legba, we must look at its mythical setting.

The origin of Fa

The Fon have three great myths telling of the origin of Fa, the first of which stresses its symbolic meanings and the other two its historical ties to the Yoruba.[17] In the first myth, divination springs from Gbadu, a mysterious primordial being, androgynous like Mawu-Lisa, whom Mawu set on the top of a palm tree to observe the earth, the sea, and the sky. She had sixteen eyes, but could not open them herself, so that each morning Legba opened them for her. Before he did so, he first asked her which eyes she wished to have opened. To prevent others from overhearing when she replied, she put one palm kernel in his hand if she wanted two eyes opened and two kernels if only one eye were to be opened. As Legba opened her eyes, he too looked about to see what was happening so that he could report to Mawu.

After a time, Gbadu bore children, but she still did not know what work Mawu wanted her to do. Legba promised to teach her the alphabet of Mawu. Later, Legba reported to Mawu that wars were raging on earth, in the sky, and in the sea because men did not know how to behave. As a result, the water in the sea did not know its place or the rain how to fall. Legba urged Mawu to send Gbadu to earth to teach men the language of their parent, but Mawu ordered Legba to send instead three sons of Gbadu to each of the three great "kingdoms." Mawu gave to Gbadu the keys of the future—a "house" with sixteen doors, each corresponding to one of her eyes. While Legba

16. See *ibid*. (my translation).
17. Herskovits and Herskovits, *Dahomean Narrative*, pp. 173–80.

would be the "inspector" of the world, Gbadu and her sons would be the intermediary between Mawu and the three kingdoms. When men wished to know the future, they were to "play" palm kernels at random. This would open an eye of Gbadu and the corresponding door in the house of the future. What lay behind each door was taught to the three sons before they were sent to earth. When they arrived on earth, they showed men how to use palm kernels to find their *sekpoli*, that soul which Mawu gave to each one, but which a man can know only by knowing which eyes Gbadu opens to name it. No shrines would be needed to worship the *sekpoli* which Fa (both the palm tree on which Gbadu sat and the process of marking the earth with the figure corresponding to her eyes) disclosed because the human body is itself the shrine of the *sekpoli*.

The cult of Fa spread, but meanwhile Legba slept with Gbadu and also with her daughter, Minona, the goddess of women. One day Legba and Gbadu came to visit the earth. They shared a sleeping-mat that night, but Legba sneaked away to Minona. Gbadu caught them out, however, and they returned to the sky to bring the case to Mawu. Legba denied what he had done, but Mawu ordered him to undress. As Legba stood before her with his penis erect, she accused him of lying to her and of deceiving Gbadu. Then she ordered that he always remain aroused, but that his sexual appetite be forever unfulfilled. At this, Legba began to play with Gbadu, and when Mawu reproached him, he answered that she herself had commanded that he be sexually insatiable. Thus it is that Legba dances as he does and tries to take any woman who is handy.

The other myths depict Legba's role somewhat differently. Fa, the second myth says, is the "writing with which Mawu creates each person," and only Legba assists Mawu in this work. Each man must know this writing if he would know how to live and which god to worship, but if he does not approach Legba first, he will remain ignorant of what he needs to know. When the people forgot what the first primordial messengers had told them about Legba's importance, others came to remind them and to teach them how to make the casts which would reveal their destiny. These messengers insisted that a shrine to Legba be placed before each house, to correspond to his position before the house of Mawu. They said too that Legba must always be "fed" first and that he must always be informed before a journey, when one is troubled, or "when one wishes anything at all in life." [18] Finally, they prophesied that soon strange men and animals would appear to create families and to give men the gods they would worship, but that even these gods and clan-founders were to have their own Legba shrines.

Much of this material requires no comment. The sixteen eyes of Gbadu, [19] the palm kernels, the disclosure of the *sekpoli* through a divinatory cast in the forest, even the presence of Legba before every house and shrine—these do not take us beyond what Fon life has already taught us. [20] The chief importance of the myths is the way in which they express the Fon understanding of Legba as the link between the ultimate shape of the cosmos and the ordinary patterns of daily life. The Fon know Legba as the primal binding force in the constellation of divination, sexuality, and language which holds these two orders in proper relationship to each other.

The master of intercourse

The first myth begins with Gbadu seated on a palm tree to observe the several realms of creation. [21] It ends with Legba, penis erect, dancing before Mawu and "playing" with Gbadu. The myth draws a vivid contrast between Gbadu's stasis and Legba's freedom of movement. She is seated; he climbs the

18. *Ibid.*, p. 178.
19. Maupoil suggests that Gbadu is simply a Fon rendering of the Yoruba *igba odu*, "calabash of Odu," *La Géomancie*, p. 84.
20. See Herskovits, *Dahomey*, vol. 2, pp. 153–56.
21. The second part of the myth unfolds the meaning of the first part even if some sort of *Redaktionsgeschichte* were to show that it had been added later.

tree. She closes her eyes, and only he can open them. She observes; he surveys and reports. Her eyes look into the future, but only he can bring the language of reconciliation and harmony into actual play. Legba possesses Gbadu as easily on her heavenly perch as he possesses her daughter in her earthly house. The one time that Gbadu moves, Legba's mastery over both her and her daughter is simply underscored by a punishment that only fulfills his nature. Gbadu's palm tree (Fa) has been transformed. The cosmic tree, whose roots are in the bowels of the earth and whose uppermost branches are in heaven, the *axis mundi*, which pierces through and joins together all levels of reality and ensures their harmonious movement around a single center, is revealed to be nothing more or less than Legba's upright penis.

But this revelation does not trivialize the symbol in the slightest. On the contrary, to identify so humorously the *axis mundi* with the erect male organ is to show how truly the language of life is human as well as heavenly. Thus, through Legba, men and women are able to know the inwardness of their social identities and the outward shapes and courses of their secret selves. As he knows the movements of Mawu herself, so he has the mastery of all human passages, inner and outer, and insures their completion. He is always the master of successful intercourse. Of even more significance socially, Legba, as Mawu's agent, has mysteriously translated her writing into the languages of all the other gods and of the great clan founders, the *tohwiyo*. Through Fa all people are assigned to appropriate gods and suitable families. Thus in worshiping the divine beings and sacred ancestors whom they know to be the sources of their most essential relationships, they must also acknowledge how Legba's utterly irrepressible mobility brings the limitless creativity of Mawu into play at every corner of life. Fa has "brought all the stories of the world from the sky," and Legba reveals how each of them is a true dance of life.

It is not enough, therefore, to say that Legba is the symbol of life's randomness or an advocate who can change the divine decrees themselves. It is true, of course, that as the Fon were able,

by means of bribery, or by the shrewd manipulation of coincidental happenings, or by exploiting the personality of those in power, to avoid the consequences of a reprehensible act or to set aside some of the less pleasant rules of the monarch, so in dealing with the supernatural officialdom, a man [could], by winning the favor of Legba, mollify an angered deity and set aside his vengeance.[22]

Such forgiveness, however, is built into the religious structure itself. Mawu, the creator, makes Legba what he is; Mawu sets him in action; Mawu bestows Fa through him; Mawu enables Fa itself to be a source of transformation and change; Mawu empowers Legba to be the special agent of the consecration of the people to her and the daily revealer of the fundamental pattern of human life. Throughout its whole range, Fon life is a crystallization of the exchange between male outside and female inside. It is patrilineal yet maternally guided, ruled (traditionally) by a king with male ministers and inwardly controlled by Mawu and a female court, shaped in the daylight by Lisa, Gu, and the pantheons of male deities and within each house subject to Minona, the goddess of the home, in the arch of the heavens and in the depths of both earth and ocean upheld and formed by Da, the serpentine force within both male ejaculate and female placenta. That exchange is acted out in the space between heaven and the bush. It has been achieved as much by the interplay between the conscious choices of history and the intuitive discoveries of history's meanings as it is formed daily by farming and cooking, buying and selling, birth, copulation, and death. And everywhere there is Legba and his penis, symbolizing that the logic of the exchange still holds, that it is a life-giving transformation, that life itself is a continuous threshold through which man ceaselessly passes from dissolution to order and from pattern to potency.

22. Herskovits, *Dahomey*, vol. 2, p. 296.

Legba is at all life's crossings, not only at thresholds, cross-roads, and marketplaces, but at every moment of meeting and commerce. It is no wonder that the Fon can say, "One is never finished telling the power of Legba."[23] Because he is the "linguist" and the intermediary of the gods, sacrifice is always offered to him before divination, to which recourse is had at every crucial moment: "No offering is ever given the great gods of the various pantheons but that a smaller offering is first given to Legba."[24] Just as significantly, Legba is intimately involved in the beginning and the end of each life. Acting for Mawu, he ensures the continuity of the clan by replacing the *se* of the dead with new souls. When a woman is in labor, no matter what other gods may be sacrificed to, sacrifice is always offered to Legba, who has a prime responsibility for the passage of a new life from the invisible world to the world of men. As we have seen, the inner and outer growth of that life is symbolized by the emergence of its personal Legba, and indeed, this linkage is so definite that in the Legba shrine of an important person "a fantastically large and erect penis is in evidence."[25] Finally, when a man has died, his "Legba" is destroyed at the same time as his *fa* and his *kpoli* are disposed of. The diviner kneels before the Legba shrine and says:

I kneel before thee, O King, Destroyer-of-all things, Who-eats-and-leaves-the-mouth-soiled. Thou-of-the-thick-lips [and here he repeats the secret, "strong" names of Legba]. . . . From the day you were brought here, you have watched over this house. You were always given food. Today we, the *bokono*, come to break you, and to take away the earth in which you dwell, for the man you have been guarding is dead. You must not remain here. You must give way to another.[26]

Then the shrine is deconsecrated by the blood of a male goat and the image destroyed before the end of the elaborate fu-

23. *Ibid.*, vol. 2, p. 238.
24. *Ibid.*, vol. 2, p. 229.
25. *Ibid.*, vol. 2, p. 224.
26. *Ibid.*, vol. 1, p. 377.

neral rituals, which guarantee the peaceful rest of the dead man and his continued availability to the clan.

Although the funeral itself and the period of mourning that follows are sad but not usually somber, filled rather with eating, drinking, and dancing, this destruction of the personal Legba is charged with a respectful awe not ordinarily associated with the trickster. Here Legba is not dancing, rutting, deceiving, or amusing. Here he stands as mute witness to the potential terror of every transformation. So blithely, so insouciantly has he wrested life out of every act of intercourse, out of every meeting between center and periphery, outside and inside, out of every exchange between the forces shaping the world, that one might be excused for forgetting that every transformation rises out of disintegration and that a false step may bring chaos and death. The Fon do not forget. They are delighted by Legba's cosmic sleight-of-hand and dazzled by his metaphysically fancy footwork just because they know that the pathways of new order that he opens always skirt the edges of chaos. If life is ruled by a dialectic of exchange, the trick is not just to keep it moving, but to keep it moving at the right speed. Balance is all. The secret of liminality lies in maintaining the rhythms of passage—in and out, dissolving and reordering, closing and opening. When a man dies, a door has shut, but if Legba were not to leave with the dead one, a door to the world of death would be left open.

Humbly, then, at this most crucial moment of all, the diviner addresses Legba as "Destroyer of all things" and asks him to depart, lest his continued presence fill the human world with death. Because Legba always leaves, the dead one can return, not as a ghost, an emissary from death, but as a *joto*, bearer of a new life for a new person and a renewed clan. Thus, although Legba causes no laughter here, he does not cease to transform the movement that is life, even the movement of life that brings death. Because he claims change for the human world, even the awful change which is death finally affirms life. If there were only stasis, there could be no transformation, and

wherever Legba moves, even where he moves away, the transformation that takes place creates a world for man. In Legba
the Fon know more than the laughter of relief or escape. They
know the laughter of a delight that is rooted in the movement
of the cosmos itself.

ESHU

Eshu, like Legba, loves contradiction, fosters intercourse,
and helps to spell out the words that disclose the inmost structures of human life. This similarity is to be expected since the
Fon have borrowed from the Yoruba both their system of divination and their understanding of the trickster-god's relation
to it. Yet this borrowing was creative, serving the special Fon
need to ratify and link symbolically their culture's inner and
outer dynamisms, so that between Eshu and Legba there remain striking differences. In a sense, this is hardly surprising.
The Yoruba, concentrated chiefly in southwestern Nigeria, are
among the most numerous, ancient, and sophisticated of African peoples, and one might expect their religious forms to reflect those facts.[27] Nevertheless, the differences between Eshu
and Legba or other trickster-figures do not arise merely because of Yoruba sophistication. We have already seen the subtlety of the Ashanti and Fon tricksters, and we will next look at
the intricacy with which the Dogon, few in number and simple
in economy, weave Ogo-Yurugu into the patterns of their
lives. What Eshu reveals is a particularly elegant yoking of the

27. See the extensive bibliographies of Ray, "African High Gods"; Eva
Krapf-Askari, *Yoruba Towns and Cities: An Enquiry into the Nature of Urban Social
Phenomena*; and G. J. Afolabi Ojo, *Yoruba Culture: A Geographical Analysis*. The
best treatments of Eshu are contained in John Pemberton, "Eshu-Elegba: The
Yoruba Trickster God" and "A Cluster of Sacred Symbols: Orisa Worship
Among the Igbomina Yoruba of Ila-Orangun"; Joan Wescott, "The Sculpture
and Myths of Eshu-Elegba, the Yoruba Trickster"; Joan Wescott and Peter
Morton-Williams, "The Symbolism and Ritual Context of the Yoruba *Laba
Shango*"; Peter Morton-Williams, "An Outline of the Cosmology and Cult
Organization of the Oyo Yoruba"; E. Bolaji Idowu, *Olódùmare: God in Yoruba
Belief*; Pierre Verger, *Notes sur le culte des Orisa et Vodun à Bahia, la Baie de tous les
Saints au Brésil et à l'ancienne Côte des Esclaves en Afrique*, pp. 109–40; and Leo
Frobenius, *The Voice of Africa*.

trickster's disruptive and recreative possibilities. In linking him to the deepest purposes of divination, the Yoruba explore the therapeutic and iconographic power embedded in the trickster's cocksure multiformity. To locate that power as the Yoruba do, however, we must first see Eshu as the Yoruba ordinarily see him.

Eshu's centrality in the daily life of the Yoruba cannot be missed. His shrines are found at the entrances of compounds (*eshuona*: "Eshu of the way"), at crossroads (*eshurita*), and in marketplaces (*eshuoja*); and at the festival of the new year he is given the first sacrifice.[28] The traditional number of Yoruba gods (*orisha*) is 401, yet Eshu, like Ifa, "is a deity universally recognized and appealed to by all Yoruba regardless of their affiliation to other cults."[29] Moreover, Peter Morton-Williams shows the mediatorial place of Eshu in the divine field that is the Yoruba pantheon.[30] Eshu can keep peace in the market and watch over the passageways and transition points in Yoruba life because his proper place is at the transcendent center of that life. Each of the larger Yoruba towns emphasizes and embodies Eshu's centrality by keeping the marketplace next to the royal compound and by seeing to it that cult officials anoint the market's Eshu pillar each day with palm oil.[31]

Furthermore, Eshu, as mediator between gods and men, plays a role in the cults of other *orisha*, especially that of Shango, the great god of thunder. Eshu's relationship to Shango is significant because Shango too is a powerful breaker of boundaries and because the representation of the dancing Eshu on the *laba Shango*, the sacred bag of cult objects carried by every Shango priest, points toward Eshu's work of imaging the Yoruba cosmos.[32] That work, as we shall see more fully later, is linked above all to divination. Although some myths stress the

28. Pemberton, "Eshu-Elegba," p. 21.
29. Wescott, "Sculpture and Myths," p. 337.
30. Morton-Williams, "Outline of the Cosmology," p. 252.
31. Krapf-Askari, *Yoruba Towns*, p. 47.
32. Wescott and Morton-Williams, "Symbolism and Ritual Context," p. 30.

creative mediation of Orunmila, who controls Ifa and shapes the world according to the commands of the High God, Olorun or Olodumare, E. B. Idowu, himself a Yoruba, shrewdly recognizes that Eshu's greater structural flexibility constantly puts Orunmila under obligation to him.[33] Thus Eshu, whose face is found on every divining tray and who receives a portion of every sacrifice commanded through divination, makes his "presence and power" known each time a diviner holds a session.[34]

The Yoruba themselves explain Eshu's power by insisting that his antics stir up all human troubles. It is he who

tricks men into offending the gods, thereby providing them with sacrifices. It is said that without Elegba the *orisha* would starve. . . . Elegba's two-way involvement prompts men to offend the gods on the one hand and aids the gods in their vengeance on the other. He is the force which makes men turn to the *orisha* both in expiation and propitiation. . . . The Yoruba say, "Eshu is the anger of the gods," and that Eshu is the first to visit the victim of an *orisha*. When men are quarreling Elegba is said to be present; when a man has done wrong, he is asked if Elegba prompted him; and when . . . a man's house is struck by lightning, the Yoruba say that Eshu provoked the sin that resulted in the man offending Shango. . . . He is thus the *agent provocateur* and, in a sense, a messenger of the gods. . . . He is superior to the others in cunning, and many myths tell of the battles he has won at their expense.[35]

Even in the apparent repose of sculpture Eshu's restless energy asserts itself, usually in phallic imagery. He is portrayed as a solitary male figure, and his sculptures emphasize his hairdressing, which is often carved as a stylized phallus. Walking, riding, or sitting, his posture expresses action, while the pipe (or whistle or thumb) he always has in his mouth suggests his insatiable orality.[36]

The Yoruba know Eshu as the embodiment of paradox. He is

33. Idowu, *Olódùmare*, p. 81. Cf. Bascom, *Ifa Divination*, pp. 107 ff.
34. Pemberton, "Eshu-Elegba," p. 22.
35. Wescott, "Sculpture and Myths," p. 337.
36. See *ibid.*, pp. 339–40; and Pemberton, "Eshu-Elegba," pp. 22–25.

"the biggest creature with big wooden stick," yet he is so tiny that he must stand "on tiptoe to put salt in the soup." He is both first and last born, old man and child, cunning and capricious. Old or young, he disregards "the normal code; he enjoys the natural licence of the innocent and the privileged licence of the aged. As a child he is the experimenter who breaks rules; as an old man he enjoys the wisdom that takes him beyond rules. Thus . . . the Yoruba say he is the youngest of the *orisha*, but the father of them all."[37] He is given the praise name used for the first born of twins and is thus an "explorer," yet among the Yoruba it is the junior who tests the path for the elder. That is his role among the gods, among the many cults, and among individual humans as well. He sets the gods in contention and reorders their relationships, just as he does among men. He is fecund and beautiful according to some praise-songs (*oriki*), sterile and ugly in others, but always he is the catalyst stimulating the deeply intended relationship between gods and humans. The "exuberance and flamboyance" of his dance, its agility and playful eroticism, embody his power to foment adultery and seduction, yet at the same time celebrate his passion to reorder the intricacies of all relationships.[38]

The similarity between Eshu and Legba is clear, but we must note carefully the Yoruba emphasis on Eshu's vengefulness in contrast to the Fon insistence on Legba's forgiveness. Both embody a pursuit of intercourse so relentless that it shatters every worn-out pattern to enlarge the space of human life. Both, therefore, are troublemakers, disturbers of the peace and disrupters of harmony, yet only Eshu is thought of as "the anger of the gods." "He is notorious for starting fights, killing people by toppling walls and trees on them, and causing calamities to deities and humans alike."[39] His myths speak of his fondness

37. Wescott, "Sculpture and Myths," p. 341.
38. *Ibid.*, pp. 343–44.
39. Bascom, *Ifa Divination*, p. 105.

for sowing confusion, and in daily life people will blame him for stirring up wrong-doing. His praise-songs also stress this theme:

> Eshu fought on Iwata street
>   like a hundred men.
> My father comes with his club.
> Eshu is a wicked child
>   who has inherited a sword.
> Eshu swings a club
>   as an Ifa priest a divining chain. . . .
> Eshu, do not deceive and harm me;
>   deceive another.[40]

Even the senior priestess of Eshu insists that he "deceives and is wicked. Olodumare, who made him, is now doubtful about his creation of Eshu."[41] Indeed, he is so vexatious, so determined to obtain sacrifice, and so vengeful when it is not offered, that Joan Wescott claims that he "is not . . . regarded as an especially humorous figure."[42]

There is, however, another side to Eshu. Wescott herself bears witness to the gaiety of his annual festival, which extends over seventeen days in late December and early January. On the sixth day of the feast, as Eshu's image is carried into the marketplace, the people sing "a gay and inviting song with a jaunty rhythm." As the Eshu-dancer whirls and spins, the song's refrain again and again compares Eshu's mischief with a broken sexual connection:

> We are singing for the sake of Eshu
> He used his penis to make a bridge
> Penis broke in two!
> Travellers fell into the river.

The dance performances . . . create an image of a spirited, jocular, and abandoned deity. His playfulness, as well as his rebellious and defiant nature, are expressed in the dance. While most of Yoruba

40. Pemberton, "Eshu-Elegba," p. 26.
41. *Ibid*.
42. Wescott, "Sculpture and Myths," p. 352.

dance consists of a gentle shuffling, in Eshu's dance there is much wide side-stepping, high kicks, and sudden and violent contractions. The intricate steps and displays of agility are not a characteristic of Yoruba dance generally.[43]

His song proclaims him as a rapidly spinning "snail-shell dancer," who dances so well that "If there are no drums/ He will dance to the pounding of the mortars."[44] That is, Eshu dances daily, not only during his great festival, to the beat that resounds through the compound as food is being prepared by the women. That beat, as ordinary as Eshu's festival beat is exotic, still insists unmistakably on the availability of his libidinal energy for the human world, but this energy can carry passengers along an open road as well as dump them in a river. Eshu's priestess sings during the weekly ritual at his shrine, after she has rubbed the floor with grass that stops bleeding:

> Eshu, I honor you because of your power.
> Eshu, you are the road maker.
> Come with kindness to me and to my family. . . .
> Eshu, you are the present giver.
> Make me rich and the mother of good children. . . .
> Come with your gorgeous appearance, you son of cowries.[45]

This is hardly the portrait of a grim avenger. Indeed, it so ironically yokes together Eshu's disruption and his creativity, and so delightedly celebrates his structural agility, that we must look beyond both the tendency to write him off as a demon and Wescott's far more sophisticated abstraction of him into a principle of social change in the tightly woven mesh of Yoruba life. She maintains that,

by postulating Eshu-Elegba, the Yoruba compensate for the rigidity of their social system . . . and externalize responsibility for any disruption that might occur. . . . Eshu is especially important to the Yoruba because what prompts them to do evil is considered to be outside themselves and they are incapable of holding themselves responsible.

43. *Ibid.*, p. 344.
44. *Ibid.*
45. Pemberton, "Eshu-Elegba," p. 22.

Thus the autonomous Eshu, a creature of instinct and of great energy and power, serves a dual role: as a rule-breaker he is . . . the spanner in the social works, . . . a generating symbol who promotes change by offering opportunities for exploring what possibilities lie beyond the *status quo*.[46]

Such an analysis is partly right, but its too simple psychological and sociological categories distort Eshu's meaning. If words such as "postulating," "compensation," "externalize responsibility," and "generating symbol" fail to describe or explain our own religious structures, as I believe they do, then they are just as unequal to the task of interpreting Eshu. To grasp how the Yoruba can combine in a single figure anger and playful dancing, disruptive and creative sexuality, we need to look at Eshu's ties to Ifa divination.

ESHU AND IFA DIVINATION

Like the Fon, the Yoruba consult diviners at certain crucial moments in their lives. They believe that Ifa, who personifies their system of divination, makes known to them the purposes of Olorun, or Olodumare, and the sacrifices that Eshu will distribute to accomplish these purposes.

The importance of Ifa divination may well be due to the fact that, except for prayers, it apparently provides the most direct access to Olorun, who controls man's destinies. It provides a knowledge of what destiny lies ahead in life, what occupation should be followed, what special tabus are to be observed, which ancestral guardian soul is to receive annual sacrifices, and which deity an individual is to worship. It provides a means of determining what sacrifices are necessary to achieve one's destiny, to receive the blessings that have been promised, and to live out the full span of life that has been assigned.[47]

In all of this Ifa divination gives the Yoruba the language of inner life which the Fon, in making it their own, call "the alphabet of Mawu."

The Yoruba stress especially the discovery through divina-

---

46. Wescott, "Sculpture and Myths," p. 345.
47. Bascom, *Ifa Divination*, p. 118.

tion of the "ancestral guardian soul." This soul, like the *sekpoli* of the Fon, is the heavenly counterpart of the person, with whom he must maintain a constant contact that he might truly *exist*, or "stand forth" in his own full being according to the divine order. But the ancestral guardian, as the name implies, is also the equivalent of the Fon *joto*. Each Yoruba, like each Fon, is known to be at least partially a reemergent clan ancestor. The discovery of this ancestor's identity, then, discloses one's place in the social scheme as well as one's relationship to the gods. Soon after a child's birth, his family consults a diviner to learn the name of the ancestral guardian soul and whatever else Ifa may choose to reveal about the child's destiny. "The figure cast on this occasion is in some ways a chart of the child's future life, and it may be carved into a piece of calabash shell" [48] to serve as an image of that life, for to live fully the child must realize outwardly this fundamental inward figure whose limits are simply the grammar of his human existence.

If these limits cannot be essentially enlarged, they can contract. The fullness of life can be choked off through the enmity of "offended deities, by evil spirits, by 'witches,' by the curses or evil magic of one's enemies, by swearing falsely, at human hands as punishment for crimes." [49] Thus divination is needed to prescribe remedies for many sorts of disorder, and because it touches and links the multitude of human and extrahuman forces present in Yoruba life, it is the practical center of Yoruba religion. Traditionally, everyone

turned to Ifa in time of trouble, and on the advice of the babalawo [diviner] all sacrificed to Eshu and through him to Olorun. This important trinity is . . . available to all, and together Olorun, Ifa, and Eshu grant and assist men to achieve the destiny which is assigned each individual before his ancestral soul is reborn.

The predictions of the babalawo also give practical advice for the client's own behavior, and give warning against slanderers, enemies, and other malefactors. Throughout life an individual consults Ifa in

48. *Ibid.*, p. 115.
49. *Ibid.*, p. 116.

case of illness or trouble, when new ventures are to be undertaken, and when important decisions are to be made.[50]

William Bascom's collection of divination verses enables us to see that Ifa divination is a true sociotherapy, renewing society and social relationships by spelling out the meanings hidden in the sacred language of social order from the beginning, yet always needing to be rediscovered in the present.

Wescott sees Eshu and Ifa as opposing principles of change and order, both needed to ensure the harmony of Yoruba society. However, it seems clear that Idowu is right to recognize in the dynamism of Eshu, which contrasts with Ifa's stasis, an intrinsic superiority. Several tales and divination verses place the work of Ifa (or Orunmila) definitely under Eshu's sway.[51] This control may not be as definitive as that exercised by Legba over Fa, but it is nonetheless operative in practice and apparent in theory. Eshu is charged with overseeing the gods on earth after he has intervened with Olorun to clear the name of Orunmila. He enables Orunmila to marry Earth and a daughter of the sea goddess, not only through the power of prescribed sacrifices, but also because of his own power of transformation. True, Ifa as a system is not the possession of Eshu. Still, Eshu's license to stir up trouble so that sacrifice might be offered to the *orisha* gives him his role as "marshal" of the divine court.[52] More profoundly, it is he who sets in motion the whole divinatory process and oversees the movement from order to disorder to diagnosis to new order. Since this power extends even to Ifa's obligation to divine for himself and to make the appropriate sacrifice, Eshu quite plainly is more than a twin principle of Yoruba divination; or at least he is a Yoruba twin principle—the elder who seems younger because he must lead the way.

The Yoruba are more definite still about Eshu's responsibility for divination. They think of him as the divine messenger, who

50. *Ibid.*, p. 118.
51. *Ibid.*, pp. 105–107, 156–61, 221–27, 553–55.
52. See Frobenius, *The Voice of Africa*, vol. 1, p. 232.

blows his whistle "to clear the way." The *babalawo* to whom John Pemberton spoke claimed that Eshu "sets the affairs of earth in order, guards and helps the children of men, . . . is so swift that he can be the messenger for many, . . . [and] can circle the earth in an instant."[53] Furthermore, Eshu has the agility to balance and harmonize the forces of good and evil:

After Olodumare had created such demons as death, disease, loss, fighting, paralysis, coughs, boils, blisters, elephantiasis, rashes . . . and deities of the hot temper, such as Shopanna and Shango, and after he had created such good things as money, wives, children, long life, and such deities as Oshun and Obatala, then Olodumare created Eshu's power. He made Eshu's power great enough to limit the wicked practices and excesses of the demons . . . [and] such that Eshu could bring to men . . . the blessings of the deities of good things.[54]

The myth telling of the origins of sacrifice also reveals Eshu's role in the creation of divination. Once the gods were hungry because men had stopped sacrificing to them. Eshu decided to put things right. He asked Yemaya for some way to change the situation. Yemaya warned him that both Shopanna and Shango had failed, and suggested that Eshu give men "something so good that they will yearn for it and want to go on living." Then Eshu went to Orungan, who told him of the "big thing made of sixteen palm nuts." When Eshu went to the palm trees, the monkeys gave him sixteen nuts. They told him to go around the world that he might hear "sixteen sayings in each of the sixteen places." Eshu did so, and then returned to the sky to tell the gods what he had learned. They agreed that this knowledge should be given to men that they might know the gods' will and how to escape evil by offering sacrifice. Eshu brought Ifa down to men, and then returned to stay with Ogun, Shango, and Obatala and to watch with them to see how the palm nuts would be used.[55]

---

53. Pemberton, "Eshu-Elegba," p. 27.
54. *Ibid.*
55. See Frobenius, *The Voice of Africa*, vol. 1, pp. 229–32. Cf. Bascom, *Ifa Divination*, p. 107; Westcott, "Sculpture and Myths," p. 337; and Maupoil, *La*

This myth may not be the only explanation of the origins of Ifa divination, but perfect consistency of belief cannot be asked of the Yoruba, among whom such consistency is not an absolute goal any more than it is among other peoples for whom orthodoxy is supremely important. Thus the significance of the myth lies in the way it pinpoints the centrality of Eshu's mediation and explains the meaning of his swiftness. Eshu is Olodumare's messenger, the myth shows, because he establishes true mutuality between gods and men. The gods were hungry, withering away into otiosity because of the forgetfulness and negligence of men. Men were dying, pursued by the anger of the gods, yet perversely unwilling to fear death. Gods and men, in short, were imprisoned by their inability to be what they were except at one another's expense. Eshu establishes mutuality between them by enabling both to become what they are. To men he gives knowledge and thus some control over destiny, in the sense that they have, in Ifa, power to work toward its shaping provided that they "feed" the gods. To the gods Eshu gives the food of homage provided that they share their divine knowledge in an effective way.

Ifa divination is this way of knowledge. In mythic terms, the knowledge of Ifa establishes the world, bringing gods and men into harmony, through three acts of Eshu—his questioning of the gods, his foray into the bush, and his circumambulation of the world. Eshu links together the transparency of the sky and the opacity of the wild, twin sources of knowledge hidden from humans, and then fashions a space that is truly neither sky nor bush because it has access to the potencies of each. These potencies are related, as we have seen before, as center and periphery. The former is too clear, the latter at once too dense and too scattered, to serve as a model for a world fit for

Géomancie, p. 77. Morton-Williams (see "Outline of the Cosmology," p. 250, n. 2) thinks that "Yemoo" (Frobenius: "Yemaya"), or Iye-Mowo, "Mother-Mowo," is the model for the Fon "Mawu." Cf. Verger, *Notes sur le Culte*, pp. 291, 449, 552.

men and women. It is Eshu, in the persistence and the agility of his movement across all boundaries, who defines the limits of this world by shaping an image of it. This image is Ifa, which both humans and gods obey that the world might continuously draw its movement from the transcendent power above it and the endless possibilities beyond it.

Eshu as troublemaker and sociotherapist

In a variety of ways Ifa divination restores order to the Yoruba world, yet the Yoruba always remember that the restoration of order begins with a dissolution of false order, passes through a phase of confusion, and ends with a "new" order, which, in its depth, is a recreation of the world. This memory focuses on Eshu, who brings to the surface hidden conflict and, once Ifa has spoken, knits together in true mutuality the relationships that forgetfulness, ignorance, passion, malice, or sheer routine have severed. The divination verses referring directly to Eshu show him at the center of every sort of disharmony—human, divine, animal, vegetable, and economic (which often draws together all the others).[56] Thus he oversees the gods, dethrones Frog and the King of the Termites, kills Dove and saves Pigeon, enters the struggles of Hyena and Cock, and decides which trees are worthy to be spared and which must be destroyed. He even intervenes on behalf of the obedient Calico, while the 165 nonsacrificing cloths must "die" with their owner. Moreover, Eshu works his will through magic powers of transformation. He claps his hands, throws dust, blinks his eyes, points his staff, and so creates beauty or ugliness, changes trees into warriors, makes paths into dead ends. Thus at every level of life—human, transhuman, subhuman, even posthuman—Eshu, the agent of metamorphosis, prepares for and completes the divinatory process as he shapes structures, rearranges hierarchies, and changes relationships.

56. See Bascom, *Ifa Divination*, pp. 105–6.

Eshu's metamorphic powers suggest just how his work is linked to the cosmic pattern of Ifa divination. As he discloses that human life lies at the center of a vast network of forces, his own activity keeps those forces flowing to reestablish this life. In this light the myths about Eshu take on deeper significance for understanding his involvement with divination. One of them, for example, tells how he persuaded the sea god, the sun god, and the moon god to exchange homes. Orishala ("the great *orisha*," or Obatala[57]) ordered them to return to their proper places, but Eshu threatened to kill the moon god if he did not try again to claim the house of the sun, and eventually set the two of them quarrelling. Eshu also threatened the sea god, and then sent him into the bush. In anger Orishala sent Shopanna, the god of smallpox, to the sea god to transform him into a hill and his children into monkeys. When Shopanna went to punish Eshu, who was in the marketplace, Eshu got the better of him. Hearing the fight, the sun god dazzled Eshu with his light so that he was at Shopanna's mercy. Orishala commanded all men to rejoice in Eshu's defeat, but Eshu fled to the river to bathe his wounds and imparted to the water the power to give smallpox to all who wash in it. "So Eshu's mischief has been handed down to mankind and remains a living thing." [58]

The importance of this myth here is that it shows Eshu as the agent of cosmic transformation. True, the sun and the moon return to their proper places, but Eshu has forced them to move in different patterns. Even more clearly, he has brought the potential of the sea into the earth itself by provoking the transformation of the sea's formlessness into the rawness of the bush. In moving this endless source of fluidity nearer to the human world, Eshu unleashes forces of destruction at the same time as he more sharply defines the boundaries of that life. Both the greater possibility of dissolution and the sharper

57. See Morton-Williams, "Outline of the Cosmology," p. 250, n. 2.
58. Frobenius, *The Voice of Africa*, vol. 1, pp. 236–38.

definition of life are symbolized by the introduction of smallpox, a kind of watery fire, which in turn is emblematic of all mischief, of all those forces which define life precisely by threatening it with dissolution.[59] Yet the myth speaks of mischief, not of evil. Like Ananse, Eshu brings disease into human life, but, because Eshu's impulse toward exchange brings about this apparent change for the worse, it creates the necessity for further transformation and opens new roads between heaven and earth.

Two other myths trace this theme in the practice of divination, the first indirectly, the second directly. Idowu relates the well-known story of how Eshu brought disharmony to a man and his two wives.[60] They had been a model of harmony, but Eshu set them at one another's throats by selling first one wife and then the other beautiful caps for their husband. Eshu kept supplying caps, each one more splendid than the last, until the wives were competing fiercely for their husband's favor. At last Eshu did not appear in the market, the cycle of competition jerked to a halt, and the family exploded in anger and reproach.

Even though the myth is apparently not a divination verse, the tale concerns just that kind of conflict which commonly brings people to seek Ifa's help. Polygyny is inherently explosive. Its potential for sexual competition is symbolized in the myth, but its explosiveness lies not merely in the dynamite of sex, but in the intrinsic instability of any three-cornered relationship. It is the chemistry of this relationship which Eshu toys with until it flashes into conflict. On the surface he is the cause, or at least the instigator, of that conflict; more deeply, he is its revealer. He exposes the instability of the superficially peaceful family by laying bare real lines of opposition that must be dealt with so that a more truthful structure—one more in touch with the forces shaping a polygynous marriage—can emerge.

59. Cf. Herskovits, *Dahomey*, vol. 2, pp. 135–39.
60. Idowu, *Olódùmare*, p. 82.

The most famous story of Eshu's exploits shows this aspect of his work even more clearly and relates it directly to divination. Once two friends owned adjoining farms. They dressed alike and were in all ways a model of friendship. Eshu decided to make them differ. He used to walk each morning on the path between the two farms, and one day set out wearing a multi-colored cap, variously described as red and white; red, white, and blue; or red, white, green, and black. He also put his pipe at the nape of his neck instead of in his mouth, and let his staff hang over his back instead of his chest. He greeted the friends, already working in their fields, and passed on. Later they began to argue about the color of his cap and which way he was going. (According to Pemberton's version, at this point Eshu returned going the other way, and the argument heated up when each friend insisted that the other had been right the first time.) Soon they came to blows. When they were brought before the king, Eshu confessed to igniting the quarrel because "sowing dissension is my great delight." When the king tried to bind Eshu, he fled, started a fire in the bush, hurled burning grass on the town, and then mixed up the possessions that the townsfolk hauled out of their houses. A dreadful row began, and as Eshu ran off laughing, he boasted that everyone had played his game well.[61]

The relevance of this story to divination is obvious. In the first place, Eshu causes trouble by walking along the boundary between the two friends, a boundary that they do not, in fact, acknowledge. They dress alike and are inseparable, yet they are not one, but two. Furthermore, neither of them can encompass the other's vision. They notice Eshu's clothing, his staff, and his pipe, but neither really *sees* his movement—or what the other sees. They are bound by habit. It is the past that holds them, not the present. Finally, their quarrel reveals all sorts of suppressed animosity. One of the sayings of the desert fathers tells how two old brothers tried, for the sake of humil-

---

61. See Frobenius, *The Voice of Africa*, vol. 1, pp. 240–42. Bascom mentions four Yoruba versions of this myth; *Ifa Divination*, p. 132.

ity, to start a quarrel, but failed because they were detached even from their own opinions.[62] Here, on the contrary, there was surface harmony, but underneath lay suspicion, anger, and violence. The friendship was held together by custom, not by mutual awareness and a willingness to undergo modification together. Thus Eshu has only to draw attention to the real boundary between them to shatter their false peace and to infect the world with their poison.

Such a story, of course, is as familiar to the Yoruba as it is to us, and its use as a divination verse shows that it is precisely this sort of commonplace disorder that brings people to diviners.[63] Simply leafing at random through the verses, one sees how aware the Yoruba are that the internal and external boundaries of their lives are charged with power, that these must be explored carefully to overcome stagnation and to deal with explosions, and that they must be constantly transformed to heal division and renew life. Insolent wives and vindictive husbands, the elusiveness of life's blessings, the power of slander or disease to destroy a family, the chanciness of public office, the arbitrary annoyance of the gods, the risks of polygyny, pregnancy, and travel, the malice of evil spirits, the dangers of growing old, the vicissitudes of sex, the touchiness of ancestors, and the inescapable dangers of the market—these are not only the symbolic settings and proverbial interpretations of the divinatory figures, but the very situations that necessitate divination. Suddenly the lines tying persons to one another, to ancestors, to gods, to groups within society either harden or crumble. Order becomes a prison or threatens to dissolve altogether. The passages of life are clogged and finally rupture, and then, in the language of the myths, all becomes as fluid as water, as random as fire, until peace erupts into violence. Divination, then, seeks to open these passages of

62. *The Wisdom of the Desert*, ed. Thomas Merton (New York: New Directions Publishing Corp., 1960), p. 67.
63. Bascom, *Ifa Divination*, p. 311.

life by transforming them into *limina*, ways out of rigidity, thresholds of larger meaning.

The *babalawo*, the "father of secrets," aims to make "known and visible . . . albeit in symbolic guise, the unknown and invisible agents of affliction" [64] in his clients' lives and to broaden for them the range of the possible. As he seeks the healing of the past and a map for the future, the *babalawo* looks to Ifa, whose servant he is, for a disclosure of the network of relationships that makes its unique epiphany in the person seated before him. In mending the breaks or in widening the scope of that network, therefore, the divinatory process is a true sociotherapy, concerned with revealing the meanings of the outer as well as the inner environment of the client. The complex symbolism of this process and its emphasis on transhuman factors cannot be sliced away, a priori, by Occam's razor as excess primitive baggage. These factors are, rather, in Victor Turner's phrase, part of a "semantic structure," which enables the diviner to reach down into the unconscious, back into the past, out into the social order, and across into that realm of the sacred which surrounds, underpins, and in some mysterious way mirrors the human world. In the living moment of a definite social order, this total analysis is the heart of Ifa divination. At this moment the language of the Yoruba is enlarged to name and to humanize an otherwise unintelligible and therefore unassimilable event. Here, at the moment of an enlargement that is also a transformation of non-sense to sense, of impasse to passage, the Yoruba see Eshu, as the Fon see Legba, working most characteristically.

It is no wonder, then, that the Yoruba say that Ifa turns feces into treasure or that "thorns turn evil into good" when Eshu interferes to make chaos out of what looked like order. [65] Eshu's "magic eyes" are transforming eyes. By a blink he makes Orunmila handsome, and so too does his "vision" expose dis-

---

64. Turner, *Ndembu Divination*, p. 3.
65. See Bascom, *Ifa Divination*, pp. 247 and 311.

order hidden beneath the appearance of order to stimulate the discovery of true harmony. Thus it is Eshu who embodies the very meaning of Ifa. It is he who reveals it as a truly liminal experience—a passage out of a structure cut off somehow from the real shape of things, into a time and a space capable of showing forth this shape, and finally back into a structure renewed and enlarged by the act of sacrifice.

As Pemberton observed so clearly, Eshu's ceaseless promotion of sacrifice is the key to understanding the way in which the Yoruba know him as a living actor in the complex drama of their lives, and not as a "postulate" or a "generating symbol" in a philosophical system.[66] An explanation of Yoruba myth leaving Eshu at the level of abstraction and mere ideology has a surface plausibility: Eshu stirs up trouble because he signifies the need for a release from social tension through sacrifice; Olorun through Ifa, his interpreter, smooths out the paths of life once again as Eshu delivers the appointed sacrifices to the appropriate gods; if the sacrifices are not forthcoming, Eshu provokes still more trouble until order is fully restored. But such an explanation reduces to soulless mechanism a vision that is insistently personal. Thus, when offering a prescribed sacrifice, one says, "Eshu, here is my sacrifice. Please tell Olorun . . . to accept my sacrifice and relieve my suffering."[67] Life is at stake, and since life is above all a web of purposeful relationships, the restoration of life means the forging of new relationships through the sacred intimacy of sacrifice:

> The world is broken into pieces;
> The world is split wide open,
> The world is broken without anybody to mend it;
> The world is split open without anybody to sew it.
> Cast Ifa for the six elders
> Who were coming down from Ile Ife.
> They were asked to take care of Mole.
> They were told that they would do well

66. See Wescott, "Sculpture and Myths," p. 345.
67. Bascom, *Ifa Divination*, p. 60.

> If they made sacrifice.
> If the sacrifice of Eshu is not made,
> It will not be acceptable [in heaven].[68]

How does Eshu make sacrifice "acceptable"? First, he embodies the liminal moment that is divination. If he did not, there would be no passage from affliction through a state of inner transformation to a social situation brought into tune again with the ultimate powers shaping it, because there could then be no meeting between those powers and the one in distress. After all, the Yoruba know how to handle disputes and problems in "secular" ways, that is, through discussions, the advice of wise men, and a system of law.[69] But in divination they experience something else: a personal partaking of Eshu's agility, which enables him to slip through invisible cracks in seemingly impenetrable structures and to speed into an endless number of presences simultaneously, no matter how great the distance separating them. In sacrifice, the offerer sacramentally travels with Eshu to the new place, the new relationship, which will restore his life to wholeness.

But Eshu's power is even more directly linked to the nature of sacrifice. Another divination verse proclaims:

Ifa says that this person should . . . put the head of a goat inside the sacrifice for Eshu. . . . Ifa says that Death is now ready to kill the person; but if he can make plenty of sacrifice, he will wriggle out of danger.

> . . . "Exchange, exchange" the Ifa priest
> Of the household of Elepe
> Cast Ifa for Elepe.
> He was told to exchange an animal
> For his life on account of Death.[70]

All sacrifice in some way is ritualized, reversed, converted loss—death transformed into life by a mysterious process of

68. See W. Abimbola, *Odu of Ifa: Yoruba Text and Translation* (unpublished), vol. 2, ch. 5; quoted by Pemberton, "Eshu-Elegba," p. 67.

69. See William Bascom, *The Yoruba of Southwestern Nigeria*, pp. 38–41.

70. See Abimbola, *Odu of Ifa*, vol. 2, ch. 10; quoted by Pemberton, "Eshu-Elegba," pp. 67–68.

exchange.[71] This is no crude bargain between man and insatiable divine powers; rather, it is a kind of ritual shortcut, a hastening of the way man always becomes man. In plants and animals the world yields itself to us; their death is our life as that very act of eating which declares our materiality, our inescapable need for something solid to fill our bellies and somewhere earthly to empty our bowels, also enables that unseeable whatever-it-is within to lift itself from this world in thought and word and silence into communion with that which has never reaped or sowed, hunted or gathered, and never will. In sacrifice this exchange happens more directly. We load our burden of death onto whatever we think can bear it, expecting that it, not we, will be consumed, hoping that through some mystery of cosmic yielding, here too our eating will lift us up into transmaterial communion. Such also is the Yoruba hope, and in that hope they look to Eshu, certainly not as the yielder of life or the source of the invisible, but as the establisher of communion, the master of exchange.

The Yoruba say, "Though the offering is difficult, it is not worse than death." [72] Eshu's power to move across the boundary between death and life and to exchange the death of the victim for increased life for its offerer is imaged in his sexual vitality. Once, a divination verse says, the sixteen male *orisha* roused the anger of Oshun, the leader of the ancestral mothers, by refusing to admit her to their gathering. Her jealousy made them impotent and brought the human world to the edge of chaos. When Orunmila divined, he learned the need for sacrifice to Olodumare to avert the world's collapse into death.

Only to the child Esu, once born of Osun and the male orisa, was the door of heaven open. When he carried the sacrifices,

> Ase spread and expanded on earth;
> Semen became child,

71. See Pemberton, "Eshu-Elegba," p. 68; cf. Lienhardt, *Divinity and Experience*, pp. 296–97.
72. R. C. Abraham, *Dictionary of Modern Yoruba* (London: University of London Press, 1958), p. 172.

> Men on sick beds got up,
> All the world became pleasant.
> It became powerful.
> Fresh crops were brought from farm.
> Yam developed.
> Maize matured.
> Rain was falling.
> All rivers were flooded.
> Everybody was happy.

Sexual vitality, while making male and female aware of their radical difference, is the mediating power which overcomes the opposition. It is a gracious power which cannot be presumed upon. The man must give of his semen, the women of herself in childbirth; each must die in a very "real" sense, if life is to be sustained.[73]

This power (*aṣe*) belongs supremely to Eshu, and whoever ignores him will experience it as frantic, wayward sexuality. But whoever pays heed to his directives will know it as the vessel of life renewed.

Eshu makes possible the discovery that a rupture in the human world implies a discontinuity also in the relationships that create and sustain it, and by redrawing the lines of those relationships he reforms the inner design of the human world as well. When a suppliant offers sacrifice, he touches his head with the victim and then sprinkles its blood on the image of the *orisha*, acknowledging his "death-boundedness," but allowing the gift of the victim's life to link his personal destiny and the power of the *orisha* in a new way.[74] Eshu's work is to bring this meeting about, thus overcoming both human death and divine otiosity. He insists on the line of division between the two friends, but if they could admit their twoness, he would make of that line a path to authentic oneness. Thus Eshu really does move two ways—shattering peace, yet dancing to the noise of mortars; stirring lust, yet enabling semen to become child— and his movement is always single and recreative. He does have two sides, but both disclose a hidden wholeness. He is

73. Pemberton, "Cluster of Sacred Symbols," p. 25.
74. *Ibid.*, p. 26; cf. Pemberton, "Eshu-Elegba," p. 70.

always betwixt and between, but even when the friction caused by his agility sets the world ablaze, its heat offers the possibility of a fusion of opposing forces.

ESHU AS ICONOGRAPHER

The Yoruba, therefore, no matter how sincerely they speak of Eshu as the anger of the gods and the provoker of disharmony, know him on a deeper level to be the reshaper of daily life through divination and sacrifice. He is the iconographer of the cosmos. The symbolic meanings of the divining tray (*opon Ifa*) give persuasive evidence of this. Eshu's face dominates the carving along the border of the tray, which is divided into four quarters.[75] According to Leo Frobenius and William Bascom, when in use the divining tray is always placed with the head of Eshu toward the east so that the quarters of the tray are in a set relation to the diviner.[76] As informant told Frobenius that, in the beginning, when all was still "in great confusion, and old and young things dead," Olodumare had told Eshu to set in order the region where the sun rose. Another informant confirmed this association of Eshu with the east in explaining the divisions of the divining tray in this way:

He put East, West, North and South together as the limbs . . . of a cross. . . . Then he called the line running East and West the "Chief Way," that from South to North the "Second Way." When asked the difference between the two, he said Edju [Eshu] met Shango on the first, and Obatalla visited Ogun on the second. Obviously, then, Edju rules the East, Shango the West, Obatalla the South, and Ogun the North.[77]

These associations were confirmed by the presence of four containers in the "caskets," or carrying cases, of the diviners, which held substances appropriate to the four *orisha*—sulphur

75. See Frobenius, *The Voice of Africa*, vol. 1, p. 248; Bascom, *Ifa Divination*, p. 34; and Maupoil, *La Géomancie*, plate viii. Frobenius claims that the diviner also places a seventeenth, or "sentinel," nut on the tray to represent Eshu.

76. See Bascom, *Ifa Divination*, p. 34.

77. Frobenius, *The Voice of Africa*, vol. 1, p. 254.

for Eshu, charcoal for Shango, chalk for Obatala, and red-
wood for Ogun—in the same relation to the cardinal points of
the compass.

Now Yoruba color symbolism is complex, but still it is fascinating to speculate, with Frobenius, that the famous story of
Eshu's passage along the boundary between the two friends'
fields may refer to this cosmic pattern.[78] Whether Eshu's hat
was red and white, or green, black, red, and white, the story
certainly hinges on a reversal of colors and of Eshu's normal
way of moving. If Eshu usually moves from east to west, bringing light into darkness, as the celebration of his great feast
shortly after the winter solstice also implies, then a reversal
of that movement would bring darkness and chaos—exactly
what happens in the story. As a two-sided figure, Eshu simultaneously dissolves and reshapes the world, but always with
the goal of reestablishing the cosmic order intended by Olodumare.

Moreover, it seems clear that the four-day Yoruba week reflects temporally the spatial organization of the cosmos. Each
day is sacred to one of the four *orisha* who reign in the earth's
four quarters. Even though the gods associated with the days
may not everywhere have been the same, the first day of the
week was always market day.[79] Thus Eshu, the god of the
market, the lord of exchange, presides over the beginning of
the week and also over its close in the market that begins the
next week, just as he does over the beginning of the day, the
beginning of the year, the beginning of the world, and the beginning of the order restored through divination. Divination,
then, can reorder the world because Ifa, as system and technique, as art and mystery, is an icon of man's place in the cosmos. Wherever or whenever that place is lost, Eshu brings

78. See Pemberton, "Cluster of Sacred Symbols," pp. 9–13, 22. Cf. Leo
Frobenius, *La Mythologie de l'Atlantide*, trans. F. Gidon (Paris: Payot, 1949), pp.
253–55.

79. Ojo, *Yoruba Culture*, p. 204. Cf. Bascom, *Ifa Divination*, p. 102.

about an awareness of the loss, sees to its rediscovery through divination, and restores it through the sacred exchange of sacrifice.

Ifa as iconography

Despite his failings as an ethnographer, Frobenius clearly saw into the heart of Ifa divination. Other studies of divination, far deeper than his, and other structures of Yoruba life, far more meticulously examined, support his realization that Ifa is a true *imago mundi*, an icon of the Yoruba cosmos. This aspect of divination both Bernard Maupoil and Carl Jung, in vastly dissimilar ways, have spotted. In linking divination to mythology, social order, and other rituals, Maupoil suggests that these help in understanding not only what a people thinks, but how; not only what they want to create and recreate, produce and reproduce, but how they want to do it. Because Maupoil locates divination within the process that shapes a people's image of their life, he discloses its iconographic purposes. Moreover, his comments on Legba support the notion of the trickster as divine iconographer.[80] Like Eshu, Legba queries, challenges, shatters, and redraws the structures of life. In so doing, both reveal the sacredness of ambiguity itself and enlarge the total pattern of meaning that is society, reshaping it more closely to the design of the cosmos itself.

Jung, on the other hand, enables us to see how a cast of palm nuts, coins, or divining chain becomes at once a part and an epiphany of the unique constellation of forces and events making up any given moment. The cast can reveal the moment because it is part of an entire system that is an image of the whole cosmos. Furthermore, Jung calls the principle behind the assumption that the divinatory cast lays bare the essential structure of a client's situation "synchronicity," and contrasts it with the principle of causality. The latter, he says, "is a sort of working hypothesis of how events evolve one out of another,

80. Maupoil, *La Géomancie*, pp. 75–84. See especially pp. 80–82.

whereas synchronicity takes the coincidence of events in space and time as meaning something more than mere chance, namely, a peculiar interdependence of objective events among themselves as well as with the subjective (psychic) states of the observer or observers." [81] The difference between synchronicity and causality lies in the evaluation of chance in human affairs. The purely empiric view admits ignorance of the totality of causal factors; the "synchronic" view looks instead to non-material causes, both spiritual and psychic, in coincidence with material causes, to account for the singular shape of a given event. In other words, to discover in this latter view why a wall falls on a man, one must know why he sat beside it as well as why it was weak.

Such is the Yoruba vision of reality, and since it immediately looks to personal situations as well as to physical causes, it is radically social in character. The man who sits beside the soon-to-fall wall belongs to a certain family and village, has certain ancestors, knows and worships certain gods, has done these things and not done those, has these friends and those enemies. He is at the center of a particular network of personal relationships; indeed, he is that network. What could be more sensible, therefore, than to describe where he has stood or sat by means of a special mode of that other network which both springs from and reflects social order itself, by means, that is, of language? A special form of language is needed because the very nature of the situation involves those—gods, ancestors, animals, trees—who do not speak in the words of ordinary Yoruba, yet the language of synchronicity will remain a Yoruba language for all that. It may originate in heaven, but it must communicate to and be passed on by the Yoruba on earth. It must provide the possibility of diagnosis and healing for them because they alone among the actors in the drama at hand are neither all-seeing nor purely instinctual.

The great genius of the I Ching is that it relates the cosmic

81. Jung, Introduction to the *I Ching*, p. xxiv.

pattern of a moment, with all that it means in terms of Chinese cosmology, social order, and psychology, to the semihiero-glyphic forms of Chinese characters. Each cast, therefore, manifests some hidden depth in the ordinary words used to speak about life, and at the same time shows forth the hidden design of the moment, so serious and so mysterious, in the sixty-four simple images in which the whole Chinese world discloses itself. Ifa lacks this linguistic elegance, yet it possesses its own complexity and powerful numinosity. In societies without an alphabet and a written language, the patterns of divination are the simplest and the most concrete abstractions of social experience. They are the language of the people reduced to its most essential shapes and revealing its most crucial meanings. Combined with the verses and the myths appropriate to the casts, these patterns give names to events that have been nameless, and form out of the previously form-less an image that embodies the world. This image has trans-forming power because it assimilates a given moment to the all-creative power that brought the human world into being in the beginning. Thus Eshu brings Ifa into play to heal the past and redefine the future by revealing what must be done—what relationships deepened, dropped, or started, what *orisha* recognized or appeased, what practices reinforced or discarded—so that this world can, again or still, show itself in the life of a single one of its Yoruba members.

Yoruba iconography

Other features of Yoruba culture confirm this vision of div-ination as iconography. In the first place, Yoruba carvings, masks, and brasses are rich and various. In this love for the plastic arts they are a typical West African people, although it seems that their art forms are exceptionally varied and their traditions especially ancient.[82] Yet this very typicality witness-

82. The Yoruba may be the "most prolific of the art-producing tribes of Africa," Bascom, *The Yoruba*, p. 108. Cf. Ojo, *Yoruba Culture*, pp. 236–68.

es to an iconographic vision, to a way of relating the most commonplace realities to the most cosmic, which the Yoruba share with other West Africans.

Denis Williams has insisted that one must draw a careful distinction between "Orisha art," which is "symbolic of the spirit," and "Ogboni art," which, "in contrast, is sacred and worshiped as the actual vessel of the spirit."[83] He opposes the descriptive and humanistic qualities of the former to the archetypal and hieratic qualities of the latter, and sees the formal aspects of Orisha art as abstract and architectonic, those of Ogboni art as iconic and linear. No doubt he is right to draw these distinctions, especially insofar as they relate to the cult of Onile, the goddess-mother who owns the earth and who, like Olodumare, is never given a human form. It is certainly no accident, furthermore, that the Ogboni images are more strictly conventional than others, and are done in metal, not in wood.

Nevertheless, certain of Williams's comparisons of Ogboni art to Christian iconography suggest that his distinction between "symbolic" and "actual" idioms is too rigid and obscures a sacramental quality common to all Yoruba art. In discussing the making of the *edan Ogboni*, the ceremonial staff of the Ogboni society, he says that its first function is

the materialization of an essence in its primary association with Earth. The image . . . is already sacred in its own right, and implies no visual referent. In the second function the image is defined as the vehicle of the spirit, a localization capable of response, standing in a particular relationship to the suppliant. . . . At its inception, then, the image is produced in accordance with observances referring to these two principal functions. Its idiom, like the Christian cross, must in the first place convey the iconic theme by which it is to be recognizable from every other plastic rendering, but unlike the Christian cross this idiom is not symbolic; it is actual, referring to nothing outside itself.[84]

However, anyone who has witnessed the "adoration" of the cross on Good Friday in a Catholic Church or who has listened

83. Denis Williams, "Iconology of the Yoruba *Edan-Ogboni*," p. 139.
84. *Ibid.*, p. 144.

to the Orthodox hymns for the Feast of the Exaltation of the Cross knows that, for sacramental Christians, the cross embodies the sacrality it symbolizes, even though it is not a sacrament in the strict sense. Moreover, when Williams says that "where the Byzantine Icon is particular and illustrative . . . , the *edan* is the actual vessel of a spirit, i.e., where the Byzantine Icon is a picture, the *edan* is an image . . . [having] no visual referent,"[85] he misunderstands the real nature of the icon and obscures the crucial connections that Yoruba iconography of every sort has with other creations of Yoruba culture.

There is no need for a lengthy discussion of the abstract character of the Byzantine or Russian icon; a single example will serve.[86] In the great icon of the Holy Trinity painted by Rublev, the three angels who visited Abraham are seated at a table upon which there is a cup of wine. Clearly, a whole theology is implicit in the icon, just as there is in the simplest *edan*, but the icon is also radically nonrepresentational. It is the visual image of a verbal image (the story in Genesis) of a bodily image (the human form of the angels) of a spiritual image (the angels in their nonmaterial nature) of God. The iconographer, like the *edan*-casters and also like the carvers of masks and sculptures, does not draw a picture of the Center of sacredness. Indeed, his objective is to create a sacred reality linking the observer with that Center through a two-fold movement—the embodiment of the mystery and the spiritualization of the human gaze. The Yoruba are also confident of their ability to manifest and maintain in iconographic form the spiritual forces that mold their world, not only in the hieratic brass figures of the Ogboni society, but in the more fluid, pic-

85. *Ibid.*, p. 162.

86. In the icons of the Christian East, "illusory three-dimensional space is replaced by the plane of reality; the connection between figures and objects becomes conventionally symbolical . . . . The artist . . . reduced forms to . . . a simplicity, the depth of whose inner content is accessible only to the spiritual eye." Leonid Ouspensky and Vladimir Lossky, *The Meaning of Icons*, trans. G. E. H. Palmer and E. Kadloubovsky (Boston: Boston Books, 1955), p. 29. Cf. pp. 201–4.

torial images of mask and sculpture. Indeed, the variety and the exuberance of Yuruba iconographic activity make it clear that Ifa divination is special, not because of its iconic purposes, but because of its universality and power.

The Yoruba city as icon

Further support for this view of the persistent iconographic tendency of Yoruba life can be drawn from its remarkably urban character and from the plan according to which Yoruba cities and towns were traditionally built. As Douglas Fraser says, "the most elaborate development toward urbanism in precolonial Africa took place among the Yoruba of western Nigeria and Dahomey. . . . [The figures] indicate that many Yoruba were already living in towns when the majority of Africans still resided in homesteads or villlages."[87] Furthermore, these ancient cities were all designed similarly.

The classical plan of a Yoruba town resembles a wheel; the oba's [ruler's] palace being the hub, the town walls the rim, and the spokes a series of roads radiating out from the palace and linking the town to other centers. Beyond the walls lie the farmplots. . . .

This form of town plan derives from the sociopolitical structure of each Yoruba kingdom. . . . The oba's palace is the converging focus of all interests; each road passes through a quarter under a quarter-chief, and all the quarters, as well as the compounds of their chiefs, look towards the palace.[88]

Each city, of course, has its own individual characteristics, but each shows this same general pattern, the significance of which has much to say about the centrality of Eshu in Yoruba life.

Frobenius reported that the design of Ife, with its four major and twelve minor "quarters," mirrored quite precisely the divine order, of which Ifa divination was a more abstract image,

---

87. Douglas Fraser, *Village Planning in the Primitive World*, p. 41. Cf. Ojo, *Yoruba Culture*, p. 104.

88. Krapf-Askari, *Yoruba Towns and Cities*, p. 39 see pp. 180–87. Cf. Fraser, *Village Planning*, plates 63–70.

but no one else seems to have unearthed the mythic model that Frobenius found.[89] G. J. Afolabi Ojo, however, agrees that the Yoruba city was a sacred microcosm. The city of Ife is unquestionably the ancient center of the Yoruba world, the navel of the cosmos, where Oduduwa, the divine ancestor of the people, established the earth, created man, and apportioned "the land surface among himself and [his] sixteen assistants."[90] Certainly four and its multiples are sacred for the Yoruba; quite evidently Yoruba cities, in their association of wards and quarters with the divine pantheon and its cults, are conceived of as sacred space; and most probably Ibadan's sixteen gates and the internal walls of other towns indicate that they reflected a mythical prototype.[91] Yet if the pattern of Yoruba towns does not mirror in any simple way the design of the mythic cosmos, it does reflect the shape of human arrangements, thus suggesting a more subtle form of urban iconography in which the town would reveal the sacredness of human space precisely in its ordering of the social, political, and economic dimensions of that space. The places where the Yoruba live, then, would be icons of the cosmos just because they are places of human relationship, power, and every sort of intercourse.

The structure of the Yoruba cosmos

Although studies that would definitively establish the links between Yoruba cities and the Yoruba cosmos have yet to be made, Morton-Williams and Pemberton have managed to break out of the frame imposed on Yoruba cosmology by the Western misunderstanding of African polytheism and to imagine, in the truest sense, that cosmology in a new way. One version of the Yoruba creation myth tells how Olorun sent Oduduwa forth in a canoe, which floated on the waters of the still inchoate earth. Oduduwa poured sandy soil on the water,

---

89. See Krapf-Askari, *Yoruba Towns and Cities*, p. 40.

90. Ojo, *Yoruba Culture*, p. 194.

91. See Krapf-Askari, *Yoruba Towns and Cities*, p. 40. Cf. Ojo, *Yoruba Culture*, p. 133, for the plan of Ado-Ekiti.

and a five-toed chicken he had brought with him scratched and spread the soil to create the earth. Then humans were made, Ife founded, and Oduduwa became its first king.[92]

In all forms of this myth the threefold structure of the cosmos is clear enough—a preexisting, primeval sky and ocean and a subsequently created habitable world. Yoruba have names for these three: for the firmament . . . , *ile orun*, house of the sky, or *oke orun*, hill of the sky; for the lowest level, *ile*, which . . . means Earth rather than water. The primeval waters must be thought of as . . . equivalent to the Earth. . . . The middle zone, the habitable land, is called *ile aiye*, the house of the World.

This term *aiye*, world, has a wide meaning: it means the civilized, ordered world, organized into states and governed by kings, the place where people live amidst their cultivated land; it includes the pattern or idea of life properly lived and . . . does not seem to include the distant uncultivated bush or the forest.[93]

As Morton-Williams says, we are not dealing here with geography, but with images of the state and the cosmic order. In fact, we are dealing with a sacred geography, with a world lying between and in vital relationship with both Sky and Earth, Olorun and Onile. Each has his or her associates through whom both involve themselves in the movements of human life so that life in the middle realm, *"ile aiye*, the house of the World, is good only when good relationships are maintained with the gods and spirits of the other two."[94]

Morton-Williams, then, has rejected the usual hierarchical model of the Yoruba cosmos in favor of a far more sophisticated, far more clearly imagined three-tiered world. He thereby gives Onile her proper place, sets the Ogboni cult in its rightful position, and broadens the symbolic meanings of the mediation of Eshu and Ifa. In addition, his system does not merely classify spiritual beings by function, but assigns them to their proper "domain." Pemberton, moreover, makes it clear

92. See Morton-Williams, "Outline of the Cosmology," p. 243. Cf. Pemberton, "Cluster of Sacred Symbols," pp. 8–10.

93. Morton-Williams, "Outline of the Cosmology," p. 244. See p. 249, fig. 1.

94. *Ibid.*, p. 246.

that these domains are more than transcendent cosmic spaces. His chief concern is to make a structuralist analysis of the Yoruba pantheon and to map it in a way that shows how the Yoruba have resolved the dangerous oppositions of life/death and nature/polity.[95] But in showing, for example, how Olorun divides his creative work between Obatala, who fashions human bodies, and Oduduwa, who founds the state, he helps us see how *ile aiye*, the physical, political world of daily Yoruba experience, holds in balance all the sacred forces that create and surround it.

Thus through the elaborate cults serving each of the great *orisha* as well as through the great cults of the Earth—Ogboni, Egungun, and Oro—the powers of Olorun and Onile are actively present in the human world. Their presence manifests itself not only in cultic activities, but in the assignment of well-defined areas of the towns as the property of the gods and their cults. Each of these areas is governed by a clan chief, and each of these chiefs belongs to a ruling body (Council of State) standing in structural opposition to the ruler (*oba*) and his palace organization.[96] The *oba*, in a sense hidden like Olorun, nevertheless possesses royal power, and his palace is located in the center of each town. Morton-Williams shows too that the Ogboni cult, which has a lodge in the palace itself and a temple just outside it, performs a mediating function between the *oba* and the Council of State.[97] Ifa divination, constantly consulted in questions dealing with public offices as well as in humbler matters, has a similar function for every segment of society. In Oyo the head diviner, the Onalemole, used to live near the palace, and in Ife the sixteen royal diviners were intimately associated with the court.[98] Finally, in each town the market just outside the royal compound has a shrine to Eshu,

95. Pemberton, "Cluster of Sacred Symbols," pp. 7–9, 23.

96. Morton-Williams, "Outline of the Cosmology," p. 253. Cf. Bascom, *The Yoruba*, p. 30.

97. Morton-Williams, "Outline of the Cosmology," p. 253.

98. *Ibid.*, p. 254. See Bascom, *The Yoruba*, p. 91.

properly attended by a special priest and priestess, who oversee the operations of the market itself.

Therefore the tightly interwoven web of political, religious,
economic, and social activities that daily shape Yoruba life is
related physically as well as theoretically to the town's design.
If that design lacks the simple elegance which Frobenius found
in Ife, it also differs from Morton-Williams' three-tiered cosmos. When the "closed calabash" of Yoruba cosmology is imaged by a Yoruba town, it looks rather like an atomic blueprint,
a physical description of the coalescence and interplay of many
forces, all held in balance by the careful distribution of the
energies of attraction and repulsion. The "atom" even has its
nucleus—not a monadic center, but a system of particles of
varying energies held together both by momentum and by delicate equilibrium. True, this human world is the place where
the realms of heaven and earth meet, but the relationship between them, which keeps on shaping that human place, has a
dynamism that is not really conveyed by the metaphor of a
closed calabash or a triple-decked universe.

Olorun and Oduduwa are, in the person of the king, not
above, but in the center. Onile, through the Ogboni cult, is not
beneath, but also in the center, yet her centrality is innately
mediatory. At the same time, both Olorun and Onile are "beyond," truly transcendent, the former in the transparency of
his own divinity and in the hiddenness of the king, the latter in
the solidity of her presence and also in her identification with
the bush. On the one hand, Olorun is the clear, fecundating
creator, who gives form to the void of the formless, watery
Onile. On the other hand, she is the pure potentiality without
which his potency would remain purely abstract and sterile.
Between them they focus and harness all other energies—
orisha, ancestors, earth-spirits, and the clans of men.

There may well be familial symbolism in Onile's power to
mediate between king and clan chiefs, as a mother smoothes
out relations between father and sons. More deeply, through
her cults Onile creates harmony because she constantly pro-

vides the very ground for the "field" that develops through the interactions of gods and men. Furthermore, she tames and makes available the dark, wild forces involved in the shedding of blood and the use of sorcery, and controls the powers of the ancestors through the Egungun cult.[99] Olorun is a true High God, and as such he is the ultimate source and guarantor of cosmic order. That order, however, must be received, embodied; to this embodiment Onile may yield herself as ceaseless potentiality, but she is never pure passivity. She is not the surface upon which the icon that is Yoruba society is drawn, but rather, through the initiative of Olorun, the actions of the *orisha*, and the restless probing of Eshu, she becomes, in the Yoruba town, the living icon of the cosmos.

Thus the imagery used by the Ogboni cult expresses a movement toward wholeness: a fascination with "threeness" suggesting a temporal completion and an as yet unrealized rebirth, the union of male and female in the *edan*, and atonement for bloodshed.[100] Moreover, the members of the cult are successful elders, "completed" men, who have arrived at a phase in life when they no longer need to differentiate themselves by patrilineal distinctions, and instead can acknowledge their oneness with one another and with Onile, the matrix of their Yoruba life. When they enter the Ogboni house, they prostrate themselves, hide their thumbs in their fists, and kiss the ground three times, declaring each time, "The mother's breasts are sweet."[101] Yoruba life has made itself in them.

Reshaping the cosmos

Eshu's role in this movement to wholeness, this work of making the earth the icon of the cosmos, is crucial. If the Yoruba leaders tuck in their thumbs and abandon themselves to Onile, they can do so because the "Mother" herself is no

99. Morton-Williams, "Outline of the Cosmology," p. 252.
100. See Morton-Williams, "The Yoruba Ogboni Cult in Oyo," p. 373.
101. Pemberton, "Eshu-Elegba," p. 69.

longer undifferentiated possibility. Through the mediation of Eshu she has acted to receive her true (Yoruba) shape, just as her successful "sons" have obeyed his promptings and received the benefits of his power. So it is that Eshu is praised as the "Father who gave birth to Ogboni." [102]

In addition to individual fulfillment, Eshu brings about the interchanges of the market, the practical heart of a town's life. His presence in the market is indeed a phallic presence, loaded with volatile, unstable energy. But if Eshu's energy can provoke disruptive connections or dump those relying on it in midstream, it is no less necessary for the exchanges that give life. Eshu embodies sexuality as unleashed desire—not lust merely, nor even avarice, envy, or greed, but that passion for what lies outside one's grasp which the Greeks saw in some sense as the sovereign mover of human life. Eshu is agile: he is moving always to challenge, break open, and enlarge every possible structure and relationship.

Eshu's sexuality, then, points beyond personal disruption and restoration and even beyond the achievement of a sort of cosmic marriage between Olorun and Onile. True, Eshu comes from above to the earth below. He exercises the High God's creative and recreative energies to probe, pick apart, and reshape the social order. Yet Eshu's mastery of the market suggests the real depth of his sociotherapy. He does more than to link the two great central forces of Yoruba life, the center above and within and the center beneath and without. Rather, he forms in complex association with them part of that center himself, in order to reveal it as a fully human center. The high seriousness of palace and Council of State and Ogboni cult, of Olorun, *orisha*, and Onile, is humanized in the tension, excitement, caginess, and sheer fun of the market that begins each week. Each week Eshu refashions the image of that cos-

102. J. E. and D. M. dos Santos, *Esu Bara Laroye* (A monograph produced at the Institute of African Studies, University of Ibadan, 1971), p. 84; quoted by Pemberton, "Eshu-Elegba," p. 70.

mic field of forces which is the Yoruba town by bringing together all those who are in fact the town to make the exchanges that create their lives.

Eshu's role in divination shows how deeply the Yoruba know this socioeconomic work to be sacred work. Morton-Williams says that in divination "the oracle replaces a dilemma with an enigma; it was the duty of the diviners at the king's court to resolve the enigma after they had produced it, the king needing information and not riddles." [103] Jung knew better, but still it is significant that Morton-Williams should have offhandedly associated the enigma of the divinatory cast with a riddle. Aristotle saw that a riddle was simply a subtle and finely-turned metaphor, really not so much a puzzling question as an oracular answer. [104] A society which produces riddles and proverbs knows that the surface hides more than it reveals and that to penetrate that surface is to discover beneath the smooth skin of everyday life systems and interweavings and connections as wonderful and strange as the circulation of the blood and the movement of neurological impulses, as grossly magnificent as the digestive tract.

Thus Eshu does not only present riddles; he is one. In a sense, he is all metaphor, all ambiguous oracle. That is his very being. The *oriki* say:

> Eshu slept in the house—
> But the house was too small for him.
> Eshu slept on the verandah—
> But the verandah was too small for him.
> Eshu slept in a nut—
> At last he could stretch himself.

> Eshu walked through the groundnut farm.
> The tuft of his hair was just visible.
> If it had not been for his huge size,
> He would not have been visible at all.

---

103. Morton-Williams, "Outline of the Cosmology," pp. 254–55.

104. See Y. M. Sokolov, *Russian Folklore*, trans. Catherine Ruth Smith (New York: Macmillan Co., 1950), p. 282.

Having thrown a stone yesterday—he kills a bird today.
Lying down, his head hits the roof.
Standing up he cannot look into the cooking pot.
Eshu turns right into wrong, wrong into right.[105]

In Jung's terms, Eshu is pure synchronicity—but a synchronicity that makes "the times" (*aiye*) possible. Unlike the complementary potencies and potentialities of Olorun and Onile, Eshu is everything at once. However, his every-which-wayness mediates inclusiveness; he embraces everything human, and everything necessary for human life. Thus he is the master of the sacred language of Ifa, in which all human possibilities are contained. He destroys normal communication to bring men outside ordinary discourse, to speak a new word and to disclose a deeper grammar to them, and then to restore them to a conversation that speaks more accurately of Yoruba life. He is both old and young. He is the twin who has first seen the world's shape and the one always traveling ahead to explore and reveal that shape. He is both small and large. He knows the innermost designs of things and their broadest scope. And always, ceaselessly, he is transforming—day into night, right into wrong, wrong into right, ugliness into beauty, and, most of all, dissolution, rigidity, and conflict themselves into new order. The pattern he endlessly recreates is ordinary rather than elegant, but in that ordinariness the Yoruba recognize the very shape of their life together.

105. Bakare Gbadamosi and Ulli Beier, *Yoruba Poetry*, p. 15.

CHAPTER FIVE

Ogo-Yurugu: Lord of the Random, Servant of Wholeness

But Love has pitched his mansion in
The place of excrement
For nothing can be sole or whole
That has not been rent.

W. B. YEATS,
"Crazy Jane Talks to the Bishop"

Jesting increases love.

DOGON PROVERB

W HEN we move to the Dogon and the figure of Ogo-Yurugu, we have traveled across the spectrum of trickster possibilities to the point which, in West Africa at least, is most remote from the classical trickster pattern so beautifully embodied in Ananse.[1] Indeed, in many important ways Ogo-Yurugu hardly seems a trickster at all. True, he is rebellious, sexually aggressive, and finally theriomorphic. His struggle with the High God, Amma, gives human life its specific shape, and he continues to mold and enlarge that life by his divinatory movements on the edges of society as well as by his subtler actions in its center. His willfulness scrambles primordial serenity only to bring order out of mere potency, and his drive to-

---

1. The most valuable works for this study of Ogo-Yurugu were the following: Marcel Griaule and Germaine Dieterlen, *Le Renard pâle*, vol. 1, "Le Mythe Cosmogonique," part 1, "La Création du Monde"; Geneviève Calame-Griaule, *Ethnologie et langage: la parole chez les Dogon*; Griaule and Dieterlen, "The Dogon of the French Sudan"; M. Griaule, *Conversations with Ogotemmêli: An Introduction to Dogon Religious Ideas*; *Jeux dogons*, and "L'alliance cathartique"; Montserrat Palau-Marti, *Les Dogon*; Michel Leiris, *La langue secrète des Dogon de Sanga (Soudan français)*; and Denise Paulme, *Organisation sociale des Dogon*.

ward wholeness fuels every sort of human initiative. Yet for all that, Ogo-Yurugu does not seem a figure of fun; he is not amusing like Ananse, bawdy like Legba, or even outrageously unpredictable like Eshu. There are hints that Marcel Griaule's team has missed this aspect in Ogo-Yurugu.[2] They have published little Dogon folklore and do not connect him very explicitly to the apparently humorous situations to which the Dogon link him, yet it is the Dogon, after all, who clearly present Ogo-Yurugu as a divine being of high seriousness, of near-Promethean ambition and failure. It is they who tell of him in nonfolkloric terms and make of him a cosmic principle of disorder, seemingly isolating his seriousness so thoroughly from any quality of delight that his tricksterhood becomes suspect.

If Ogo-Yurugu is not in the middle somehow, not betwixt and between, not the engagingly cocksure contradictor of contradiction, can he be an embodiment of liminality and a witness to the potentially human in all that has calcified or is still wild? Is he, then, as Ugo Bianchi thinks, simply a proto-gnostic demiurge, an intellectual principle lightly veiled in mythic imagery?

OGO-YURUGU AND DOGON MYTHOLOGY

Such questions always lead back to the nature of the language of myth, and the summary of this book will explore further the way in which the trickster pattern sheds light on this issue. Here, faced with Ogo-Yurugu's mythic seriousness, we will do well to look at him through the lens of his power to shape human language. Ananse wangles from Nyame posses-

2. See Mary Douglas, "Dogon Culture—Profane and Arcane." She believes that the research of the Griaule team would have profited by joining the "high metaphysical subtlety of the French" to the "low sociological cunning of the Anglo-Saxon" (p. 23). However, in *Ethnologie et langage* Calame-Griaule does stress the explicit link the Dogon make between various kinds of joking and sexual love. Her analysis shows that Dogon laughter is associated with both Ogo and Nommo. See especially pp. 257, 282, 303–6, 320–23, 375–82, 401. Cf. Germaine Dieterlen, "Le rire chez les Noirs d'Afrique."

sion of all Ashanti tales. Legba is the master of the alphabet of Mawu, the divine linguist who interprets and translates the languages of gods and men to make the human story possible. Eshu disrupts communication by laying bare its hidden gaps so that through the language of divination and sacrifice he can overcome death and refashion the icon of life. By placing Ogo-Yurugu at the center of their great myth, the Dogon insist that his being and his actions are the hinge on which their own story hangs. No matter what we may lack of Dogon folklore, we do have, thanks to Griaule and his friends, the great tale that the Dogon tell about themselves, about their world and its inner form, about its meanings and workings, about its origins and possibilities.

In this story Ogo-Yurugu reveals a uniquely Dogon way of seeing and handling liminality. The key to this understanding of the passages into greater life is, as Griaule has said, the Dogon sense of the cosmos as a "vast system of correspondences" made up of interrelated signs and images belonging to categories that both reflect and reverse one another. Social institutions themselves "constitute a scheme of representations," which in turn is reproduced in myth, "but with persons, places, times, and functions transposed."[3] The several levels of meaning, like the various planes of personal, social, ancestral, and cosmic life, interlock, mirror, and comment on one another. Stories known to the whole people, more esoteric myths possessed by elders like Ogotemmeli, and an intricate system of designs and symbols making visible the whole network of relationships that is Dogon knowledge—all these are connected, not like the floors of a house, but like the curves of a spiral.[4] The movement creating each curve and the entire spiral is the movement of life itself. It is the movement of Amma in the seed of the universe, the movement in the first star and the first grain, and the movement of the fetus both in his or her

3. Griaule and Dieterlen, "The Dogon," p. 83.
4. *Ibid.*, p. 84. Cf. Griaule and Dieterlen, *Renard pâle*, p. 101.

own being and in the mother's womb. This movement establishes the many levels of the cosmos, and, by linking them in a ceaseless process of creation, brings forth the continuing correspondence among them.

The "word of the world"

This process of creation and correspondence has a word-dimension. The Dogon understand creation to be the work of a "word," and they believe that their mythology reveals that same word. The Dogon term for symbol is *aduno so*, "the word of the world"; for myth, it is *so tanie*, "amazing word"; and for the whole mythology that is their sacred history, *aduno so tanie*.[5] Thus the Dogon know well that the story of their existence embodies that existence. This story manifests the life of the world because, in some deep sense, it *is* the world itself in human speech. The unending spiral of interconnection[6] is reflected in its verbal representation, which is at the same time one of its "curves." Ogo-Yurugu is so central to this symbolic system that Germaine Dieterlen gave his name—*Renard pâle* ("pale Fox" or *Vulpes pallidus*)—to the book that summarizes and integrates thirty-five years of research among the Dogon. His centrality in the myth faithfully mirrors his place in the social order. He is at the heart of the Dogon story because his actions make possible the movement which opens the planes of existence to one another and which, therefore, creates the process of life itself.

The mythical system of the Dogon, like every other aspect of their culture, has four levels of expression, moving from more to less abstract.[7] Corresponding to each level are graphic symbols, which are displayed everywhere and range from nonrepresentational "traces" through "images" and "figures" to realistic "designs." These symbols constantly find expression

5. Griaule and Dieterlen, *Renard pâle*, pp. 41, 43.
6. In which "each element, each event . . . is linked to and interacts with all others both in space and in time." *Ibid.*, p. 43 (my translation).
7. See *ibid.*, pp. 73–94.

in constellations of patterns, dances, festivals, masks, wall-paintings, daily customs, household objects, and sacrifices. Because this intermeshing of meanings and symbolisms speaks so strongly for them, the Dogon do not need to repeat in sequence *aduno so tanie*, the whole history of the cosmos. As a result, the fragments of this all-embracing myth have had to be pieced together with painstaking care during two generations of fieldwork. Yet the Dogon always remember that "the condition of the person mirrors the condition of the universe, [and] everything which affects the one has repercussions on the other; . . . in some way all a man's actions and . . . circumstances must be conceived as closely connected with the functioning of things in general."[8] The Dogon know, then, that the conflicts expressed in their mythology and those experienced in their lives work together to tell the story of their being in the world. The primordial struggle to create that world is recapitulated in the life of each individual and, on the other hand, the personal achievement of a fully human life discloses the creative movement of the whole cosmos. The symbolism of ritual passage is very much intact for the Dogon. At each great crossing in their lives, at each liminal moment, the narrative of the myth and the symbolic meaning that Ogo-Yurugu embodies join to open the passage to deeper life, while that successful passage reconfirms the meaning of the myth.

The relationship between myth and daily life links great primordial events to the ordinary crises of infancy, childhood, adolescence, and later life. Ogo fears that Amma, "his father," will deprive him of the feminine partner whom he needs to become a creator, and this fear leads him to struggle to possess his placenta, the matrix of creativity. The Dogon cosmogony, in fact, which records this struggle as it leads to incest, Ogo's loss of the power of self-expression through circumcision, and the castration of Nommo, his twin, seems in many ways to present an African variant of the myth of Oedipus.

8. Griaule and Dieterlen, "The Dogon," p. 88.

Some scholars, in fact, have objected that the Griaule-Dieterlen version of Dogon mythology and a classical Freudian interpretation of human development match too neatly. However, while it is necessary to ask whether or not European preconceptions have distorted Dogon thought and to test the conclusions of *Le Renard pâle* against all the evidence available, too much fuss about eisegesis and exegesis, methodological weakness and information gaps misses the real problem. That problem is, very simply, the difficulty of grasping how the Dogon themselves understand the relationship between myth and life. After all, Freudian theory is itself a way of doing hermeneutics, and if that method has intruded too far into the interpretations of Griaule and Dieterlen, the only corrective is to dig more deeply into Dogon mythology for its meaning.

As we do, we need to remember that the Dogon insist that the world is a system of correspondences, in which the "amazing word of the world" is also the story of each man's existence. It is they, consciously and intentionally, in daily actions and at special moments, who read that story as the inner design of each life. Thus the myth calls on us to take it seriously as a psychosocial paradigm of some sort, and in doing so, we begin to see both the ambivalence and the contemporaneity of Ogo-Yurugu. Even though Amma totally defeats Ogo, banishes him from the divine and human communities, and establishes his obedient twin as the founder and lord of humanity, Ogo's rebellion has determined the shape of creation. In defeat, as Yurugu (the Fox), he continues to reveal the secrets of life. He may resemble Satan or Prometheus, but his far greater ambiguity suggests that we cannot understand his mythic meaning unless we look at the specific ways in which the Dogon experience him at the liminal moments of life.

We must also ask, even more carefully than we did in regard to the Fon, how far the entire mythic structure of the Dogon can be seen as a projection of familial experience. With the Fon it was enough to point out that the use of familial symbolism in speaking of the ultimate forces of the cosmos cannot be considered, *of itself*, either unconscious projection or unsophisticated anthropomorphism—what is commonly called "animism." With the Dogon too that use arises from the conscious conviction that the cosmos is at its very center a human place, that the true face of the universe is a human face, that even the vastest and most elusive energies of existence are related to and disclosed most completely by human life. It is true, of course, that this conviction is at bottom a theological statement. As such, it can be opposed to the aniconism of Islam or Buddhism, compared to the several ways in which Jews, Christians, or Hindus both affirm and deny the humanity of God and the sacrality of creation, or tested by the post-Enlightenment doctrine of the historical immanence of every mode of transcendence, however modest. Yet the religious creativity of the Fon or the Dogon vision goes beyond their awareness that the divine and human worlds do not mirror each other in any univocal way. It lies instead in their ability to imagine, in word and action, their discovery of a far more mysterious mirroring that reveals ordinary, historical experience as sacred and of a symbolism that expresses, molds, maintains, and enlarges this sacredness.

Because the Dogon relate this symbolism—whether verbal, graphic, ritual, or customary—so deliberately to the everyday processes of psychosocial growth, it will be necessary to grasp the full intentionality and richness of the language they have devised to speak of their world in order to respond fully to the question of projection. Although Mary Douglas is right in saying that the Dogon have not produced "a modern linguistic philosophy in a primitive setting," she misses the mark when she claims that they have created "a totemism of linguistics."[9] What they seek, rather, is the way in which individual and social process is also a language of ultimate purpose, so that their achievement needs to be compared not to our linguistics, but to our psychology at just that point where it remains open to

9. Douglas, "Dogon Culture," p. 20.

symbols of transcendence. For this the work of Erik Erikson will be most useful because it avoids Freud's rigid positivism while retaining his keen sensitivity to the biological and familial roots of the loftiest reachings of the human mind.

The Dogon, of course, do not speak of "mechanisms of repression," the "transpersonal psyche," or "ego synthesis." Yet they know their world is always becoming what it has been made to be, always realizing itself in a movement—at once parabolic arc and ever-turning spiral, precarious yet certain—enfleshed in each Dogon life. Both their mythology and their daily life show their understanding that man both has and is a body, possesses and is possessed by his sexuality, is shaped by and shapes his parents, moves outward as he moves inward, receives and creates both past and future, ends and extends the cycle of generations. They use other words, but for them the symbolism of ritual passage is *praxis* as well as *theoria*, an enterprise sacred as both work and revelation. It is truly the "word of the world," both breath and earth, both inmost design and most concrete act.

At the heart of this symbolic movement the Dogon see Ogo-Yurugu. As we look first at a summary of those portions of Dogon mythology which speak of him directly, and then at his role in the daily life of the Dogon people, his imaginative and intellectual significance for them will become clear. At the same time, this significance discloses the way in which the Dogon link the commonplace and the transcendent and thus points to further dimensions of the trickster pattern.

A summary of the Dogon cosmogony

In the beginning, there was Amma, "he who holds all in place." [10] In him were both the one and the many, for he was in the form of an egg with four parts. His first creation, like all that followed, embodied "signs," which he had already con-

10. For this summary I have relied on Griaule and Dieterlen, *Renard pâle*, especially pp. 61–384.

ceived mentally. The first thing made was the *sene*, a seed from which Amma planned to create the universe, but his plan failed. He put more into it than it could hold, and at its first turning, water left it, making it useless. Amma then destroyed the universe that had begun to take shape, preserving only the *sene* and the four essential elements.

Next, Amma began a new universe by preconceiving its designs and correspondences. Then, moving in a spiral, he left the egg-form and created a new seed, the *po pilu*, the "littlest thing," which was the image of Amma, for "he himself was not large." From the *po*, which was equivalent to the word, Amma proceeded to create a double placenta, from which would be born the *nommo anagonno*, heavenly images of the life-giving water and of the fish that live there. They would be Amma's helpers in perfecting creation and the progenitors of the human race.[11] Each half of the placenta contained a pair of male twins, for, although the *nommo* were meant to be androgynous, their female halves were to be created later. In the upper half of the placenta were the *nommo die*, who would become Amma's vicar in heaven, and the *nommo titiyayne*, who would become the sacrificer and the guardian of the spiritual principles. In the lower half of the placenta were the *o nommo* (referred to hereafter as Nommo), who would later be sacrificed, and Ogo, who would become Yurugu. Amma intended to produce four pairs of androgynous twins who could give birth to perfect beings like themselves and who would both express and elaborate his own multiplicity in unity. Created reality would be rooted in twinness.

Ogo found himself alone. Amma would give him his female partner in sixty "periods" (the universe being as yet extratemporal and extraspatial), but Ogo was anxious and impatient. In his desire to possess his partner, Ogo began to think that she would not be given to him. Amma assured him that he would

11. See *ibid.*, pp. 106, 129–46, 170–73. Cf. Griaule, *Conversations with Ogotemmêli*, pp. 18–19.

have her at the moment of his birth, but Ogo did not believe him and began to seek her without waiting for Amma's plan to unfold. His search took the form of a walking tour around his placenta, the vast distance he covered equaling the future distance between the earth and the sun. As he moved clockwise, as opposed to Amma's counter-clockwise movement, Ogo prefigured the ultimate arrangement of space by his steps and of time by the "periods" in which he walked.

After his tour, Ogo claimed to be as wise as Amma and capable of creating his own world. He said, "Amma, I have seen the world you have made." Amma challenged him to create neither in sun nor in shadow, hoping to defeat him at once by giving him an impossible task. But Ogo stole the "nerves" that were supposed to open up into four clavicles and wove them into a kind of basket in which he enclosed himself. Since Ogo was now in a place without shadow or light and had begun to move as Amma had at the beginning, Amma responded to the threat by cutting the "vein" of Ogo's tongue so that he was deprived of part of the timbre of his voice. He could still speak, but Amma had shown his dominion over Ogo's creative powers.[12]

However, Ogo wanted to equal Amma. Thus he tried to steal the *sene*, Amma's first creation, in an attempt to possess the source of fecundity. Although he could not gain mastery over the *sene*, it joined him in rebellion, and when Ogo broke loose from his placenta, it descended with him. Ogo, born out of due time, left the womb with "his eyes closed," in primordial darkness, tearing away a piece of placenta and leaving a hole, which would become the moon. With man's navel, the moon therefore witnesses to Ogo's prematurity, the restlessness and haste from which all disorder has sprung.

In tearing the placenta, Ogo thought that he would take his female partner with him, but Amma had removed her spiritual principle and had entrusted it to the other *nommo* for safekeep-

12. Griaule and Dieterlen, *Renard pâle*, p. 179.

ing. All of Ogo's future attempts to gain her would fail; he would never find her. On the other hand, Ogo had overturned Amma's plans since he had not waited for his proper twinness. Although he was to remain alone, weak, and frustrated, his rebellion continued to shape the universe.

The torn piece of placenta served Ogo as an "ark" on which he descended, as the *sene* helped him by moving like a whirlwind. Amma would not allow Ogo's disorderly initiative to give the world its form; he properly oriented the ark, stabilized it, and transformed it into the earth. When Ogo saw that its soil was damp and muddy because of the moisture that the placenta still retained, he thought the earth held no place for him, but Amma dried it, making it heavy and sandy. Ogo first tried to hide himself from Amma, attempting to separate himself from Amma's creation. Then he tried to find his female partner in the earth. He penetrated the placenta-made-earth, and inscribed a spiral in its interior, making a tour as he had done in "heaven," again trying to imitate his father and to make the placenta fecund by restoring it to wholeness. In the process he dug sixty holes, which would serve for the sowing of grain to "complete the incomplete earth."

But in penetrating the earth, Ogo united himself with his mother. The people say that he entered by her mouth and left by her vagina, a twisted sort of incest that resulted in the birth of Yeban, little beings with big heads, discolored bodies, and frail limbs. Ashamed of their origins, they hide in holes, and when they mate, they produce the still smaller Andoumboulou. All of them are born single, and the male Yeban mate with their daughters. Witnesses to Ogo's failure and lost twinness, they fill the interior of the earth. Ogo tried to make his mother his wife, the equivalent of his female half, but this disordered union brought only single, incomplete, defective beings. Ogo's first attempt to equal Amma had failed spectacularly.

Ogo's search for his partner had been fruitless. The earth's soil was becoming drier, and Ogo judged that the earth was useless as it was. He decided to return to heaven to continue his search. Seeing the increasing gravity of Ogo's efforts, Amma turned what remained of Ogo's placenta into a blazing fire so that Ogo, in grasping at it, burned his hand. He managed to grab a small piece of it, but the rest Amma transformed into the sun, into which he placed the spiritual principle of Ogo's female half.

Now Ogo decided to steal the *po pilu* and the other grains, the foundation of creation, and so to gain possession of the universe. He also wanted the milk teeth of his male twin, for these were associated with the word. They would become symbols of parenthood, and Ogo desired to assure himself of descendants. However, even though Ogo thought that he possessed all that he needed to make the earth fruitful, in fact he had only the male *po pilu*. Amma had kept the female *po* and the female grains, and had thus preserved for himself all possibility of reproduction. Nevertheless, in stealing that which was the "littlest thing," the image of Amma, so sacred that some priests will not pronounce its name, Ogo had penetrated the secret of all beginnings.[13] Although Amma would permit Ogo to prepare the earth for the coming of men, Ogo's attempt to become Amma's equal led Amma to replace him as the ancestor of humanity with Nommo, his male twin. As a sign of this decision, Amma cut Ogo's tongue, depriving him of his power to express the word.

With the help of the second piece of placenta and the male *po*, Ogo again descended to the earth. There Ogo found that his disorder had spread. The soil was drier, and the *sene* had, despite its own incompleteness, taken root and grown into a great tree. Wanting not only to imitate but also to oppose Amma, Ogo decided to sow his newly-stolen grains. He placed then in the first hole he had made and put the second piece of placenta over the hole, thus adding a second act of incest to the first. Amma, however, had sent the ant, the termite, and the spider to help combat Ogo. The ant entered the hole

13. *Ibid.*, p. 107, n. 1.

and stole back all the grains except the male *po*, while the termite diverted from the remaining grain the moisture of the first piece of placenta (the earth) to prevent its germination.

Amma then directed the *nommo titiyayne* to seize the second piece of placenta. Ogo tried to defend it, but he could only rescue a small piece. As the Yeban and the Andoumboulou fled, the penis of the latter was crushed. This led to his death and foreshadowed the death of men. In the beginning, Amma had created the *po* by starting with the formation of its sex. The destruction of the Andoumboulou's sex and his consequent death showed the primacy that Amma had given to the organ of reproduction and fertility, and hinted that only death could revitalize a sterile world.

The sway of death was extended by the actions of the spider and the *sene*. The spider had betrayed Amma and had entered the *sene* tree to weave for Ogo a new expression of the word, while the *sene* was also trying to create its own world, but could not because its fruits lacked the element of water. The *nommo titiyayne* tried to reclaim the *sene* itself, and could not, but he tore from it its leaves and fruit. These would later become wild vegetation and wild animals, witnesses to the disorder that Ogo and the *sene* brought into the world. The spider also failed because of its lack of water, and thus the word of Ogo would remain a "dry word," destined to be the language taught to the initiates of the Society of Masks. In further contrast with the complete word of the sacrificed and risen Nommo, Ogo's word would be convoluted, a fallacious, treacherous word. Thus when he later "speaks" with his feet as the Fox, his "word" will often be incomplete and false.[14]

Now Amma determined to repossess creation and to correct its disorder by an act of expiation. This act would renew the world, for Amma planned neither to begin afresh by reintegrating the placenta made impure by Ogo's incest nor to abandon it. Thus the sacrifice would be a purification, enabling

14. *Ibid.*, pp. 215–16.

Amma to repossess in the body of the victim the created centers of the word and to rework the plan that Ogo had destroyed. It would also prepare for the descent of an ark containing all the principles and agents needed for the reorganization of the world, and it would ensure the expansion throughout the universe of the powers of Nommo, who would become its master.

Since Nommo was formed in the same section of the placenta as was Ogo, and thus shared in some way the responsibility for his rebellion, Amma designated him as victim. Amma first separated into two parts the four souls of Nommo; this prefigured the creation of sex, which would be necessary for the multiplication of the human race. The separation also averted the danger of the souls' mating with Ogo's female half, a mating that would have produced triplets. Amma wanted to protect against either deficiency or excess, for both of which Ogo had become the symbol. Next Amma castrated Nommo, and the blood from the severed parts purified the placenta.

At this point the Dogon cosmogony reaches a peak of symbolic intensity. The castration gave birth to Sirius the star, the center of the universe; symbolized menstruation (a kind of purification of the womb) and the separation of the sexes, for Nommo was sacrificed an androgyne and arose male and female; marked the interdiction of twin incest, which is acted out at every birth, and thus sealed the end of Amma's first plan and began the present order; created the planet Venus; presaged every sacrifice; and, in providing Amma with the "contents" of the severed parts, gave him the materials out of which he would elaborate the new order. Finally, as the castration divided the human race into male and female, it also foreshadowed circumcision and excision, which would be necessary for the firm definition of the sexes.[15]

Ogo's part in this drama was also essential. At the moment of castration, he again returned to heaven, still looking for his

15. *Ibid.*, pp. 233–38.

female half. This time Amma hid the sun as well as Ogo's partner, and when Ogo could not approach the sun, he went to the castrated Nommo to steal the "sex-souls" contained in his foreskin. As he took the souls and put them into his own foreskin, he also managed to get a little semen into his mouth. As he fled, the *nommo titiyayne* tried to stop him. He was unable to, but he did circumcise Ogo with his teeth, regaining the sexsouls and establishing the pattern for human circumcision. To get back the stolen semen, the *titiyayne* broke Ogo's teeth, tore his tongue, and wounded his throat, depriving him even further of his capacity for expression. Then Ogo chased the *titiyayne* near the sun, into which the latter threw the foreskin. There it was transformed into a lizard, which proceeded to excise the clitoris of the sun. Thus Ogo was finally and fully deprived of the female principle that was meant to complete him.

Ogo again returned to earth, but his role in creation had been played out. Now everything in the primordial womb Amma had made was ordered and classified. Amma proceeded to sacrifice the castrated Nommo to purify the placenta, and parceled out his body to renew the universe. His blood ran like rain, and after five days Amma raised him up to become the symbol and support of the reorganized world. The ancestors of the Dogon, bearing the embryonic forms of their beliefs and practices, would spring from the risen Nommo, and the people would order their lives in five-day weeks to commemorate Nommo's death and resurrection. Amma's last act would be to bestow the female *po pilu* upon men so that they, by agriculture, could complete the work of creation. Then, reserving for himself alone the care of the dead, he would hand over his powers to all the *nommo* and remain enthroned in the very center of the universe, from which point he would watch over his creation.

As Ogo came to rest for the third time upon the earth, his lack of movement symbolized the exhaustion of his power and the finality of this descent. He wanted to continue his "work," but Amma forced him down on all fours, and he became

Yurugu, the pale Fox. His new name suggests his thievery, his furtiveness, his incompleteness, and above all, his aloneness. He had lost completely the power of speech and now could talk only with his paws, on the ground. He was destined to remain an exile, to live apart because of his impurity. However, he had been a necessary agent in the development of the world. The Dogon say that Amma provoked the acts of Ogo to experiment with the universe. Even today Yurugu's presence in the uncultivated bush favors the expansion of humanity, for with the seeds given by Amma man follows him to extend and purify the world.

Even before his birth, Ogo had shown a lack of discipline and had refused to bend to the designs of Amma. His role, according to Dieterlen, was both cosmic and personal: he sought to create a new world so that he might develop fully. He failed, yet his rebellion was somehow necessary since it brought to both the cosmic and personal domains "the beneficent ferment of opposition." Foreseeing everything, Amma had prefigured the dual universe in creating the double placenta, but in order that this duality be wholly expressed in the world of men he needed both Ogo and the obedient Nommo.[16]

OGO-YURUGU IN THE DOGON LIFE CYCLE

The area of southern Mali and north-central Upper Volta where the Dogon live is savannah, broken by gorges, hills, and rocky outcroppings. The land—at least until the droughts of the 1970's—has been able to support small-scale grain cultivation, which is the foundation of their way of life. The openness of the savannah and the regular alternation of two six-month seasons, wet and dry, shape both their agricultural methods and their vision of the world. The terrain is generally flat, yet it is rougher, more broken by valleys and escarpments, than, for example, the plains of North America.[17]

16. *Ibid.*, pp. 269–70.
17. See Leiris, *La langue secrète des Dogon*, p. 4; and Griaule, *Jeux dogons*, p. viii and plate 8.

The Dogon cluster in small, distinct villages, each of which is surrounded by cultivated fields. Many villages are built against the sides of rock formations, but even where they are not, there is a clear demarcation between the village, with its carefully tilled fields, and the surrounding land, with its sparse vegetation and boundless expanse. The alternation of wet and dry seasons reinforces this sharp contrast between what is orderly and life-sustaining and what is uncultivated and sterile. The rhythms of the earth, to which all agricultural peoples must attend with the greatest care, are here neither the more gradual but more extreme swings of the temperate zone, nor the steadier and more lavish flow of the tropics. For the Dogon the seasons swing unendingly from wetness to dryness and back, so that they experience this movement too as an aspect of the inner design of their cosmos. When they "remember" the meaning of their existence, their myth reflects this design, and not their probable origins in the ancient empire of Mali or their migration to avoid conversion to Islam.[18] It is, then, not history that they remember, but the work of cosmic creation and recreation.

Childhood

The Dogon reexperience that work of creation and recreation especially in the great turning points of the spiral movement of life, which brings about the system of correspondences that is the entire universe. Thus even before a child's birth, the Dogon link his behavior to the pattern of their mythology. When the baby moves in his mother's womb, they say that he has begun to move in a spiral, like a whirlwind, and that he does so because Amma too moved this way at the beginning of his creative work.[19] Yet Ogo also moved in a spiral, both within the placenta and when he descended in his ark, so

18. See Griaule and Dieterlen, *Renard pâle*, pp. 14–18.
19. *Ibid.*, pp. 374–75; cf. pp. 101, 112–18; the "spiraling wind" is the equivalent of Amma himself.

that even in the womb the child reflects both poles of creation. Sometimes, as here, an explicit comparison with Amma or, more usually, Nommo is made, and the comparison with Ogo remains implicit, while at other times the converse is true. Discerning the pattern of these comparisons will show how Dogon myth and practice together shape a single language of meaning.

When the child is born and his placenta expelled, it becomes clear, the Dogon believe, that the infant is not like Ogo, who left the womb without the placenta, but like Nommo, who reached full term and was not born alone.[20] After holding the newborn child over a design on the ground that represents both man and woman, the women in attendance rejoice because, even though the child is not a twin, he possesses both the masculine and the feminine principle, unlike Ogo.[21] On the other hand, the child's navel will always witness to Ogo's premature departure from the primeval womb. Furthermore, even if the child does possess twin principles, he is very evidently not a twin. Yet as Ogo's rebellion and search for his lost twinness may "explain" the reason for single birth, it also illuminates a far more mysterious loss.

This loss is not the trauma of birth, as the myth might seem to suggest, but rather the expulsion of the child from an infantile paradise. The Dogon mother nurses her baby for at least two and a half years, through two rainy and three dry seasons.[22] For all this time, he is never separated from her. All day she carries him with her, and at night he sleeps with her. If his mother should have to leave him for some important reason, she always leaves him with a relative so that he is never alone. His father does not even acknowledge him until he begins to crawl, but even then, he is very much his mother's child, and will remain so, continuing to sacrifice at her family altar until

20. *Ibid.*, p. 180.
21. See Palau-Marti, *Les Dogon*, p. 62.
22. See Paulme, *Organisation sociale*, pp. 459 ff.

she dies, although he is officially a member of his father's family.[23] Significantly, even though his parents do begin to share their food with the child after about six months and often play with him, he normally does not stand until the age of two and does not speak until three. Then, suddenly, everything changes. When he begins to walk, he is weaned, and his mother ceases to carry him on her back. Soon she will be pregnant again.[24] Relatives and other children enjoy holding him as he learns to walk, but their span of interest is short, and they usually leave him after a brief time. It would be false to say that he is now left to his own devices, for he is always surrounded by a crowd of children and elders who treat him with affection and kindness. However, he has moved out of a world of the profoundest intimacy into one where the care of others substitutes adequately for his mother's care without replacing the totality of her embrace, and he has likely done so shortly before she will give birth to another child.

One culture's trauma is another's tenderness. The transition here is indeed abrupt, but the Dogon would no doubt be shocked to see a nonnursing American mother toilet train her child. Nevertheless, deepening the sense of Freud's much-disputed aphorism that anatomy is destiny, Erik Erikson has suggested that the bodiliness of all humans requires them to pass through definite stages of development, each of which is related to two other processes of organization, one shaping experience within the individual ego and the other drawing the person into full membership in his or her society.[25] More-

23. G. Dieterlen, "Parenté et mariage chez les Dogon," p. 142.

24. Geneviève Calame-Griaule, Review of *Die Weissen Denken Zuviel: Psychoanalytische Untersuchungen bei den Dogon in Westafrika*, p. 281.

25. Erikson's depth psychology does not treat religious phenomena as regressive fantasies dealing with infantile fears or wishes. He sees childhood as a dynamic, reciprocal movement, constantly being created by and recreating the adult world of family, society, and sacred cosmos. The processes of growth—the various physiological changes, the organization of experience within the ego, and the assimilation of the child into historical and geographical groupings—are so intertwined that the child grows on different levels at the same time he or she responds to challenges to the physical, reflective, and social self. See especially Erik H. Erikson, *Childhood and Society*, pp. 21–108.

over, each of these stages has its own constellation of meaning centered upon certain bodily zones, the configurations of which become symbolic systems available for the assimilation and interpretation of later experience. Erikson, then, recognizes what the Dogon also know: that the processes of human development are a symbol-creating enterprise, as the child learns to associate certain images, not merely with certain needs or conflicts, but with growth itself and his increasing involvement with the world.

In the first stage of life, in which the infant experiences life largely through his mouth and skin, the Dogon mother, by her prolonged and intense intimacy with her child, teaches him a deep trust that the world is ultimately nourishing and caring, that everything will surely come right.[26] Indeed, because the early intimacy of nursing continues past his development of teeth, despite the difficulty this must cause, and delays his assertion of selfhood in walking and speaking, the Dogon child surely feels his relationship with his mother to be a paradigm of paradise, which, even when lost, has promised so much that it must be reattainable.

The myth reflects such an understanding. In the beginning Amma himself, the source of creation, is indistinguishable from his "egg," and Ogo knows that, if only he can steal his placenta, he can make with it a new and perfect world. In the end, despite the dislocations of his revolt, the two parts of the primordial womb become the earth and the sun, the continuing ground and source of life.

Yet both the myth and customary symbols are ambiguous. The heart of the myth is Ogo's rebellion, and in the way in which the Dogon associate that rebellion with the pattern of their lives they show that the myth is a discovery of meaning, not a projection of repressed conflict. In the first place, the milk teeth are, for the Dogon, symbols of the "word" and of parenthood. They are comparable to those of Nommo, and when

26. See Peter L. Berger, *A Rumor of Angels: Modern Society and the Rediscovery of the Supernatural*, pp. 67–71.

they are lost, they are said to "return to Nommo."[27] The appearance of these teeth is the sign, then, of growing social and religious potential as well as the mark of biological development. However, their appearance also signals the approaching separation from the mother. In this sense they witness, covertly, to the permanent loss of twinship that Ogo's revolt has brought about and to the human sexuality that has taken its place.

But if milk teeth symbolize rebellion as well as compliance, the change that occurs in the Dogon child when he leaves his primal paradise reveals that this paradise is also an ambivalent symbol. On the other hand, his parents say that he used to be "good," but now he is "bad."[28] On the other hand, as he begins to play with dirt, they laughingly say that he is like Ogo-Yurugu trying to make the world. In fact, the Dogon associate all children's games, at least indirectly, with Ogo. They claim that very young children have a joking relationship with the Fox so that, in playing with "his earth," they both seek him and chase him; like him, their "work is to amuse themselves with the earth." When they fashion animals and other objects out of dirt, they act like the Fox, who "scratched" to tear his placenta, while in one game (called *sey*) they take the place of Nommo pursuing his twin.[29]

Thus the Dogon relate the playfulness of children to the twin creativity of Ogo and Nommo. If Erikson understands play to be "a function of the ego, an attempt to synchronize the bodily and the social processes with the self,"[30] the Dogon see it as a symbol of creation itself. The difference springs out of the difference between a reverent, but still secularized, vision of the world and one that knows the human world embodies transhuman presences. True, Erikson has expanded the Freudian

27. Griaule and Dieterlen, *Renard pâle*, p. 202.

28. Calame-Griaule, Review of *Die Weissen*, p. 281.

29. Griaule and Dieterlen, *Renard pâle*, p. 269. See Griaule, *Jeux dogons*, p. 172.

30. Erikson, *Childhood and Society*, p. 211.

notion of the ego so that this "inner institution" not only safeguards the individual from the excessive demands of primordial desire, parents, and society, but also weaves inner and outer experience at each level of development into a present that is successful because it finds a meaningful use for the past and promises a fruitful future. The child, as he moves in his play from the cosmosphere of his own body to the microsphere of toys to the macrosphere where he meets and becomes involved with other children, plays to gain mastery over his world. In play he leaves the world and creates a counterworld so that he might return to ordinary existence better able to discover in it the harmonies and meanings he has discovered in himself.[31] Certainly the Dogon are aware that play takes the child outside the restrictions of everyday space, time, causality, social reality, and bodily needs so that he might come to know these restrictions more as horizons than as absolute limits. Yet by associating play with the rebelliousness of Ogo, the Dogon intentionally mythicize it. Because for them children's play reflects the first fumbling efforts to shape the cosmos, it becomes the symbol of all creativeness, and thus links the everyday human shaping of the world to the sacred events standing at its origins.

Moreover, such a mythicization of play implies that childhood itself is a sacred symbol at the same time that it is a stage in the process of human growth. As children play, they simultaneously become the Fox and pursue the Fox, and thus their "work," their most commonplace activity, reveals that their "badness" is inextricably bound to their creativity. Their rebelliousness, like Ogo's, takes them beyond what is already settled and sure, yet the delight they inspire suggests that, like Nommo, they obey not simply impulse but the deep designs of Amma himself. The counter-world that Dogon children create, therefore, is more than a playground. It is an early experience

31. See *ibid.*, pp. 209–14.

of liminality, which shows that their personhood bears the impress of all creation.

Furthermore, if the mythicization of play discloses the true nature of childhood, it also sheds light on the meaning of the cosmogony. It suggests that Ogo's "badness" is as ambivalent as that of children, for it is as necessary and, somehow, as playful—despite its apparently tragic character. This implied playfulness of Ogo begins to show us why the cosmogony is something more than a mythic image of the oedipal conflict.[32] True, Ogo's desire to take his own initiative arises from his fear that he will lack a feminine half with which he can realize his creative potential. Like a child, Ogo (he is, after all, within the primordial "womb") boasts to his "father" that he is capable of equaling his work, and in his first attempt outwits him. However, when he tries to establish himself as Amma's equal by stealing the placenta, his "mother," he fails dismally. When his "incest" also fails and results only in the creation of monsters, he returns to steal the "seed" that will make the placenta fertile. The significance of this seed is made explicit in Ogo's second ascent, when he seizes a little of his castrated twin's semen in his mouth. He is incapable of creating a fruitful world with his "mother," one part of which mocks his incapacity by giving birth to the Yeban, while the other part scorches him when he

32. Erikson's understanding of the oedipal conflict focuses on the changes in familial relationships stemming from internal patterns of growth. Developing powers of movement and speech, he believes, enable a little boy to "intrude" himself in new ways into others' lives. This new power is directed especially to the mother, with whom he has always first played out and ritualized new-found abilities. Conflict arises, however, because the boy is smaller and weaker than his father and because "not even in the distant future is [he] ever going to be the father in sexual relationship to the mother" (*ibid.*, p. 87). Thus his body, his ego, and his parents push him out into the larger world, but at the same time he learns that such initiative is paid for by a loss of primal intimacy. While Erikson's view sheds more light on the Dogon myth than does Freud's, it seems likely that the "object-relations" theory of personality development, which stresses the ambivalences of a child's psychic separation from its mother, would provide additional insight into this and similar myths. See Margaret S. Mahler, Fred Pine, and Anni Bergman, *The Psychological Birth of the Human Infant: Symbiosis and Individuation* (New York: Basic Books, 1975).

gets too close. In desperation, he seeks to possess the fecundating power—the "seed" of his father. Yet the ensuing failure, which ensures that the "sons" of Amma will exercise their creativity only by submitting their sexuality to him, is highly ambivalent. In one variant of the myth, Amma refrains from killing Ogo because the latter convinces him of the future worth to men of his "word" in divination.[33] Even in the better-known version Ogo has shown that the primordial state cannot be equated with paradise, has forced Amma's hand, and, most mysteriously of all, has in his twin's victory become himself a coshaper, if not the master, of creation.

Thus the "untiring solicitude" for children which Griaule saw in Ogotemmeli,[34] together with the amused indulgence with which their playful independence is treated precisely at the moment of its mythicization, gives the myth a lighter, though not less serious, tone than is first apparent from its cosmic complexity. This lightness—really a subtle lightheartedness—becomes more noticeable as we hear the myth played through the system of Dogon life, but already we can begin to sense the way in which the Dogon transform their experience into sacred symbol. That this transformation is too intentional and too sophisticated to be simply a process of unconscious fantasy is shown further by the way in which they relate the cosmogonic events to the human world. Amma and Ogo struggle over possession of the placenta and the life-giving seed, but their battle is also carried on for the word. It can hardly be coincidental that the Dogon associate mythically placenta, seed, and word, when in childhood their first speech is so closely linked to the time of their first separation from their mothers. In the myth, however, the conflict over possession of the word does not mask the sexual dimension of the struggle, but adds to it a further, more deeply social dimension. To create a world, the myth says, one needs more than

33. Griaule and Dieterlen, *Renard pâle*, p. 230.
34. Griaule, *Conversations with Ogotemmèli*, p. 155.

a womb, a penis, seed, and semen. One needs the word. Without it there is only isolation and exile. Therefore to submit to the socializing process is to gain the word, the truly self-expressive, world-creating element, of which the myth itself is the prime symbol.

In accordance with the pattern of the myth, it is not surprising to find that the Dogon divide all speech into forty-eight categories, half belonging to Nommo, half to Ogo-Yurugu. What is surprising is that the division does not place only "clear" forms of speech with Nommo and only "mute" or divinatory forms with Ogo-Yurugu.[35] "The world of the Fox," as Douglas says, "inverts the associations and values of the world of Nommo by means of a very complex parallelism of opposites. It is too simple to say that the Fox has the world of night and death and obscurity, Nommo [that] of day and life and clarity."[36] For example, as one might expect, to Nommo belong judgments of old men and priests, names, last words, numbers, traditions, circumcision and excision, purification rituals, and prayers, and to Ogo false promises, contradiction, stuttering, dream speech, insults, children's first speech and their ritual games of theft, ill-fortune, burial and death, boasting, and irrelevancies. However, Nommo also possesses such forms of speech as riddles, scolding, threats, and trivial, angry, and divinatory words, while Ogo's categories include truth, both expressed and unexpressed, marriage congratulations, courtship, formulas of healing and sorcery, and the lovemaking of husbands and wives.

Some of these apparent contradictions are not difficult to resolve. Thus Ogo's association with words of love and marriage has its origin in his inauguration of human sexuality by his rejection of the primordial plan of twinship, and his possession of the formulas of healing and the categories of truth is, as Geneviève Calame-Griaule suggests, related to his knowledge

35. See Calame-Griaule, *Ethnologie et langage*, pp. 174–80.
36. Douglas, "Dogon Culture," p. 21.

of what is beyond everyday experience.[37] More problematic is Nommo's possession of apparently disruptive or inconsequential modes of speech and the "convoluted" words of riddles and divination. The thread that draws this fascinating taxonomy together seems to be that of outward social utility. That is, as Ogo is the master of divination in its origins and its mystery, Nommo possesses its words as necessary tools of social construction. So too, riddles, anger, and triviality are forms of discourse clear in their ordinariness if not in their implications.[38]

Yet even such an explanation reveals the two-sided character of both Ogo and Nommo at the same time that it at least partially accounts for the double doubleness of human speech as the Dogon understand it. If every form of speech not only has a parallel, but is itself at once "dry" and "wet," clear and obscure, then Nommo is not univocally a victor-hero, nor is Ogo merely the defeated agent of disorder. The Dogon call woven cloth "the spoken word" (soy),[39] but conversely, it is evident that the intricate tissue of language of which Dogon life consists is a fabric woven by Ogo as well as by Nommo. The achievement of speech, then, by an individual as by the world, involves learning many sorts of delicate distinctions and acquiring the wit to balance in speech, as in deed, what is said and not said, what is meant and what is implied, what seems to be so and what is so. The process by which the child acquires the word and becomes a social being is, therefore, like the work of both Nommo and Ogo. It is not a submission, but a true education, which imparts to the potential for sacred style living flesh.

Adolescence

Despite this emphasis on the significance of the word, the Dogon never forget that the sexual symbolism of their myth

37. Calame-Griaule, *Ethnologie et langage*, pp. 182–84.
38. See *ibid.*, pp. 107–11.
39. Griaule, *Conversations with Ogotemmèli*, p. 28.

has important meanings for their communal life. The myth states clearly that Dogon society came into being as the result of the payment exacted for Ogo's rebellion and incest. With the castration and sacrifice of Ogo's twin the world is purified, made fertile, and prepared for the creation of mankind, and with the circumcision of Ogo the threat to Amma's power is ended. Here, however, the myth is ambiguous. It is not at all clear why Nommo instead of Ogo should be castrated, nor why the former's castration should lead to the renewal of the earth, while the latter's circumcision, a less radical operation, should render him forever impotent. The explanation that in being circumcised Ogo lost the sex-souls he had stolen from his twin brother, and thus the hope of finding the female principle that would make him whole, only serves to emphasize the myth's ambiguity, for it is Nommo's castration that leads directly to the end of androgyny and to the separation of the sexes. One can see easily enough that submission to Amma makes the sacrifice of the sexual organs effective, while the lack of submission produces permanent alienation. Yet it is most telling that Amma finally confirms Ogo's rebellion by making the separation of the sexes, not androgyny, the foundation of the human world.

The ambiguity of the myth becomes deliberate ambivalence in the light of the event that marks the turning point in the life of the individual Dogon, the rite of circumcision. At the age of twelve or thirteen, the young Dogon boys are circumcised. With the loss of their foreskins, they are fixed in their masculinity and become apt for procreation, since they have lost the symbol and lodging place of their "femininity." Before, they were considered androgynes; now they are counted as men and are ready for marriage.[40] In submitting their sexuality to the control of the community, they have re-presented the castration of Nommo, and thus have insured the recreation of the

40. Griaule and Dieterlen, *Renard pâle*, pp. 257 ff. Palau-Marti reports that the excision of the clitoris establishes the femininity of girls; *Les Dogon*, p. 62.

race. They, like Nommo, do not submit out of guilt, but with a kind of generous obedience to the nature of things, and, like him, they become worthy to found the people. On the other hand, in forfeiting the primordial bliss of androgyny, they become like Ogo-Yurugu. They will always experience their sexuality as the drive to rediscover a lost unity, to find that feminine half which life's beginnings promised them.[41]

From this point of view, the myth becomes an immensely sophisticated reworking of early life and a means to ease the passage into adulthood. In the myth, Ogo and Nommo are twins, the one forever degraded for his rebellion and incest, the other castrated and sacrificed in atonement—both punished by an almighty father. They are punished, but not destroyed, for out of the sacrifice comes the existing order of reality, while out of the rebellion comes the impulse drawing that order into being. In Dogon life the very act that marks the paternal triumph and seals for all time the gates of paradise also thrusts the boy into society and thus hallows and redirects the creative yearning that never will be satisfied.

The Dogon awareness of this interpretive interaction between mythology and daily life can be gathered from the way in which they imagine and structure the adolescent period following circumcision. The boy spends a large part of his time with his age-mates and develops an extraordinary relationship with the wife of his mother's brother. The basis of this relationship is the boy's likeness to Ogo-Yurugu, who, in stealing a fragment of his placenta, remained one with his "mother." The boy is considered to be so linked to his mother's body that, as Griaule says, he belongs to her generation. He is, then, equivalent to his mother's brother and, "as it were, a substitute for his maternal uncle—the ideal husband of his mother." Thus

the child . . . unconsciously preserves toward its mother the attitude of Yurugu. But since she cannot commit incest, the wife of the maternal uncle replaces the mother. This transference is explained by the

41. Griaule and Dieterlen, "The Dogon," p. 93.

fact that the couple who engendered the child must represent the original twin Nommo. . . . The genitors should be brother and sister and the child can regard his real father as a stranger and his maternal uncle . . . as his ideal genitor.[42]

In imaginative play, therefore, the uncle's wife becomes the boy's "mother," and is allowed to act out with her the desires he had for his actual mother. Yet this "acting out" is in fact a mythicization of adolescence and of the socialization of sexuality. The boy calls his aunt "my wife," and she refers to him as "my husband." Sometimes this joking relationship even becomes explicitly sexual, and, in any event, the boy is allowed to plunder his uncle's household. He has become Ogo-Yurugu seeking his female soul, and his thefts are symbolic of his deeper desire. His uncle, who becomes symbolically both Amma and his father, has the special responsibility of finding the boy a wife—ideally, his own daughter.

Here we have a delicate meshing of the symbols of personal growth and sacred transformation. Erikson calls the time that most cultures give to their adolescents before the establishment of adult identity and the entrance into full participation in the society a "moratorium," a time of personal testing and experimentation. It is more than a psychosexual safety valve, a way of releasing excess and immature energy. This period gives the younger man or woman a chance to fit odd pieces of self-experience, new energies, and images of the future into various experimental selves in preparation for the full synthesis of adulthood.[43] The Dogon sense of adolescence as a time of identity testing moves beyond the notion of moratorium to that of sacred but still playful passage. Dogon adolescence is directly, if imaginatively, related to the story of Ogo-Yurugu's rebellion so that each illuminates and enlarges the meaning of the other. On the one hand, the myth places the young man's need for separation from the matrix of childhood, for sexual experimentation, and for the establishment of his own adult

42. *Ibid.*, p. 92.
43. Erik H. Erikson, *Identity: Youth and Crisis*, p. 132.

world in a framework of cosmic creativity. On the other hand, the social institution that makes the mother's brother a substitute father and transfers the adolescent's unattainable desire to "reenter" his mother to an ironic relationship with his uncle's wife reveals that from the whole range of Ogo's rebellious efforts to create a counter-world issues the space needed for the creation of a world structure both open to the High God and truly separate from him.

What we have, then, is a distinctly Dogon way of expressing, in word and social structure, the availability of life-creating possibilities of transformation. Both myth and social order play with and ritualize the biosocial passage from womb to special intimacy, to preliminary independence, to age-group identification and circumcision, to full-blown adolescence, to marriage and adulthood. In both, the difficulty in leaving behind the primordial wholeness and in pressing on to a mature creativity is transposed into a search for twinness. In both, Ogo's mistrust of Amma and his persistence in claiming possession of his "mother" is seen as both necessary and willful, destructive and life-giving. Yet myth and social pattern stand in relation to each other, not as script and drama, not as model and image, but as twin symbols of the liminality of childhood and adolescence. Ogo is more than a symbol of infantile fear and guilt, of adolescent rebellion and defeat. He is an embodiment of the possibility of moving beyond these negations to a life-creating synthesis. The Dogon are not so much "working through" a psychological crisis as "playing out" the meaning of human growth. The myth emphasizes the cosmic necessity of Ogo's unrest for the establishment of the whole cosmos in its astral, mineral, vegetable, animal, geographic, spiritual, and human dimensions. It reveals that the struggle to discover the true shape of sexuality brings forth all structure. The interpretation given to adolescence by the Dogon social pattern makes of that period a true passage from androgyny to adulthood in which repressed oedipal conflicts become games of transition. These games are played in a time apart from ordinary social order, a time that, in preparing for fully adult life, transforms sexuality into an interiorized and ever-present limen. The "inner institution" of the ego is, for the Dogon, itself the threshold where separateness is always passing into community and where order is continually queried and reforged.

Adulthood

The adults who emerge from the passage through the adolescent limen are, by all the evidence, mature persons. According to European psychological studies,[44] the Dogon live in their familiar environment with less anxiety and guilt than we experience in ours. They have a profound trust that all their wishes can be satisfied, although, not surprisingly, they have some fear of abandonment and adjust less well than we to strange surroundings. Still, Dogon adulthood is by no means a regression to the placidity of infancy. As Erikson points out, the maturity of so-called primitives is a real maturity even in our terms, enabling them to establish an identity leading to the intimacy of genital love, to the care of parenthood, and to the wisdom of a final integrity.[45] Thus the adult Dogon has neither fled from conflict nor arrived at his destination. His maturity is, above all, a time of openness to the sacred; it too is a ceaseless process of transformation and cosmic re-presentation.

During adulthood, then, the Dogon discover further significance in Ogo-Yurugu, meanings relevant to the life of the adult member of society, even though that society is understood in one sense to be the result of Ogo's defeat. At marriage the Dogon enter a highly complex social system based in the minutest detail on the first five mythical generations of the human race.[46] Since these generations sprang from the sacrifice and the resurrection of Nommo, marriage symbolizes the

---

44. See Parin et al., *Die Weissen Denken Zuviel.*
45. Erickson, *Childhood and Society*, p. 112.
46. See Dieterlen, "Parenté et mariage," pp. 108–28.

fixing of the Dogon identification with Nommo, the "good" twin. However, as with circumcision, so with marriage: the same act also consecrates the darker or less controllable side of man, that side which mirrors Ogo-Yurugu, so that his sexuality will always be a re-presentation of Ogo's search for his twin, and his performance of sexual intercourse a reenactment of Ogo's primordial act of incest. Even the place of the marriage bed in the house and the very positions husband and wife assume during intercourse symbolize both Ogo, the initiator of human sexuality, and Nommo, its transformer.[47] The root of sexual awakening is acknowledged by linking Ogo and the shrine of the ancestors. At the same time, the whole house symbolizes Nommo, who enabled this potential source of destruction to become the very pattern of creation and the guarantee that the fundamental order of the world will continue.

A similar two-fold symbolism occurs in Dogon agriculture, which is the source of life in another way. The agricultural symbolism of the myth forms part of a constellation including sexuality and speech. To create a counter-world, Ogo must possess the *po pilu*, the seed of creation, as well as his placenta and the word. When Amma crushes his rebellion and finally establishes the world from the sacrificed Nommo, he reconsecrates this constellation. Thus the whole process of Dogon agriculture—from the sowing at the beginning of the rainy season to the harvest at its end—is associated with Nommo. However, even though Ogo's sowing was unproductive and was superseded by that of the mythical ancestors; even though he became Yurugu and was banished to the dry lands beyond the fields marking the edge of the world, Ogo-Yurugu is still linked to the creativity of work. A young man, for example, must work for three days in the fields of his prospective father-in-law: one day in the rainy season with his age-mates, one day in the dry season (associated with Ogo) with a friend,

47. See Griaule and Dieterlen, "The Dogon," pp. 97–98.

and another day in the next rainy season.[48] In the Bulu festival, which celebrates the harvest and thus the beginning of the dry season, Ogo's rebellion is remembered and acknowledged as part of the primordial rhythm of life. Furthermore, the Dogon stress the dual roles of the placenta of Nommo and of Ogo, now transformed into cultivated land and the sun, for both have shaped the world and both make possible the growth of grain.[49]

The Dogon recognize that agriculture depends on both sun and earth, wetness and dryness, work and rest, communal compliance and individual initiative. One will say, moreover, that "the man who gives me a field is the same as a man who gives me a wife."[50] Agriculture is identified with marriage, for both are made possible by transforming the creative image from a yearning to turn inward in incest to a true movement outward. The world, that great matrix of life, becomes fruitful ground both through the submission of Nommo and through the drive of Ogo. In other words, the field of Dogon existence comes into being by means of the interplay of forces emanating from two poles. Without both poles that existence would dissolve.

This theme of doubleness, so evident in the myth and apparent from the first moments of a Dogon child's life, manifests itself in every adult social institution. The regularity of the rhythms of Dogon life contrasts sharply with the institution of divination. Every detail of their lives is prescribed and given meaning by sacred tradition, yet they consult the Fox as a matter of course to discover the hidden shape of their lives. To conduct affairs properly, they say, and "to organize the country, the first [thing is] to practice divination."[51] Even more explicitly than the Fon and the Yoruba, the Dogon assert that

48. Dieterlen, "Parenté et mariage," p. 139.
49. See Griaule and Dieterlen, *Renard pâle*, pp. 228, 384.
50. Dieterlen, "Parenté et mariage," p. 137.
51. Griaule and Dieterlen, "The Dogon," p. 90.

divination reaches beyond individual and social therapy, that to order rightly a single life or the life of the village is to show forth the order of the cosmos. They also know that their trickster-figure possesses the secret language of the world and spells out for them the words that continually spell out human life. "Under the movement of the Fox's paws," they say, "the earth turns." [52]

The Dogon make the iconographic purpose of their divination tables so explicit that one cannot mistake it. [53] Both sorts of divination table, one for actual divination and the other for the instruction of future diviners in the deeper meanings of the art, are icons whose design represents the ultimate mythic form of the world and whose momentary meaning is "spoken" by the action of Yurugu on the underlying pattern already created by Amma. The divination table is drawn on the sand beyond the fields of the village, that is, on the boundary between the human and the wild. It is a six-paneled rectangle, an image of the field in which Ogo tried to sow the stolen grain on his second descent to the earth. In each of the panels, which render schematically heaven and earth, Amma's work above and below, and the movements of Ogo, the diviner traces figures dealing with the questions of his clients. These figures are linked to the roamings of Ogo within the placenta and on the earth.

The diviner—like the Fox—pursues a quest; for the figures that he draws on the divining table are like images of the eternal quest of the rebel seeking to recover the rest of his placenta and his lost female twin. Likewise, he "reads" the tables from right to left: the succession of the basic figures constitutes an image of Ogo's . . . alternating "descents" and reascents between heaven and earth, the third of which led him to his death. Of the zigzag thus made . . . he says: "The path of death is twisted, the path of life is straight, the path of death is three." [54]

52. Griaule and Dieterlen, *Renard pâle*, p. 280.
53. See *ibid.*, pp. 274–83.
54. *Ibid.*, p. 276 (my translation).

Thus even though Amma has deprived Ogo of his power of speech and has degraded him from *nommo* to Fox, his word, twisted and false though it often may be, still continues to disclose the path of the world. When a fox walks across the divination table at night, and when the diviner reads Yurugu's message, the wholeness of life that Ogo sought is drawn out of the very disruption that has led to the divinatory moment.

This exploitation of ambiguity and incompleteness becomes even more explicit in the symbolism of Yurugu's altar and the table for instructing novice diviners. The name of the altar, *yurugu lebe*, is popularly understood to be a contraction of another word meaning "two together," thus referring to the dual state of him who is simultaneously Ogo and Yurugu.[55] The table of instruction "witnesses to the reorganization of the universe by Nommo and to his mastery over the Fox,"[56] but it also symbolizes the continuing presence of Ogo-Yurugu and his never-ending role in ordering the world. This table, a twelve-paneled rectangle, traces the movement of creation from the opening of Amma's "clavicles"[57] to the "entombment" of Yurugu. It is drawn in an east-west orientation, and the movement from panel to panel is a zigzag, or spiral, representing the movement of the sun through twelve lunar months. The last six panels symbolize the story of Ogo's female partner, Yasigui, so that even the more hidden part of the myth, that which reveals its significance for women, is also manifested to the novice diviners. The table of instruction, then, is quite simply an *imago mundi*, an icon of the cosmos in its spatial and temporal movements, which are in turn images of the sacred history of the Dogon. Each act of divination recreates this image, revealing that its inner structure is brought forth by the insatiable craving of Ogo as well as by the obedient

---

55. *Ibid.*, p. 277. The name more properly refers to Lebe Serou, the great mythic ancestor, and to the cult named after him. Cf. *ibid.*, p. 31.

56. *Ibid.*, p. 280.

57. The clavicle is the place where each human body, the Dogon believe, begins to be formed. See *ibid.*, p. 150.

submission of Nommo. This redrawing of life, moreover, takes place on the boundary between human society and formless nature, to show that the movement away from ordinary space and time necessitated by every mishap or danger ends in a return to an ordinariness that now brings to light formerly shadowed paths of transcendence.

Furthermore, divination reveals that Ogo—defeated, degraded, cast out, speechless, even "dead"—still moves and speaks so that the story of life might continue to unfold. Each year the diviners offer a sacrifice to Yurugu and pour out to him libations of beer. The following morning they gather to read the divination tables on which they have posed their questions and to drink the rest of the beer. One of them prays:

O Yurugu, praise for your going-and-coming. Because of your gentle foot, we follow [your going-and-coming] morning and night. Thank you for your gentle foot. Show us who will die and who will be healed. We will go forth to raise grain in the bush; tell us if we will have ripe grain or not. The world that Amma made is molded out of forty *yala* of the sun, fourteen of the earth, six of Yurugu. . . . O Yurugu, those who consult you praise you for your going-and-coming.[58]

Ogo failed in his rebellion, and men base their lives on the pattern of Nommo. Yet as Yurugu he guides them, through divination, into and out of darkness, disruption, and formlessness so that the human world might always encompass both order and accident, clarity and darkness.

The Society of Masks, to which all males belong "from the time their beards first appear until they turn white," extends still further the meaning of Yurugu's divinatory movements.[59] The origin of the society is tied to the death of the Andoumboulou and to the first instance of death among men—both the

58. *Ibid.*, pp. 278–79 (my translation). The *yala* is a second-level sign, the "mark" or "image" of a thing. Cf. *ibid.*, p. 75, and Leiris, *La langue secrète des Dogon*, p. 148.

59. *Ibid.*, p. 9. See Germaine Dieterlen, "Les Cérémonies Soixantenaires du Sigui chez les Dogon."

result of Ogo-Yurugu's revolt. Its language is secret, the heritage of Ogo, and its chief public functions are the performance of funeral rites and the celebration of the Sigui festival. Since this festival is held only once every sixty years, the time symbolizing the period of creation, the Society of Masks is charged with renewing the life of the whole community, both when an individual life runs its course and when the "period" of communal life has played itself out and needs renewal.

The masks worn on these occasions represent spirits, the primordial ancestors, man in his fetal state, and the animals brought to earth by Nommo but vanquished with Ogo when they followed him in rebellion.[60] These images of animals and fishlike fetuses directly or indirectly embody the wildness of man's beginnings and point toward his birth into true humanity. At the crucial points of death and communal renewal they appear, disclosing the face of primal nature at the center of human life and holding out the promise of rebirth by a repossession of the first moment of transformation just when it is most needed.

Certainly the Dogon understand that the dances of the Society of Masks have their beginning in that moment. As Ogotemmeli explained to Griaule, ritual dance began after the "jackal's" incest with the earth had enabled him to possess her fiber skirt and had made him Amma's enemy. Amma was asleep, but Ogo, his "son" and rival, thought that he had died. Dressed in his mother's skirt, Ogo went up to the roof of Amma's "house" to mourn him. As he danced, "he spoke, for the fibers were full of moisture and words." Simultaneously honoring and scoffing at Amma, Ogo traced the shape of the world and the future in the dust of the roof as he invented the divining table that men would later copy.[61]

60. See Palau-Marti, *Les Dogon*, pp. 70, 75. Cf. Griaule, *Conversations with Ogotommêli*, pp. 128, 189–91; and Dieterlen, "Cérémonies Soixantenaires," p. 4.

61. See Griaule, *Conversations with Ogotemmêli*, pp. 186–87. Only after many years did Griaule discover that this "jackal" was the "pale Fox."

The ambiguities that abound here express the many-sidedness of death, Amma's relationship with Ogo and the relationship of a man to his father, and the mysterious interweaving of water, words, sex, and fiber. The men of the Society of Masks may dance at the funerals of elders in guilt and exultation because their oedipal fantasies have come true, but they also dance in grief and reverence, for they too are fathers. Ogo, after all, was wrong. Amma had not died. If the High God truly did go away and fatherhood ceased, there could be no world. Furthermore, Ogo did not retain possession of his mother's skirt. Its fibers crumbled, its moisture dried up, its words were stilled, and its sexual potency left him forever, so that divination would always symbolize man's unending need to search for wholeness.

Thus when the men reenact Ogo's dance, they are exploring the meaning of his discovery of death. First, then, they dance both to mourn and to rejoice, for the death that ends an elder's life and prefigures one's own certain death also ensures the movement of the generations, that everlasting cycle which constantly renews the world. Second, if Amma did not die, he did fall asleep. By calling attention to Amma's otiosity, Ogo goaded him into action, just as by giving Ogo his head, Amma initiated the movement of life. Third, even though his mother's fruitfulness turned sterile in his grasp, Ogo joined irrevocably, if inadequately, the human patterns of weaving, speaking, sex, and dancing. The Dogon say that " 'cloth is the center of the world,' that it expresses everything since the originating signs of all things were traced in it." [62] Ogo's skirt was fiber, not cloth, but it foreshadowed the revelation of "signs" through weaving. Once revealed, these signs could be reshaped, but never again hidden. Finally, Ogo's dance, however misconceived, did indeed lay bare the future of the world. That future, which is also an eternal re-presentation of the beginning, is manifested in each act of divination, but it is shown forth

62. Griaule and Dieterlen, "The Dogon," p. 107.

too, as a ceaselessly reborn cosmos, in each funeral. The dead are included in a living network of five generations, which reflects the first mythical generations. They will pass on one of their souls to a descendant so that when they are finally assimilated to the mythical ancestors, they will have recreated the order forged by Ogo's revolt and Nommo's sacrifice.

It was Nommo who, in union with the primal ironsmith, purified Ogo's dance as he purified the abortive first world. According to Ogotemmeli, the first dances took place in front of the smithy in the space prefiguring the village square. The smith's transforming hammer provided the music.

Now the team of dancers, the orchestra, and the setting all reproduce the scene and the actors of the original dance. To recall the mingled ringing sound of the iron and the muffled breathing of the bellows, small bells are attached to the drums; and when the drumstick, a symbol of the hammer, smites . . . , the roll and reverberation of the drums recalls the noise and clamour of the mythical smithy. . . .

And the team of dancers, the Society of Masks, is a picture of the whole world, for all men, all activities, all crafts, all ages, all foreigners, all animals, can be represented in masks. . . . The masked dancers are the world; and, when they dance in a public place, they are dancing the progress of the world and the world-order.[63]

There, in the center of the village, as the world dissolves in the death of a single person, the world is danced into life again, the rhythm of its movement refashioned from every sort of creature, each finally given its proper place and name, each becoming what it truly is. The dance is the risen Nommo's, but the impetus remains Ogo's.

The serpentine movement of the dance, whether at a funeral or at the Sigui festival, symbolizes and renews the fundamental spiral of life.[64] Yet there is a homier, earthier ritual especially emphasized during Sigui, which shows how the life cycle both reveals and renews the world. The very infrequency with

---

63. Griaule, *Conversations with Ogotemmêli*, p. 189.

64. The order of the celebration of the feast also moves in a certain helical pattern from village to village. See Dieterlen, "Cérémonies Soixantenaires," p. 2.

which Sigui is held suggests the key part that the elders of the community must play in its celebration. Yet it is not as masters of ceremonies that the elders chiefly perform during the feast. Like Ogotemmeli, they are living embodiments of the tradition of the people. It is their ordinary responsibility to hand down this tradition and the mythology giving it a voice. During this extraordinary feast, however, they have an extraordinary role.

Old age and death

During Sigui, all males consecrate themselves and the whole community to the new Great Mask, the symbol of their world, by a ritual of beer drinking. Seated on special "mask-seats" as they drink, they represent the mythic ancestor who helped to purify the world after the first human death.[65] But this drinking of beer is itself a cleansing ritual. The elders often drink too much during funeral rites and great feasts, but their drunkenness is looked on with affectionate amusement. It is the drunken elders, on the contrary, who berate passers-by, telling them, "The dead are dying of thirst," thus warning that the dead will remain in a radically unstable situation until their memorial altar pots (from which the child who inherits part of his ancestor's life force will always drink) are consecrated.[66] Since the prescribed funeral rites are very expensive and this final ceremony even more so, families often delay until there are several altar pots to be set up. This delay, however, leaves the dead in mid-passage and produces a two-fold disorder in the village. Because the dead have not been fully assimilated to the generation of ancestors, they seek to regain their life among the living, and their unsettled condition leaves the living unable to move forward into the next figure of the pattern of life. In Erikson's terms, the "cogwheeling of generations" has jammed.

The dead reveal the structural disorder caused by the delay

65. Griaule, *Conversations with Ogotemmèli*, p. 176. See Griaule and Dieterlen, *Renard pâle*, p. 366.
66. See Griaule, *Conversations with Ogotemmèli*, pp. 179–80.

in setting up the altar pots through their interference in the fermentation of the village's millet-beer. It is they who introduce into the beer its disordering quality as a sign of their own lack of wholeness and the resultant imbalance in the village. As the old men drink, their being resists the impure element and finally casts it out in words "disordered but effective," returning it to those who have made the dead wait.

The words find their way over walls and through doors till they reach the people responsible for the delay. The men staggering in the streets may stutter meaninglessly, sing, or shout insults; but their words are heard by all, and some will certainly have an end of mourning ritual to perform or a funeral account to pay. Even if the words of the drunkards are uttered indistinctly, they are clearly understood by all those careless people whose granaries are not full enough to start the rites.[67]

Illness, of course, misfortune of every sort, and more death are further warnings, and in such cases divination may lead the sufferers to do what the drunken elders could not persuade them of. Yet clearly the elders in their drunkenness have a unique power to oversee the passages from life to death to life. In their disorder they become the vindicators of order. Their drunkenness very literally renews the world as their distorted words help the dead pass on to ancesterhood. Thus Ogotemmeli could say that "for the old, drunkenness is a duty; it seems like disorder, but it helps to restore order."[68] The elders are so in tune with the cosmos that their very license discloses its deepest structure. Each old man, sloppy and abusive, dissolving in mind and body, becomes a living witness to communal renewal. Each is simultaneously the obedient, resurrected Nommo and the rebellious, defeated Ogo-Yurugu, both of whose actions shape and reshape the world.

The final stage of life is the time when one stuggles to achieve, in the face of death, a wholeness that gives meaning to all of life.

67. *Ibid.*, pp. 182–83.
68. *Ibid.*, p. 183.

Strength here takes the form of that detached yet active concern with life bounded by death, which we call *wisdom* in its many connotations from ripened "wits" to accumulated knowledge, mature judgment, and inclusive understanding. Not that each man can evolve wisdom for himself. For most, a living *tradition* provides the essence of it. But the end of the cycle also evokes "ultimate concerns" for what chance man may have to transcend the limitations of his identity.[69]

Thus there is marvelous irony in the Dogon understanding that the behavior of old men at Sigui—or even at an ordinary party—dramatizes the deepest wisdom of the society. In their drunken resurrection they incarnate that amazing word which speaks through their myth and which bestows on Ogo-Yurugu his sacred power, less soberly than when they instruct children, but far more vividly. The apparent mental and spiritual dissolution of the old men in the grip of the death-produced powers of beer mirrors the physical and mental decay of their old age. Yet the Dogon see that decay as the first bloom of new life, as they know that the intoxicating force of beer finally brings harmony out of ferment. More deeply still, as they believe that drunkenness, in its isolation and incoherence, is the fertile soil of a more coherent society, they understand that the long withdrawal of old age into the utter singleness of death is inwardly a movement into the center of life, where community is always being reborn.

OGO-YURUGU: COSMIC PARADIGM OF IRONY

The wisdom symbolized by Ogo-Yurugu throughout the Dogon cycle of life proclaims that the world comes into being and life achieves wholeness through conflict, disorder, and even death, as well as through obedience, harmony, and birth. Amma remains the creator, but his pure energy becomes visible through the crazed lens of Ogo's rebellion. His drive toward a wholeness that is also separation brings death and sex into creation, those dual powers which make the world truly human, even though both must be purified by Nommo.

69. Erikson, *Identity*, p. 140.

Ogo calls forth the sacrifice out of which human society comes into being, provokes the creation of the heavens, and outlines the careful ritual forms through which the Dogon order their lives. It is he, in short, as the cosmic antagonist, who stirs his protagonist twin to accomplish the great *agon* of Amma, the world's completion.

The imagery of drama is fitting here, for Dogon custom and myth mean to insist that life is a story always being told—beginning, developing, climaxing, ending, and beginning again. This story is embedded in the very structure of the human personality. With Nommo, Ogo is both the aboriginal source of that personality and its present inmost shape—its entelechy, its irresistible force and goal. Ogo's persistent attempts to gain control over his own destiny have not become a model to imitate; they have molded the human psyche itself so that, willy-nilly, man must experience Ogo's aloneness, anxiety, and search for wholeness. Especially in his sexuality, man relives Ogo's anguished search. Although his efforts to create a counter-world failed, the pattern of Ogo's cosmogonic odyssey was stamped on the human self and is felt as an insatiable concupiscence that Nommo must weave into livable form.

Each person manifests this form. Each is composed of the body; the *nyama*, a vital force partly received and passed on through the father's lineage; eight "grains" implanted in the clavicles and symbolic of the four elements and four points of the compass; and the four "body-souls" and four "sex-souls." [70] The body-souls are divided into two pairs of "twins" of opposite sex. One pair represents the twin placenta of Nommo, while the other pair represents both the part of Ogo's placenta that he stole and the greater part that he could not steal, which was transformed into the sun. The four "sex-souls," like those Ogo stole from Nommo and lost when he was circumcised, are given to each person at birth. However, even though Nommo's sacrifice made them available to man-

70. See Griaule and Dieterlen, *Renard pâle*, pp. 36–37.

kind, Ogo's rebellion foreclosed the possibility of human androgyny, so that after circumcision or excision only one pair of sex-souls remains. Thus the very defeat of Ogo ensures that each man or woman will bear in his or her inward self that incompleteness which Ogo experienced in the beginning and which led him to rebel. True, each person also receives the wholeness of Nommo so that he or she is an image of the restored cosmos. Yet the cosmos itself, in sun and earth, indeed in every part, reflects Ogo's struggle. The inner being of each person, then, reflects a primordial metamorphosis that has left it forever open to metamorphosis. Ogo has implanted the threshold to death and to life firmly within each individual.

The achievement of twinness

For this reason Ogo remains for the Dogon, even after his degradation into the Fox, a revelatory being who spells out the secrets of existence. Dogon thought and daily life are rooted in a conviction that human twinness was meant to express the creative wholeness of Amma, yet it is obvious that most Dogon are born and die alone. Their myth explores that vast gap between wholeness and aloneness. In spite of their tightly-knit community, the Dogon too must cope with solitude, sexual anxiety, and death. They do not, however, look at these experiences or at the rebellion that caused them as univocally evil. Without Ogo's search for his female twin nothing would be what it is, and even as Yurugu, he continues to reveal and enlarge the boundaries of life. The "beneficent ferment" of Ogo's opposition complements the orderly graciousness of Amma. The "space" between Amma's carefully balanced movements and Ogo's frenzied search finally became the hierophany that is the world, whose human dimension mirrors all its other faces.

Ogo draws forth Amma's creativeness, for Amma could not be fully the sacred center without a periphery having its own mode of being. Nor could the full range and depth of twinness be expressed without Ogo, and without twinness nothing could exist. For the Dogon, therefore, twinness is not at bottom a given, but an achievement, and man's aloneness is only a beginning. In most of his existence he attains twinness, wholeness, through the patient observance of the rhythms of the seasons and the years in ritual and custom. Yet in the most intimate areas of his life, those of generation and death, he must always embody Ogo's relentless thrust beyond the borders of the planned. Life in its fullness, as the celebration and the renewal of the cosmos, only happens where twinness has not yet been fully realized, but must be sought. If there were not two —really two, two to oppose and modify as well as to reflect— there could never be one or three.

In the deepest possible sense, then, Ogo-Yurugu is the agent of social and personal synthesis, in the present as well as in the beginning. With Amma and his own twin, Nommo, he helps to create the world by making true twinness possible. At each critical stage in Dogon life, his craving opens the passageway leading into that further communal life which more closely expresses cosmic wholeness. At each of these liminal moments Ogo-Yurugu enables the individual to recapitulate his past experience, to realize its transformation, and to link it to more levels of being. The Dogon male, for example, never leaves behind his early experience of oneness with his mother. As his identification with Ogo and Nommo becomes progressively deeper, however, it enables him to recognize increasingly larger meanings in this experience and its loss. His striving for an individuation that also inserts him into the patrilineal cycle of generations brings him a solely male identity through circumcision; tests the purpose of that identity during adolescence in the joking relationship with his uncle and aunt; unites the ambivalent forces of sexuality in marriage; discloses the social and sexual meanings of everyday work in the fields; and nurtures future generations by dancing out the recreation of the world with the Society of Masks. Thus the individual Dogon grows old and faces death knowing that the wholeness he has always sought has come to dwell in his own body.

Drunk or sober, alive or dead, he gives flesh to the creative reciprocity of yearning and fulfillment.

Discovery or projection

Ogo-Yurugu, with his twin, is the embodiment of an "epigenesis" that recreates Dogon society even as it draws forth the self through a spiral of interlocking challenges and promises, which is the process of bodily, psychic, social, and spiritual growth.[71] Additionally, Ogo links inner development and socialization by offering the individual and the whole community symbols, roles, and actions that turn conflicts into moments of communion and renewal. It would be wrong to say that this transformation takes place as the mythic conflict is internalized and Ogo vanquished by a triumphant Amma, the symbol of the Dogon superego. Nor does the prescription, "Where there is Ogo, there shall be Nommo," convey the subtlety of the Dogon perception of things. Partly, of course, this is so because the Dogon recognize and accept more easily than Freud the permanently analogical character of life and language; for them the many-layered quality of mythic speech is an advantage, not a liability. Moreover, the Dogon do not restrict the meaning of Ogo-Yurugu to that aspect of their lives which is unconscious, instinctive, literally primordial. Rather, they know that he symbolizes and discloses the doubleness of reality at every level, from the beginning to the present, from the public to the most inward, so that he touches every aspect of divinity, society, and personality.

Here Erikson's perspective can help us to look beyond Freudian categories and even beyond the Eriksonian school of

71. Erikson's most useful contribution to understanding the symbolic processes of religion is probably his notion of "epigenesis." Epigenesis refers to the "proper rate" and "normal sequence" of each stage of human growth, but it also underscores the interlocking of each stage with those which precede and follow it. For students of religion the importance of this concept lies in its implication that each stage in human life reimagines those which have preceded it. See *Childhood and Society*, pp. 65–72, 269–74; also "The Ontogeny of Ritualization."

psychohistory. It is certainly true that Ogo-Yurugu and the whole Dogon mythical system mirror as well as facilitate Dogon ego-synthesis and public order. Is he, then, a projection into a sacred cosmos of internal and communal processes? Is this not especially likely because of the social sophistication of the Dogon and the elegant fit between mythic narrative and daily life? After all, Erikson believes that any people—Sioux or American or Dogon—deliberately, if intuitively and unconsciously, shapes its children according to its social assumptions. Such intentionality seems to imply a conscious or unconscious creation of myth based on psychic and socio-economic requirements.

This question is in the end both metaphysical and theological. As usually posed, it tends to assume the unreality, or better perhaps, the purely metaphoric character of mythic and spiritual beings without challenging the adequacy of the linguistic and conceptual framework of the social and human sciences. Thus such a question calls for an examination of the epistemological underpinnings of these modes of thought (which include most of the psychoanalytical theories of religion) and a keener look at the issue of transcendence—its possibility, knowability, and articulation. In the summary we will have to face not only the Freudian reduction of religion to projection, but the various denials of transcendence made by Kant, Feuerbach, Lévi-Strauss, and others. Here the point is simply that Ogo-Yurugu has several sorts of meaning for the Dogon: he is spiritual being, symbolic paradigm, and principle of inner life. A uniquely Dogon image of the self as a meeting-place for all the forces of the cosmos (very much like Jung's identification of Jesus with the Self of Western man without Jung's subjectivism), Ogo-Yurugu makes possible that seizure of meaning and experience of transcendence which is the discovery of the sacred. He brings the cosmogony to bear on life in a recapitulative, integrating, freeing way, which may not rule out the possibility of projection, but which contrasts sharply with the self-estranging flight of neurotic projection. Ogo-Yurugu enables the Dogon to shape a livable present not by encouraging the repression of past conflicts, but by mastering their meaning; not by thwarting personal autonomy in the name of an externally imposed, abstract ideal, but by disclosing the link between the concupiscent itch and social order; not by pointing to a transcendence out in the future or up in the sky, but by revealing final meanings in daily time, ordinary space, and the most tangible happenings of the individual body.

In his openness to the possibilities of discovery, Erikson, in spite of his ambivalence about the ultimate nature of the religious quest, helps us to recognize the radical nondeterminism of a society as tightly woven as that of the Dogon. Thus the play of Dogon children and adolescents experiments with modes of transcendence. Dogon ritual embeds transcendence in everyday life. And the controlling aim of the Dogon life cycle is transcendence. For the developmental process moves through productive work and genital love toward a wholeness lying beyond both self and society.

If, then, in tying together inner growth and "social metabolism," [72] Ogo-Yurugu mirrors the experience of these two movements as they create the spiral of life, he mirrors also the experience of that final wholeness. To decide whether he is a projection or a revelation may be a theological question, but even as projection he reveals the discovery of transcendent identity. To see, as the Dogon do, the universe as a system of correspondences is to be free of our post-Enlightenment embarrassment at the meshing of the sacred and the secular. The Dogon have experienced the creation of their communal life as a disclosure of the inmost meaning of their place in the world. They know how that world comes into being between the poles of wetness and dryness, field and bush, work and rest, light and dark, male and female, submission and conflict, weaving and forging, animals and gods, divination and

72. See Erik H. Erikson, *Young Man Luther* (New York: W. W. Norton, 1958), p. 254.

everyday speech. They see that their world *is* geographically and historically because space and time too are the projects of a weaving and a forging that are more than human just because they are truly human. For the Dogon sacred cosmos and human world are not contradictories, but reciprocal symbols, each an epiphany of the other. Similarly, the process of ego-synthesis is itself a cosmogony, the work of the same polarities shaping the world into a life both given and made, both commonplace and transcendent. If, therefore, Ogo-Yurugu is a projection of Dogon experience, he is so precisely as the revelation of that experience of meaning, at once gift and discovery, on which Dogon existence is ceaselessly being founded.

Ogo-Yurugu as Dogon hermeneut

There are four ways in which Ogo-Yurugu discloses and interprets a specifically Dogon vision of the process of human growth and, at the same time, enlarges the range of the trickster pattern of which he is such an ambiguous embodiment. First, he provides an insight into early childhood experience that may rival Freud's in subtlety and wit. A brilliant section of *Dahomean Narrative* takes issue with the Freudian emphasis, drawn from the myth of Oedipus, on the "unconscious wish to kill the father or father-surrogate" and to seize his authority and sexual power.[73] This critique by Melville and Frances Herskovits, based on Otto Rank's methodologically careful study, *The Myth of the Hero*, rather than on the much shakier *Totem and Tabu*, suggests that the classical psychoanalytic approach to myth neglects the themes of paternal hostility and sibling rivalry in favor of the son's desire to vanquish and replace the father, because its proponents are "not accustomed to think in comparative, cross-cultural terms."[74] An analysis of Dahomean tales in the light of the polygynous Dahomean family shows how inadequate as a hermeneutic tool is a one-

73. Herskovits and Herskovits, *Dahomean Narrative*, pp. 85–95.
74. *Ibid.*, p. 88.

way application of ancient Greek tragedy to the West African situation. It is true, of course, that the usual application in our culture also oversimplifies both the Oedipus trilogy and the events of childhood, but the root difficulty is the methodological distortion that results from accounting for a complex effect by positing a single cause and from an unacknowledged ethnocentrism wearing the vestments of scientific universalism.

The Herskovits' study of the family life of the Fon leads them to place great weight on sibling rivalry as a key to the interpretation of myth. They insist that the hostilities between parents and children "are not unidirectional." Both in myth and in everyday life these hostilities reflect an "intergenerational competition," which takes different forms in polygynous and monogamous societies, but which is nonetheless rooted in early childhood rivalry for the attention and affection of the mother.

This rivalry sets up patterns of reaction that throughout life give rise to attitudes held toward the siblings . . . with whom the individual was in competition during infancy, and it is our hypothesis that these attitudes are later projected by the father upon his offspring. In myth . . . we must posit that the threat to the father or father-surrogate is to be seen as a projection of the infantile experience of sibling hostility upon the son. It may be said to be the response to the reactivation of early attitudes toward the mother under the stimulus of anticipated competition for the affection of the wife.[75]

Such elements are present in myth, however, not as they would be in a clinical report, nor even as they appear in dreams or fantasy. In the Dogon myth, for example, the rivalries of polygynous life have been so transmuted that they disclose the blessing as well as the blight of division, from the first painful separation from the mother at age two to the final separation from human life itself.

Thus the chief usefulness of the Herskovits' hypothesis for us lies in the way it gives deeper access to the creativity of the

75. *Ibid.*, pp. 94–95.

Dogon myth. Ogo is not simply jealous of Amma, his "father"; he knows that his anxiety is grounded in his utter dependence on the will of the one who does not unequivocally desire his independence. Furthermore, Ogo is vulnerable on two opposing counts: he is both the youngest and the first-born, the first really to emerge from the divine oneness. His situation is inherently ambiguous. He belongs to two generations, his father's and his own (as Griaule saw), and also to two worlds, the divine and the created. Thus the High God's otiosity—whether experienced as neglect or "sleep"—becomes for Ogo a hostility against which he must act to ensure his own fulfilled existence. His need is especially acute because of the possibility that he may be replaced by his twin, whose very priority (he has already received his female half) has given him, paradoxically, the security of a younger son.

It is no wonder, then, that the Dogon understand Ogo's increasingly erratic frenzy to be a misguided movement toward freedom, not a wish to slay or even to supplant his father. Moreover, his act of incest altogether lacks the horrific quality of Oedipus' marriage to Jocasta. The aura of tragedy is missing; the incest, such as it is, is truly *overcome*. True, Ogo is degraded and condemned to solitude and Nommo is castrated and sacrificed, but in bearing together the burden of Ogo's rebellion, they become the twin founders of the world. This absence of the tragic is something other than the mere lack of cosmic remorse or stoic *apatheia* in the face of implacable and incomprehensible destiny. That absence, rather, signifies the Dogon conviction that reality is always moving in a spiral of growth drawing even rebellion, incestuous desire, paternal rage, murderous jealousy, and death into the service of life.

This, of course, is the real point of the Dogon myth, its creative center. In spite of the conflict present in their lives, the Dogon do not see human existence as a grim struggle among competing autonomies, ending in total victory and unconditional surrender. The witty playfulness of the adolescent boy's relationship with his aunt represents more than a double displacement of his feelings of aggression and sexual desire, for it further transforms a search for wholeness that is already regarded, with amused respect, as both normal and sacred—in the nature of things. In the language of the myth, Amma is neither tyrant nor victim. He sets in motion the spiral of life and ensures its final establishment. He both upholds and stands back from an order that continues to be reborn through the unexpected as well as the customary, through divination as well as Sigui, through drunkenness as well as piety, through concupiscence as well as communality. The Dogon father, then, carries in the depths of his selfhood the whole cast of mythic figures in constant interaction. Within him are Amma —generating, delaying, opposing, shaping, growing silent; Ogo-Yurugu—itching, rebelling, losing, still leading; Nommo—obeying and achieving dominion, dying and rising, castrated and endlessly fecund; and not least of all, the primordial matrix itself—torn and whole, sun and earth, both memory and hope. It is this manifold being which he, together with his wife and all the people, imparts to his sons and daughters.

Thus the second way in which Ogo-Yurugu discloses the Dogon vision of human life is that he makes human bodiliness a specifically Dogon experience. Many, if not most, African societies are patrilineal and polygynous, give children an intense experience of maternal intimacy and then break this intimacy abruptly, practice circumcision, and encourage cross-cousin marriage.[76] Yet, unlike the Dogon, few of these societies know their social structures so completely as a network of many-layered analogues, while none of them, of course, uses the same imagery to express the underlying patterns of their lives. To question this difference is, in one sense, to ask why the Greeks created great philosophy and the Romans did not; almost any answer can assume some semblance of probability. Asked in another way, however, such a question can lead to an

76. See, for example, Marja-Liisa Swantz, "Organism and Symbolism," *IDOC-International* 26 (May 1971): 49.

awareness of how a people, in this place and in these bodies, are at home in the world. Certainly there seems to be a relationship between the clear boundaries of Dogon life and their vivid sense of man as an image of the cosmos, from his toenails to his skull and from his liver to his fingertips.[77] Furthermore, the pattern of the human body is represented at every level of social order, from homestead to village-quarter, to village, to district, so that every organ or segment is imaged ever more broadly in organizations of the body social. The intensity of this Dogon insistence that the organic character of their life corresponds to the shape of the human body unquestionably creates as well as springs from that character.

Thus the link between body and society is discovered inwardly as well, in the very processes molding both person and community. The formation of children within the womb is symbolized by figures that are at once the "forms" of fish and easily recognizable drawings of the male and female sexual organs. These figures are assimilated to that part of the person's "body-souls" which signify Nommo's section of the primordial placenta. At death the person, through a complex series of ritual transformations, becomes again a "fish"—both the fetal form and the person's inner pattern—representing the dead and resurrected Nommo, whose members give birth to social order.[78] As we have seen, Ogo-Yurugu continues to shape the physical and social bodiliness of human life. Each soul reflects Ogo's divided yet transformed placenta, while men especially are drawn forth into life by the same solitariness and drive for their complementary female self by which Ogo began to prod creation into being. "He was alone from birth," says Ogotemmeli, "and because of this he did more things than can be told."[79]

Ogo-Yurugu, then, provides the Dogon with an image of man's radical aloneness, but it is a vital image empowering

77. See Griaule, *Conversations with Ogotemmèli*, pp. 50–55.
78. See Griaule and Dieterlen, *Renard pále*, pp. 367–80.
79. Griaule, *Conversations with Ogotemmèli*, p. 23.

Dogon life to achieve its own specific density through him. The Dogon story is not tragedy, though it contains tragic elements —incomplete or flawed characters; irresistible desire and struggle, dread and retribution; an irretrievable shattering of harmony resulting in suffering and death. Genesis moves beyond tragedy because of Yahweh's fidelity to man, the image of his own being, a fidelity experienced by mankind as mercy, but the Dogon transcend both the moral and the metaphysical categories of tragedy in another way. The symbol of this transcendence is the two-sidedness of Ogo-Yurugu. He has been defeated and degraded, yet he lives on as a revelatory being who continues to help mold the cosmos. He is speechless, yet continues to speak, sexless, yet ceaselessly engendering the sexuality of the whole human race. He was a divine being and is now an animal, yet his passage from one state to the other makes possible that being who seems both and neither. He is the very incarnation of aloneness, yet his revulsion against that solitude helps to shape human community and even the bonds tying man to the rest of creation. In Ogo-Yurugu, therefore, the Dogon look at what things are and reach past sadness, past pity and terror, even past *apatheia*, to an explanation of the world where each thing has its place and man himself is at home.

Synchronicity and humor

Griaule's portrait of Ogotemmeli—shrewd, contemplative, gracious—gives a clear image of what this Dogon sense of at-homeness looks like in the flesh. To ask what that sense *feels* like leads to a consideration of the third and fourth ways in which Ogo-Yurugu specifies Dogon life and suggests the inward quality of the Dogon personality. These are Ogo-Yurugu's simultaneity and the revelation he makes of Dogon irony.

By simultaneity I simply mean the dual, contemporaneous presence of Ogo-Yurugu to the Dogon as both primordial *nommo* in the process of rebellion near the center of the divine order and defeated Fox in endless movement on the fringes of human society. Ogo-Yurugu's two-sidedness has its roots in this simultaneity. Just as the High God is not really a god who went away at some historical moment, but the-god-who-went-away, so the Dogon do not know Ogo-Yurugu in two states separable in time, but as the *nommo*-who-lost-his-status-and-lives-as-Fox. Such a distinction helps to break down our excessively linear way of thinking so that we can capture some sense of mythic synchronicity. For the Dogon, Amma is at once near and remote, active and retired, transparent and opaque. Likewise, Ogo-Yurugu is always lusting and always impotent, always in the center and forever on the margins, always seeking and never truly exhausted, always deep within and still most public, always revealing and ever speechless and hidden. This contemporaneity of both Ogo and Yurugu finds its most powerful expression in divination and human sexuality. In divination, he is the Fox who is endlessly going and coming to sketch the living pattern of the world and to disclose how men must move to bring that pattern forth. In human sexuality, Ogo-Yurugu establishes that pattern in the center of each person. If "the sexual organ is the high altar of man's foundation,"[80] then Ogo-Yurugu is the instrument by which Amma gives that inmost place of offering and communion its true shape. Yet the organ itself is only the outward sign of an inward movement. That movement symbolizes both man's aloneness and his coming together with woman, for both are needed to produce the never-ending spiraling of generation, which the Dogon know as the final structure of reality. Present as the hidden ferment of the divine center and as the boundless potency of the still formless bush, Ogo-Yurugu goes and comes within each person to create—always with Amma, Nommo, and the earth itself—not just any life, but that life, reflected throughout the universe, which the Dogon recognize as specifically their own.

80. *Ibid.*, p. 159.

What we are speaking of can have no other name than irony, the yoking of opposites in an act of imagination that brings them together without absorption or mixing, holding them in perpetual interaction. We do not know as much as we would like to know about Ogo-Yurugu and the language of Dogon delight. Yet we do know a few things: the story of the Fox's dance when he believed that he had vanquished his father; the amused attitude of adults toward a child's early misbehavior and their insistence that children have a joking relationship with Ogo-Yurugu; the similar relationship that an adolescent boy has with his maternal uncle's wife and that adult males have with their counterparts among the Bozo people; the link between raillery and sex; and the amusement created by the drunkenness of old men. At least in these instances, we can see the Dogon imagination using humor as an image of the creative necessity of disorder. In each case the Dogon know Ogo-Yurugu as the living paradigm of that disorder, a disruption that is, finally, not merely unavoidable and beneficent, but delightful.

Moreover, especially in the joking relationship, laughter itself becomes a mode of liminality, a reversal of order for the revelation of deeper order, an abolition of time for the capture of time. "This form of alliance, using . . . laughter, insult, and mockery, abolishes the generational system and the ties of relationship, denies the reality of the passage of time, and in a word turns the world upside down to enable it to proceed rightside up."[81] The Dogon call the joking relationship *mangu*, and Griaule has shown how they and the Bozo use it to achieve a mutual catharsis that is also an affirmation of their separate identities.[82] When Dogon and Bozo meet, each insults the parental sexual organs, the religious practices, or the sacred customs of the other before engaging in normal conversation. The basis of this practice is the belief that in their inmost being each

81. Calame-Griaule, *Ethnologie et langage*, p. 401 (my translation).
82. See Griaule, "L'Alliance cathartique," pp. 246–48, 256–58.

possesses an element belonging to the other so that both persons "are complete only in each other's presence." [83] Thus, as with an adolescent boy and his aunt, a kind of twinship, in which the partners simultaneously accept and deny both their separateness and their oneness, comes into being. The Dogon elders insist that the insults are directed to that part of oneself which lives in the Bozo; in this way a man cleanses himself by loading his impurity on a more distant "self," even as he affirms that the line between him and that other self is both bond and boundary.

In an important essay, Mary Douglas has applied to ritualized joking Freud's notion that jokes use anomalies—conflicts in form and meaning—to give the id a romp and to save the ego psychic energy. [84] She expands that notion to give joking an even more creative purpose, for she sees that the meeting of nonform with form is, usually, a disclosure of new form, new life, hidden in the old. Energy is not simply saved; it is released in a recreation of the habitual world. Where ritual says that social patterns are inescapable and jokes claim that they are escapable, joking rituals insist, in Douglas's words, that "anything is possible" [85]—that, in fact, the inescapable is always pregnant with escape. In this perspective, ritual joking is necessarily a liminal experience, a passage beyond order through antiorder to transformed order. As the Dogon know, it is this ironic imagination embodied in Ogo-Yurugu that gives joking the power to maintain, restore, and enlarge personal and communal worlds.

Dogon irony ends in delight because Ogo-Yurugu and Nommo, as agents of Amma, have seized disorder on behalf of life in such a way that nothing can ever finally be lost or wasted. The Dogon are not stupid. They weep at death, get angry at their children, fear the powers of the new generation

83. *Ibid.*, p. 257.
84. Mary Douglas, "The Social Control of Cognition: Some Factors in Joke Perception."
85. *Ibid.*, pp. 370, 373.

and the destructiveness of sex, and suffer with the pains of disease and age. Yet the elegance of their system of thought, the wisdom and dignity of an elder such as Ogotemmeli, and the coherence of their social system show the confident grasp of the present that only comes from an ease with the past and a hope for the future. Such an ease and such a hope can spring from many sources, but Ogo-Yurugu, the chief actor in the Dogon mythic drama, suggests that here they spring from a radically ironic imagination, capable of an act of communal oxymoron linking death and dancing, disobedience and tradition, play and social order, absurdity and wisdom, aloneness and twinness. Because it is above all Ogo-Yurugu who embodies these linkages, the pattern of wholeness that emerges from them ensures that nothing will be lost since nothing has been swept under the rug of forgetfulness. Childhood especially is neither repressed nor clung to, but through the mediation of Ogo-Yurugu becomes an endlessly widening hierophany unveiling the interrelated meanings of every plane of existence.

Both as *nommo* and as Fox, Ogo-Yurugu shuttles between worlds, joining the world above of Amma and the world beyond of the bush to the world of man. More deeply still, he moves within each person to link the private world of childhood with the social world of adulthood. In the process he reveals that creative wholeness, of which twinness is the symbol, lies in a thrusting outward—in work, in sex, in ritual—which at the same time reaches inward to manifest one's identification with the cosmos. This discovery of incarnate transcendence orders society and makes adulthood possible even as it shows that man himself is the threshold where what can be passes into what fully is.

We would like to know more about Dogon laughter, but Griaule has given us one especially significant glimpse of it.

[The Hogon's wife] was an old woman with a gentle voice, which broke at certain words because of palpitations of the heart; bending her small round head forward, wide-eyed and open-mouthed, she listened intently to what the European said to her.

"God brings you!" she said. "Give me a cure for my heart!"

"It is old stuff," he explained. "How can one make a new heart out of an old one?"

He repeated this joke to her every time they met, because he knew it made her laugh till she cried.[86]

New hearts from old stuff, laughter and tears: Griaule repeated his little joke because he was kind, but the old lady knew a joking relationship when she was in one and understood that Griaule's "insult" was actually a healing riddle. Her laughter was both her solution to his riddle and her acceptance of the cure he offered her. A guess perhaps, yet we know that few peoples have been as fascinated with the possibilities and the metaphysics of irony as have the Dogon.

I think of the funeral they held for Griaule when they learned of his death in France.[87] They prepared an image of him, dressed in European bush outfit, notebook in hand, and set it in place to watch and record the rites of his own properly Dogon funeral. It was surely a mark of respect for a fascination that matched their own, but just as surely the funeral displayed Dogon irony at its keenest pitch. This irony, as far beyond mockery as it is beyond stoic resignation, is in the end simply delighted amazement at the "astonishing word of the world" that is the story of human life, whose secret was very probably disclosed in the laughter of the Hogon's wife. Ogo-Yurugu's name is bestowed on that story because, revealer of riddles, himself all synchronicity, all irony, he especially knows the trick of harnessing dissolution to rebirth, of bringing new life from old stuff, of yoking in a single dance the twin movements of life and death. He above all embodies the endless retelling of that story which is all that is and whose every repetition answers the riddle of the world in a burst of joy.

86. Griaule, *Conversations with Ogotemmêli*, pp. 59–60.
87. See *The Illustrated London News* 231 (August 24, 1957): 287–89.

CHAPTER SIX

Toward a Theory
of the Trickster

And what is "common" about "the common life"? What if
some genius were to do with "common life" what Einstein
did with "matter"? Finding its energetics, uncovering its
radiance.

SAUL BELLOW, *Mr. Sammler's Planet*

Genius is nothing more or less than childhood recovered at
will—a childhood now equipped for self-expression.

BAUDELAIRE

SPEAKING OF THE SACRED

THE TRICK now is to bring these four trickster-figures
into relationship with one another without freezing them into
an abstraction or blurring their differences. If we began by em-
phasizing the hermeneutic value of a pattern open to a broad
range of symbolic expressions, it will not do to end in slavery to
a tidy structure that satisfies our logic by denying the trickster's. The task seems like the challenge given to Legba—to
dance while playing gong, bell, drum, and flute. Fortunately,
the trickster's agility, the quality that makes definitions of him
seem so clumsy, is supremely verbal. Words are what he juggles best, and Legba's dance—clanging, ringing, thumping,
fluting as he leaps and whirls in perfect step and exact
rhythm—expresses his linguistic deftness. We have just seen
how Ogo-Yurugu embodies that amazing word of the world
which discloses the personal and communal, human and divine movement of life in Dogon speech. Eshu, the cosmic
iconographer, shatters every worn-out image of life so that the
language of Ifa divination may call forth the sacrifice that

brings once again into intimate conversation the world's every part. Legba knows the words creative of intercourse, sexual and heavenly, ritual and economic, and everywhere his phallus stands as a symbol of muteness overcome and communion reestablished. Because Ananse can "read" the words hidden in Nyame's mind, and because he proves himself the master of all discourse, his name is given to the stories the Ashanti tell to remember and thereby to recreate their life together.

The task of discerning the pattern revealed in these figures, therefore, becomes lighter because each of them, in his mastery of symbolic and mythical language, symbolizes that very multivalence which Eliade has recognized as inherent in every religious image and structure. The linguistic nimbleness of these tricksters shows how each image gathers together a "whole bundle of meanings" and encloses "many frames of reference." To translate any such "image into a concrete terminology by restricting it to any one of its frames of reference is to . . . annihilate, to annul it as an instrument of cognition."[1] A fortiori, then, the translation of the translator of the sacred cannot aim to confine him within the boundaries of the univocal. To have all sacred words is to be capable of all sacred moves; the trickster can change forms as easily as he can tell lies. To pin him to one meaning is to annul his power to link the many levels of experience and to destroy the imaginative irony that he incarnates. His dance pulverizes the univocal and gives voice to each of the "surprises of the actual."

As Hans Penner has pointed out, however, every theory is a reduction, or, in the words of Meyer Fortes, a "breaking up of the vivid, kaleidoscopic reality of human action, thought, and emotion."[2] Thus even if the trickster's dance is intrinsically elusive, we must find a way to draw ideas from process or end in mere description. It is here that Ricketts has made a real contribution to understanding the trickster. By insisting that the

1. Eliade, *Images and Symbols*, p. 15.
2. Meyer Fortes, *The Dynamics of Clanship among the Tallensi* (London: Oxford University Press, 1945), p. vii.

trickster in his wholeness combines the "elements" of trick-ster-fool, transformer, and culture hero, he makes the question of the trickster pattern a matter of discovering the logic holding together disparate and even contradictory aspects of a single figure. Yet these aspects of the trickster's structure must not be imagined as elements in the sense of impermeable monads, but as fluid constellations of meaning. To look at them this way has the advantage of granting at once the trickster's multivalence and of enabling us to compare Ananse, Legba, Eshu, and Ogo-Yurugu with one another and other tricksters without collapsing them into a single form or reducing the cultural logic upholding them to a single dialectic.

From this angle, each element of Ricketts's pattern has several meanings, and each shades off into the other to suggest at the start the dynamism holding them in balance. Thus Ananse appears as a trickster-fool in the grip of a ravenous concupiscence that drives him through every ordinary barrier in search of—what? Not sex or food, really, but the very rub of life. That is his project, and he launches himself for the sake of his trajectory regardless of its target. In this sense his trickiness cannot be assessed in terms of his own "victory" or "defeat." In his dealing with enemies, friends, animals, gods, spirits, his own family and body, Ananse embodies transaction. For this reason he is a mediator specializing in "exchanges"—a perpetually open passageway. He transforms by no plan except the shape of his own urge to realize the act of dealing, yet because this drive necessarily creates intercourse, he establishes the social geography of the world in the very process of playing out his own inner design.

Still, to call him a culture hero is to speak too loftily. Neither a mythic nor a social entrepreneur whose self-determination determines the world under the guidance of some invisible hand, Ananse is far more ambiguous. He does not impose his form on the world, but spins out a web of purpose, a network of relationships, in which the given reality of others—Nyame, Asase Yaa, women, the wild—is as significant as his own. The pattern comes full circle if we see that Ananse's creativeness is linked to his funniness. He is "wonderful" because his trickiness, his innate ambiguity, captures contradiction for human life, yet he is most wonderful of all just because this trickiness does not spring from heroism, but from insouciance. He amuses as he shapes and shapes as he amuses because his disclosure of the juncture of order and disorder reveals that what is given is truly a gift.

Legba, Eshu, and Ogo-Yurugu similarly open up the pattern of trickster-transformer-culture hero. Legba's lust may appear to be a more conventional engine of disruption than Eshu's desire to "feed" the *orisha* and Ogo's craving for perfect twinness, but each of these revives every process clogged by human impotence and stupidity or by divine indifference and envy. Each of the three is driven past the boundaries of original order— Ogo past those of the primordium itself, Eshu past those of social habit and forgetfulness, Legba past those of primal inertia and contemporary impasse. Each sets his own desire in opposition to a cultural or cosmic order, but each moves for the sake of movement itself. Thus all three show their trickiness more by their agility than by their pranks. People may or may not laugh at their wiles, but they know their slipperiness as that of sacred transactors, middlemen whose power lies in their capacity to face every way at once.

Eshu's stroll on the boundary and Ogo's dance on his "dead" father's roof sketch with particular sharpness their liminal power. All three transform because they touch all forms and all times simultaneously. And because each embodies synchronicity, each continually reconnects the present moment with the moment of his society's beginning by means of divination. Here, however, we can see how specifically the trickster works. He makes possible not simply an abstract system of binary oppositions, but a speech sacred because it is spoken just here and just now. Thus Ogo-Yurugu's power to connect is the chief disclosure of that spiral movement which precisely establishes the correspondences of Dogon life. Legba at each

threshold symbolizes the historical imagination of the Fon discovering the two-way cosmic exchange between old and new,
inside and outside. Eshu in the marketplace or at the divining
tray recasts each event to image the whole Yoruba universe.

Each society knows that its trickster-figure, whether non-
chalantly, implacably, or rebelliously, has brought forth its
visible form as he deals on every plane of being and juggles
every manner of relationship. Furthermore, each knows that
he helps to forge its inward and unseen order, the process by
which a person becomes a living icon of the network of divine
and human exchanges that make up communal life. Is such a
forging heroic? It seems both more and less. Its very depth
—its intimacy, its ordinariness—shows that the dazzling boldness of Legba and the passionate willfulness of Ogo are expressed accurately, not in grand symbols of "titanic insub-
ordination," but in a moment of initiatory hilarity and in the
drunkenness of old men—that is, at the heart of ritual and
social absurdity. Still, the social density that these tricksters
achieve in the continuing commerce with others so fittingly experienced in the market suggests the greatness of their ac-
complishment. These apparent individualists become sources
of community because they join the transcendent and the
daily, the center and the circumference, the formed and the
formless in their revelation of man himself as the confluence of
the same forces that are shaping his world. They are not so
much the heroes of a culture as its exemplars.

Again the pattern returns to its beginning, for the exemplar-
ity of Ananse, Legba, Eshu, and Ogo displays itself in a delight
evoked by story, "forgiveness," riddle, and adolescent joke.
Moreover, this circularity of the trickster pattern points to its
own deepest meaning: the unveiling of the imaginative process that is able to marry disorder and transformation and social order, foolishness and wisdom, history and timelessness.
Thus the answer to Ricketts's question about the kind of logic
that combines the elements of the trickster into a single structure is, on one level, simply this: it is the logic of sacred mul-

tivalence. But we cannot end there. We must next examine three attempts to express that logic in other terms and to substitute more univocal language for its "bundles of meanings." The attempts fail, I think, but the questions they raise will give greater resonance to the analogous use of language that the trickster exemplifies so boldly and that is the most useful way of speaking about him—or about any other religious fact.

THREE EXPLANATIONS OF THE TRICKSTER

The Jungian hypothesis

When reading Carl Jung's essay on the trickster,[3] one is struck at once by the breadth of learning and the keenness of mind he brings to his analysis. As we have noted, however, this analysis is undermined by too close a reliance on Radin's collection of the Winnebago trickster cycle. Jung simply assumes that this cycle is normative and that its trickster's movement from an undifferentiated psychic state to an adult capacity for differentiation represents a pure survival of an archaic form. Critics have pointed out that Jung's lack of contact with the lives of traditional peoples can give his interpretations "an air of fantasy,"[4] yet his sensitivity to the symbolic meanings of the trickster suggests that his opinions cannot be dismissed out of hand. Jung's intent, of course, is to establish the trickster as an archetype still lurking in the sophisticated psyche of Western man.

In picaresque tales, in carnivals and revels, in sacred and magical rites, in man's religious fears and exaltations, this phantom of the trickster haunts the mythology of all ages. . . . He is obviously a "psychologem," an archetypal psychic structure of extreme antiquity. In his clearest manifestations he is a faithful copy of an undifferentiated human consciousness, corresponding to a psyche that has already left the animal level. That this is how the trickster figure originated can hardly be contested.[5]

3. "On the Psychology of the Trickster Figure."
4. See Herskovits and Herskovits, *Dahomean Narrative*, pp. 95–103.
5. Jung, "On the Psychology," p. 202.

Jung identifies this "archetypal psychic structure" with his notion of the "shadow," that component of the personality which
represents an earlier, prerational level of life, but which is still
present, though hidden in or repressed into the unconscious.
This "puerile and inferior" personality reveals itself in irrational, nonsensical behavior, at once masking and pointing
toward an even deeper aspect of the self, the "anima"—all
"that a man can never get the better of and never finishes cop-
ing with."[6]

For Jung, then, the trickster symbolizes both a potential for
regression into unconsciousness and a call toward true wholeness. Even in his still incompletely evolved state, the trickster
holds forth the possibility of transforming the "meaningless
into the meaningful." His very objectification in mythic form
reveals movement from primordial unconsciousness toward
integrated consciousness. His buffoonery is partly the mockery with which this more mature state looks at the ignorance of
the past, partly a promise that the dark side of life still holds a
blessing for the future. This duality is embodied in the trickster's "*divine-animal* nature, on the one hand superior to man
because of his superhuman qualities, and, on the other hand,
inferior to him because of his unreason and unconsciousness."[7] Thus Jung sees that the very act of retelling the myth of
the trickster is a "therapeutic anamnesis," a means both of
holding the shadow figure in the light of consciousness and of
challenging the hearer to reach toward the fullness of "relatedness" that only the embrace of the anima can bring. For
the individual as well as for the collective, the growth of consciousness "brings liberation from imprisonment in *agnoia*,
unconsciousness," and bestows both light and healing.[8] As
the trickster gradually sheds his gross, antinomian aspects, he
becomes a savior figure, "in confirmation of the mythological
truth that the wounded wounder is the agent of healing, and

6. *Ibid.*, p. 210.
7. *Ibid.*, p. 204.
8. *Ibid.*, p. 211.

the sufferer takes away suffering."[9] He becomes his opposite as unconsciousness becomes consciousness and unrelatedness becomes relation.

Others have tied this hypothesis to the procedures of Jungian analysis, but have held firmly to Jung's belief in the psychohistorical genesis of the trickster.[10] It is this belief which weakens Jung's hypothesis and lessens its value as an interpretive tool. Karl Kerényi's essay, however, which appeared as a companion to Jung's, shows the two major flaws in his approach. In the first place, Kerényi sees that the trickster has a "greater consistency, an unchanging, indestructible core that not only antedates all the stories told about him, but has survived in spite of them."[11] Jung is so fascinated by the possibility that the trickster will demonstrate how personal psychic ontogeny recapitulates the collective phylogeny that he can only regard the trickster-figure as a moment in an evolutionary process, never giving enough weight to his irreducible ambivalence. Certainly Jung would be comfortable with the notion of the "two-way mind,"[12] which Ananse and Eshu exemplify, but his evolutionary focus makes it difficult for his theory to absorb the Ashanti and the Yoruba awareness that this two-wayness is a goal, not a stage.

In the second place, Kerényi shows the reason why Jung's hypothesis does not really fit even the less episodic, more narrative myths of Legba and Ogo-Yurugu. That reason is Jung's inattention to the social context and intent of the myths, a neglect that finally exposes the shakiness of his approach. Kerényi recognizes that the trickster is both radically social and the "enemy of boundaries." Within the strictness of "archaic social hierarchies," he says,

9. *Ibid.*, p. 196.
10. See John Layard, "Critical Notice of *The Trickster*, by Paul Radin" and "Note on the Autonomous Psyche and the Ambivalence of the Trickster Concept"; and Philip Metman, "The Trickster Figure in Schizophrenia."
11. "The Trickster," p. 174.
12. Layard, "Note on the Autonomous Psyche," p. 26.

nothing demonstrates the meaning of the all-controlling social order more impressively than the religious recognition of that which evades this order, in a figure who is the exponent and personification of the life of the body: never wholly subdued, ruled by lust and hunger, forever running into pain and injury, cunning and stupid in action. Disorder belongs to the totality of life, and the spirit of this disorder is the trickster. His function in an archaic society is . . . to add disorder to order and so make a whole, to render possible, within the fixed bounds of what is permitted, an experience of what is not permitted.[13]

Kerényi denies any mythic evolution of the trickster, therefore, because the contradictoriness of the trickster is rooted in the social patterns out of which his imaginative forms spring. The myths of the Fon, for example, show Legba distancing himself from his mother, Mawu, and becoming progressively absorbed in the affairs of men, yet he remains Mawu's interpreter. His disruptions of the human space he has helped to create turn dead ends into crossroads and depend on his never-relinquished intimacy with Mawu. Legba both goes away and stays home so that he can reflect and make possible the daily Fon passage from inside to outside and back again.

On an even deeper level, Ogo-Yurugu reveals a theory of human growth that differs from Jung's despite many points of agreement. Like Jung, the Dogon know that "each man is his own primitive ancestor,"[14] but their view of time diverges from his. Aware of synchronicity, Jung still believes that linear history is paramount. Although he sees that the personal and collective past is present in each individual, Jung's comments on the trickster show that he thinks of wholeness as the fruit of an evolution away from certain irrational, animal-like states for which he finds the trickster a fitting symbol. The Dogon, on the other hand, believe that time is radically synchronic. Of course they experience its passage and even recognize a cer-

13. Kerényi, "The Trickster," p. 185.
14. Karl Stern, *The Third Revolution* (New York: Harcourt, Brace, & Co., 1954), p. 207.

tain nonrepeatable quality to the events of the first times. Yet Ogo is present to them even in his defeated state as Yurugu. He continues to draw forth the pattern of personal and social reality within the body-souls of each person and upon the divination tables on the periphery of the village, especially at each passage into larger life. He thus remains a perpetual image of the simultaneous presence of all time, especially the beginnings, those most elusive moments of all.

What Jung sees concerning the trickster's transformation of the meaningless into the meaningful, above all in the therapy that takes place whenever he is remembered, the Dogon—as well as the Ashanti, the Fon, and the Yoruba—see too. Yet, as Jung realizes, they do not see their trickster as a "remnant" of an earlier level of consciousness.[15] They know him, rather, as a ceaseless revealer of their human situation. This is a delicate point, for certainly Ogo is in some way experienced by the Dogon as the dark image of Nommo, the manifest paradigm of the human ego. Moreover, the Dogon recognize that the struggle for wholeness necessitates a movement beyond the primal oneness with the mother toward a mode of relatedness stimulated by Ogo, but only achieved through the submission of Nommo. The difference between the two views lies in the Dogon belief that this movement is truly recapitulative—not linear and evolutionary, but spiral and epigenetic. Ogo is always becoming Yurugu; he is always past yet still present, always transformed yet still transforming, always transcended yet never superseded. It is just this conviction of the simultaneity and correspondence of all planes of being and consciousness that enables the Dogon, like the other peoples we have studied, to see their trickster-figure as the embodiment of the passage out of an incompletely realized center, into the wild, and back into a center enlarged by both departure and return. To remember Ogo is to perform sociotherapy because

15. Jung, "On the Psychology," pp. 200–201.

in re-membering every dissolution becomes a potential re-newal, and contradiction itself is included in the social order.

Finally, of course, Jung's assessment of the trickster does not square with our four societies' understanding of him because he differs with them about the nature of social order itself. When Jung claims that "outwardly people are more or less civilized but inwardly they are still primitives," [16] he is lump-ing together three processes—biological evolution, sociolog-ical change, and individual psychological development—which are analogous but not synonymous. Lacking a principle such as Erikson's epigenesis, one will almost inevitably blur this distinction and end by simply identifying past and present or by denying any real inner link between them. Jung, then, for all his respect for the dark, chthonic forces of the uncon-scious, imposes an identity of meaning on "primitive-archaic" man and "undeveloped-unconscious" man that rests on a faulty parallel between pretechnological society and child-hood. This belief that an earlier—in time, in size, in economic specialization—form of social organization is equivalent to a simpler, childlike form of mental organization produces a view of the trickster at variance with his *intended* complexity.

There is more here than first meets the eye, for of all modern thinkers Jung has most insisted on the individual as an epiphany of collective mankind, a theme that the Dogon elabo-rate endlessly and that is clearly emphasized by the diviniza-tion practices of the Fon and the Yoruba. Yet where the latter three, with the Ashanti, see the body social as an image and pattern of the individual and the cosmos, Jung seems to think of any particular social form as a mere ripple on the surface of human consciousness. Unlike Eliade, who also recognizes a certain transcultural, transhistorical permanence to patterns and images that first come to light at very definite cultural and historical moments, Jung does not seem interested in the social

16. *Ibid.*, p. 208.

specificity of his archetypes except as a metaphor for a particular stage in the development of consciousness. The social order that he accepts as a given, though he decries its illusions of pure rationality, is our own secularized world, where all sacralities—the cross of Christ and the enlightenment of the Buddha as well as the antics of the trickster—are dissolved into their conceptual content, all religious phenomena reduced to psychic noumena, all religious systems chased into the sacristy of the individual mind and restricted to the task of arranging quietly its furniture. This order, like the universe it perceives beyond it, is essentially boundaryless, always expanding, wholly centrifugal. Its only fixed point is personal consciousness in constant evolution; and thus it is really no order at all, but an external alliance of finally incommunicable centers, themselves nuclei that are only transitory happenings.

Jung, then, can accept the trickster's movement outward as a symbol of a movement inward, but he cannot take seriously the trickster's irreducible grossness as the representation and reaffirmation of social concreteness.[17] Ananse *incorporates* contradiction, disease, and jealousy into Ashanti order, as Eshu incorporates disorder, Legba concupiscence, or Ogo-Yurugu contempt for preconceived wholeness into Yoruba, Fon, or Dogon order. They transform the meaningless into the meaningful, not by becoming saviors, but by remaining ambiguous, facing both ways on every boundary. Indeed, they are transformers just because their passage beyond these boundaries continually provokes intercourse between what is outside man and what is inside him.

Strangely—strangely because one can guess how Freud would have dismissed the trickster, with far less sensitivity than Jung, as the image of repressed libidinal and aggressive

17. Jung tries to resolve the difficulty by stressing the "tension of opposites" between "two dimensions of consciousness." He insists that "there are no general psychological propositions which could not just as well be reversed; indeed, their reversibility proves their validity" ("On the Psychology," p. 209). However, it is not the abolition of logic that the trickster represents, but the expansion of its categories.

energies—Freud's pessimistic, even tragic, vision of human culture is more open than Jung's optimism to this attempt to construct and renew the boundaries of social life. For Freud, human hostility always threatens to destroy civilization because "instinctual passions are stronger than reasonable interests. Civilization has to use its utmost effort . . . to set limits to man's aggressive instincts" and to restrain them by imposed psychic checks.[18] One of the most persistent of these efforts is religion and its symbols, and though Freud's disdain for its "illusory" and "regressive" character is well known, he had no doubt that some vast restraining enterprise was necessary if human culture were to be sustained and the human self achieved. For him,

> both civilization and ego are denials, are denatured nature. Civilization is the repression of instinct, a trade of happiness for longevity. Ego is a "shrunken residue" of a more inclusive feeling. Neither man nor his culture is "natural."
> . . . The suggestion that ego and civilization are . . . against the original nature of man does not mean that they are artificial in any effete sense. The very fact that they are sustained in a tension against nature means that they are profoundly related to it in a kind of longing and hostile embrace.[19]

Now the kind of mind that experiences and imagines the trickster is largely in agreement with this vision of Freud's. The Ashanti, the Fon, the Yoruba, and the Dogon know that they need boundaries to live and that these boundaries are at once fragile and oppressive. They know that the individual ego, the social order, and all that is beyond both are held apart and brought together in an intricately managed embrace. Yet they do not know this embrace as hostile, nor do they experience their separation from both primordial selfhood and nature as "denaturing." It might be argued that the roots of such alienation are there, waiting to grow as the social order itself ramifies. However that may be, these societies do recognize the

18. Sigmund Freud, *Civilization and Its Discontents*, pp. 86–87.
19. Samuel Hux, "Culture and the Abyss," p. 56.

possibility of repression and denaturing, of coming to be cut off from the deeper sources of being. They recognize too that the mere existence of the divine order will not prevent such estrangement. The High God, who symbolizes this order's center, is not simply otiose, but transparent; his designs need constantly to be spelled out, his creative purposes brought down to earth. For these peoples it is the trickster, above all, who weaves the web of purpose that is their life together. He is the mediator who spells out cosmic designs in human language, who opens passageways into all that is still wild, and who transforms social boundaries into modes of intercourse. Their vision, unlike Freud's, is not tragic precisely because their irony assumes that the yoking together of all antinomies is as possible as it is necessary, whereas his assumes only that it is necessary for man to think it possible.

The trickster as structuralist cog

It is just here, in the recognition that at least in his function the trickster represents an imaginative principle creative of man's social universe, that we confront Claude Lévi-Strauss's contention that he is an interesting, if slight, cog in a vast intellectual machine of mediations. Lévi-Strauss places his brief but fascinating remarks on the trickster at a crucial point in his discussion of the study of myth. He sees the fundamental problem in understanding the nature of myth as the seeming contradiction between the radical contingency of myth, operating without any recognizable logic and dependent on arbitrary psychocultural associations, and the similarity of myths found in widely separated areas of the world.[20] He rejects attempts to resolve this contradiction by psychological and functionalist explanations or by assertions of the primitive inability to deal clearly with empiric reality because all such explanations and assertions rest on a logic—our own—which simply assumes its own completeness. The typical approach to

20. See Lévi-Strauss, *Structural Anthropology*, pp. 202–28.

mythology, he believes, has failed because it has tried to force mythical thought into our categories "instead of trying to enlarge the framework of our logic to include processes which, whatever their apparent differences, belong to the same kind of intellectual operation."[21]

Lévi-Strauss seeks, then, to use the discoveries of modern linguistics as an analogy to show how myth, like all language, can be both historical and ahistorical, diachronic and synchronic, but as "an absolute entity on a third level."[22] The language of myth is a grammar of the mind in which pattern is all, like a sea voyage made for its own sake so that "sea routes are replaced by the rules of navigation."[23] This grammar can be grasped only by an exhaustive analysis of its components ("mythemes"), not the isolated motifs in encyclopedias of myth and folklore, but "bundles" of relations disclosing the simultaneously diachronic and synchronic meaning of the myth. Lévi-Strauss compares this analysis to the discovery by extraterrestrial archeologists of a musical score, which must be read both horizontally (diachronically) and vertically (synchronically) to learn its harmonics as well as its melodic line. In the Oedipus myth, for example, the correlation of two sets of contradictory relationships—overrating of blood relations/ underrating of blood relations and persistence of autochthony/denial of autochthony—links cosmology and daily life structurally as well as causally. Thus the myth suggests that, although the experience of human sexuality contradicts the belief in autochthony, the experience of family ties means that "social life validates cosmology by its similarity of structure."[24]

Lévi-Strauss treats the trickster in the context of his analysis of the Zuñi emergence myth, whose aim, he believes, is to mediate the fundamental contradiction between life and death. The Zuñi experience this contradiction through their

21. *Ibid.*, pp. 202–3.
22. *Ibid.*, p. 206.
23. Lévi-Strauss, *The Raw and the Cooked*, vol. 1, p. 25.
24. Lévi-Strauss, *Structural Anthropology*, p. 212.

involvement with plant life in agriculture: plants live, then die, and agriculture is similar to hunting and warfare, which nourish life through death. Thus the variants of the myth introduce mediating pairs to make possible a final correlation of change/death and death/permanence. Once again Lévi-Strauss insists that mythic and social order affirm each other by their mutual structural affirmation of the possibility of holding the ultimate pair of contradictories together in life-giving tension. The real "story" of the myth is its chiastic structure, while its "meaning" is the logical process creating the "double, reciprocal exchange of functions" that is also the inner purpose of the social order.[25]

Lévi-Strauss believes that the trickster exemplifies this logical process. In explaining why in North America the trickster's role is given "practically everywhere to either coyote or raven," he maintains that to "resolve" oppositions Zuñi myth has replaced two opposed terms with no intermediary (life and death) with "two equivalent terms which admit of a third one as mediator"—agriculture, hunting, and warfare. Then this triad is replaced with a second—herbivorous animals, carrion-eating animals (e.g., raven and coyote), and beasts of prey. The hidden argument is this:

Carrion-eating animals are like beasts of prey (they eat animal food), but they are also like food-plant producers (they do not kill what they eat). Or to put it otherwise . . . : ravens are to gardens as beasts of prey are to herbivorous animals. But it is also clear that herbivorous animals may be called first to act as mediators on the assumption that they are like collectors and gatherers (plant-food eaters), while they can be used as animal food though they are not themselves hunters.[26]

Lévi-Strauss then uses this model of mediation to account for a vast range of mediating symbols and personages, including the trickster, whose inherent ambivalence reflects his function

25. See *ibid.*, pp. 216–24.
26. *Ibid.*, p. 221. It is not true that the trickster is almost everywhere in North America a coyote or a raven; see Ricketts, "The North American Indian Trickster," p. 328. A theriomorphic trickster may represent other forms of mediation than those discovered by Lévi-Strauss.

with great clarity. "Since his mediating function occupies a position halfway between two polar terms, he must retain something of that duality—namely an ambiguous and equivocal character." [27] If he is both harmful and helpful, it is because he participates in the values of both of the contradictory poles that he bridges in his own being.

Flawed though it may be by a startling optimism of technique, which looks to mathematics and the computer for the discernment of mythic structure beneath the shifting surface of multiple variants, Lévi-Strauss's hypothesis is still enormously attractive. Clearly, it calls for a study of sacred mediators encompassing the elaboration of his theories in *The Savage Mind* and their still more complex application in the *Mythologiques*. [28] Even this brief overview sheds light on Ananse's theriomorphic structure: the spider is suspended between heaven and earth, a nondomesticated creature, yet a dweller in human houses. Moreover, Lévi-Strauss's references to Griaule's work among the Dogon suggest that an examination of Dogon taxonomies as an especially well-wrought "science of the concrete" might reveal exchanges, relationships, and transformations which the Dogon myth deals with on a level beneath that of its narrative line. [29] It seems certain, for example, that the opposition between oneness and twoness (which the Dogon recognize as the root contradiction out of which their life springs) embodies itself in Ogo-Yurugu as the symbol of both the struggle to link diachronicity and synchronicity and the very process of logic by which that link is forged. Yet above all else, Lévi-Strauss's remarks affirm that the trickster's place on the boundaries of every sort of relationship is no accident, but a profoundly intended design. The boundaries themselves are symbols—social images of deep structural rules governing the processes by which continuity and order are maintained in the

27. Lévi-Strauss, *Structural Anthropology*, p. 223.
28. See particularly *The Raw and the Cooked*, vol. 1, pp. 332–33. Eliade has handled religious dualism in a very different way; see *The Two and the One*, pp. 78–124.
29. See Lévi-Strauss, *The Savage Mind*, pp. 5, 39, 163, 231.

face of historical pressure and the life/death dichotomy, which is the most evident result of that pressure.[30] The trickster reveals the elasticity of those boundaries; or better, reveals that they are membranes through which life passes into the future and death, and at the same time flows back again to its beginnings and new life.

Nevertheless, in spite of the importance of Lévi-Strauss's thought and the sheer pleasure it might give to use the trickster to probe his own ironic joining of the Marxist and the Buddhist ways of overcoming history, there are reasons for refusing to accept his method and theory as the most appropriate tools for handling the trickster. Those reasons spring from his corrosive Kantianism, in which the living flesh of the world dissolves, leaving behind only the mind's bare bones. If, as he believes, "the unconscious activity of the mind consists in imposing forms upon content, and if these forms are fundamentally the same for all minds—ancient and modern, primitive and civilized . . .—it is necessary and sufficient to grasp the unconscious structure underlying each institution and each custom, in order to obtain a principle of interpretation valid for other institutions and other customs."[31] No matter how enticing structuralism might appear to the historian of religions seeking to avoid the pitfall of homiletic description, if he takes this Kantian path, he must prepare to end in the self-contained space of the mental category out of which philosophy has been trying to escape for nearly two centuries. Lévi-Strauss is not coy about his assumptions. He holds them, after all, because he thinks that they are true, the heritage of Marx more than of Kant. He does not shrink from the accusation of studying men as if they were ants, or from the prospect of understanding "life as a function of inert matter," or from a vision of all meanings that insists "super-structures are faulty acts which have 'made' it socially."[32] For him it is simply a fact that all human

30. See *ibid.*, p. 234; cf. *Structural Anthropology*, pp. 290 ff.
31. Lévi-Strauss, *Structural anthropology*, pp. 21–22.
32. See Lévi-Strauss, *Savage Mind*, pp. 246–48, 253–54.

works are mental constructs, myths in every sense, whose "faultiness" will soon appear, causing no alarm "to those whose thought is not tormented by transcendence even in a latent form."[33]

The thought of Lévi-Strauss can hardly be rejected, a priori, on the grounds that he is a neo-Kantian stoic agnostic, especially in a culture whose intellectual life flows in exactly the same direction. Yet he can be faulted for the blitheness—the ethnocentrism, if you will—with which he takes up his position and for his lack of interest in the similarities between his structures of the mind and Platonic forms or Hegelian categories.[34] However, it is not Lévi-Strauss's insouciance toward the philosophical ground on which he stands that chiefly concerns us here. His "materialistic reductionism," as Eliade calls it, fails to seize the trickster's meaning because it finds trivial just that "hum and buzz of implication" (in Lionel Trilling's phrase) which is his project as well as his matrix. Thus Eliade claims that Lévi-Strauss has replaced "hermeneutical effort" with "demystification" and has failed to respect the "specific mode of being" of the "spiritual creations" he studies.[35] Lévi-Strauss would answer that he does indeed recognize the authentic inwardness that these creations possess and has devised a method to grasp it. But even if Eliade does not provide a metaphysical rationale for his objections, he points to a serious methodological issue: to disdain the religious symbols and practices of human life as "surface structure" and "mere content" and to reject analysis of them as a hankering for the transcendent is finally to disembody man altogether. Spiro Agnew's flippant dictum, "When you've seen one slum, you've seen them all," puts crudely what every idealist doctrine im-

33. *Ibid.*, p. 255.

34. See Robert L. Zimmerman, "Lévi-Strauss and the Primitive," in *Claude Lévi-Strauss: The Anthropologist as Hero*, ed. E. Nelson Hayes and Tanya Hayes (Cambridge, Mass.: M.I.T. Press, 1970), p. 231.

35. Eliade, *The Quest*, pp. 132–33; cf. p. 158, and *The Two and the One*, p. 191. For a telling exposition of the reductionist tendencies of Lévi-Strauss's method, see Mary Douglas, "The Meaning of Myth."

plies: that only essences are real. If that is the ultimate epistemological truth, then mathematics becomes the only valid analytical language, and one need waste as little time on giving words to mental processes as on deciphering the symbolisms that those processes create.[36]

Eliade's call for hermeneutics is apt here because the West African trickster is the exemplar of the language of cultural interpretation. Brandon's shrewd supposition that the trickster represents some sort of radical irrationality in human life seems very close to the mark. Certainly Lévi-Strauss sees the trickster as a figure who is both structurally and symbolically *ab-surdum*, the response to irreducible contradiction. Yet this stands the truth as traditional peoples see it right on its head, for they know their tricksters as the very revelation of intelligibility. Lévi-Strauss's comments about raven and coyote suggest this conclusion, but, given his assumptions about the gap between mind and world, he cannot take it seriously. The four West African societies we have studied, on the other hand, take this revelation so seriously that they find it hilarious. Ananse is "wonderful," the namesake of the people's wisdom, because he links heaven and earth, the manifest male and the hidden female dimensions of social order, domesticity and nature, center and periphery, divinity, humanity and animality. In him they become a true language, a pattern of intelligibility that crystallizes the hidden shape of the universe. The Dogon, the Fon, and the Yoruba celebrate the endless branchings of this pattern in divination, and with the Ashanti they know that the trickster brings to light all non-sense so that all might become language and therefore human.

In contrast to Paul Radin's suggestion that civilization is an

36. See Clifford Geertz's important essay, "Religion as a Cultural System." Note the epigraph from George Santayana's *Reason in Religion*: "Any attempt to speak without speaking any particular language is not more hopeless than the attempt to have a religion that shall be no religion in particular. . . . Thus every living and healthy religion has a marked idiosyncrasy. Its power consists in its special and surprising message and in the bias which that revelation gives to life."

account of man's efforts "to forget his transformation from an animal into a human being," [37] the trickster recalls that transformation and, by asserting its reversibility, transforms the transformation. Contrary to Freud's belief about the link between myth and repression, the trickster brings out in the open conflict, lust, and dread that they might become agencies of communion, not disunion. And in opposition to Lévi-Strauss's stoic pessimism, the trickster represents a blatant insistence that those very moments of disjunction which seem to deny transcendence altogether weave it into the daily fabric of human life. Thus the trickster is hermeneutics in action, creating language out of his own body like a spider spinning its web, spelling out the ways of intercourse with upright penis, probing ceaselessly all opacity for hidden designs, and forever rejecting every form of muteness. One is permitted to believe that he, like every hermeneut, is doomed to failure, but not before immersing oneself in the specific language of his dance.

A neo-Durkheimian approach

Despite his rejection of their transcendent aims, Lévi-Strauss possesses great sympathy for the social enterprise of traditional peoples. By what he believes to be a foreshadowing of the Marxist overcoming of historical necessity, these societies seek to "annul the possible effects of historical factors on their equilibrium." [38] The resulting effort to recreate the "prior" stages of their communal life requires a procedure that will break up patterns of change before they threaten the order of society or even before they form. This procedure "consists not in denying the historical process but in admitting it as a form without content. There is indeed a before and an after, but their sole significance lies in reflecting each other." [39]

This awareness of the social order itself as the chief project of

37. Paul Radin, *The World of Primitive Man* (New York: H. Schuman, 1953), p. 3.
38. Lévi-Strauss, *Savage Mind*, p. 234.
39. *Ibid.*, pp. 234–35.

premodern societies ties Lévi-Strauss to the thought of Durkheim, to whom he has paid such forthright homage[40] and whose followers have sought in other ways to work out the methods by which society is maintained as the unique experience of the holy. The trickster so clearly works to shape and reshape this experience that we must consider carefully Laura Makarius's examination of his social function from a point of view enabling her to take advantage of Durkheim's inquiries into the meanings of social order, yet not encumbering her with the weight of his early-twentieth-century psychology and ethnology.

Makarius has observed that even the strictest taboos are deliberately violated at certain times by those in search of some benefit that this violation promises. She argues that taboos have their origin in the "danger of blood," especially in the potential destructiveness of blood connected with female sexual functions. However, just because this blood must be avoided to prevent injury, it can also be *used* to ward off evil and thus finally comes to be regarded as the source of luck, power, prosperity, and success. To gain possession of this source of power, therefore, it becomes necessary to break the taboo against contact with blood, especially female blood. Yet because this taboo is tied so closely to the most intimate social boundaries, above all to the prohibition against incest, any magical use of the power of blood, no matter how beneficial, has an aura of illegitimacy and must take place only rarely and hiddenly.[41]

There is an obvious difficulty in identifying a notion as complex as that of taboo so narrowly with the "danger of blood" and, even more, in linking it to a supposed mode of reasoning that seems much like *participation mystique*. Nevertheless, Makarius makes an excellent case for the simultaneous rupture and healing of the social order that takes place when bound-

40. See Lévi-Strauss, *Structural Anthropology*, dedicatory note.
41. Makarius, "Le Mythe," pp. 19–25.

aries are intentionally transgressed by a "magician" who seeks to benefit the whole community. The individual who assumes this dangerous task appears "as a transgressor who separates himself from society and rises above its law through devotion to the human cause. He assumes the guilt of all, and is condemned . . . to atone that the social order may triumph and that the contradiction which has put it temporarily in peril may be resolved."[42] The trickster, then, becomes a "mythical projection" of the magician who violates the order of society to benefit it, an image of the "founder of society's ritual and social life." His apparent contradictions—his largesse and his spitefulness, his individualism and his social creativity—are rooted in the ambivalence of his role as the heroic violator of all that is forbidden.

To support her hypothesis, Makarius discusses three tricksters—Manabozo of the Algonkians, Maui of the Polynesians, and Legba. All three are originators of magic, and their stories ring with their mocking disdain for the ordinary prohibitions of their societies. They help found their peoples' modes of life and mediate between gods and men precisely because "trickiness" unites sacrality and profanity. Thus it is that he who knows the "trick" of magic "may also give to men the most ingenious tools and the most useful instructions, that the giver of magic medicine . . . assuring the well-being of the group may also provide all other benefits, and that the one who can change the states of things . . . by magic may also modify present circumstances and transform nature."[43] The trickster's doubleness becomes both the source of his transforming power and the reason for his banishment from the community; as profaner of the sacred he becomes a sacred being, yet remains an outsider, the victim of his own violations. Radically impure by reason of his unbounded sexuality, gluttony, and mendacity, the trickster nonetheless helps to give the indi-

42. *Ibid.*, p. 25 (my translation).
43. *Ibid.*, p. 40 (my translation).

vidual access to the sacred power by which his society is built. Finally, then, Makarius believes that the trickster's many-sidedness is determined by a social structure that, expressing itself mythically, needs both to insist on the immutability of its patterns and to affirm the possibility of transcending those patterns.

The merits of this view are plain. Makarius can recognize in the trickster an "organically structured personage" rather than a dissolving god or an evolving hero because she sees how he embodies ambivalences inherent in every traditional society. She sees too that these ambivalences arise from the nature of the sacred order, at once firmly marking the limits of ordinary life and insinuating itself more deeply into that life,[44] so that the trickster can both dissolve and reinforce sacred boundaries. Certainly she is correct in judging that Lévi-Strauss fails to see that the trickster only synthesizes because he first disrupts.[45] Moreover, Makarius properly rejects those aspects of Radin's interpretation which link the trickster with a supposed incapacity to differentiate human and animal, self and world, since the trickster's talent for blurring such distinctions suggests a most vivid awareness of them.[46]

In the end, however, Makarius has not quite shaken herself free from an evolutionary theory of the trickster, although her view is superior to that of Radin or Jung because it is firmly grounded in an awareness of the trickster's relationship to society. Thus she speaks of the trickster's appearing at the moment of social evolution when taboo was no longer absolutely necessary for social cohesion and bearing within himself "in germ the atoning being who takes the sins of humanity upon himself."[47] Such an assertion lacks the support of historical evidence, but it also seems unlikely because it imparts to the

44. See Emile Durkheim, *The Elementary Forms of the Religious Life*, pp. 256–65.

45. Makarius, "Le Mythe," p. 42, n.1.

46. *Ibid.*, pp. 44–45.

47. *Ibid.*, p. 41.

trickster a titanic quality suited to a suffering mediator but alien to a trickster. The symbolic languages of each have their similarities, and one day it may be possible to show how history has affected the forms taken by mediators and to speak of "seed" and "fruit"; but fidelity to that organic structure of the trickster perceived by Makarius herself forbids a premature linking of his gross and foolish bursting of boundaries with the struggles of epic heroes and redeeming saviors.

Makarius's espousal of this modified evolutionary view is due, I think, to her underrating of the trickster's ironic humor and an important distinction toward which it points. She rejects the overly philosophical opinion of Melville Herskovits that Legba personifies a "way out" in a world controlled by destiny, because it does not take sufficiently into account his mastery of magic,[48] but she accepts for Legba the title of "arch-individualist." However, no matter how relentlessly Legba pursues his own ends, he not an individualist. His whole work is to shape and renew the human world, a work that establishes within each Fon the image of cosmic and social order. Legba is the opener of passages, but these passages lead always to the center of the social world with all its density of clans, lineages, and customs. Even Legba's incest and his deflowering of the king's daughter, which Makarius cites as violations of taboos, give access, not to the world of magic, but to the *daily* potencies of women and household life. Furthermore, he is the associate of Mawu, not her rival, for it is not autonomy that Legba is after, but intercourse, the life-giving exchange that stretches beyond the barter of goods and the sharing of bodies to become the double movement between bright male outside and dark female inside, characterizing for the Fon the dialectic implicit in every individual and institution, in the world and the divine pantheon itself.

What Makarius seems to miss is the trajectory of the trickster's movement outside the sacred order. Even in the rather

48. *Ibid.*, p. 39, n. 1. See Herskovits, *Dahomey*, vol. 2, pp. 222–30.

different case of Maui, that trajectory is closer to the elliptical sweep of a boomerang than to the one-way arc of an arrow. The trickster violates boundaries to humanize them, but the "new" shape that the world assumes is its present one. This is one of the points of the trickster's irony: all that wheeling and dealing, that endless juggling, simply keeps new balls flying through the air in the same order and at the same speed. Even where his only ritual is the telling of his stories, his work is, above all, synchronous. His transforming power has worked in the past to create the present, and it works in the present to make the future reflect the past. He moves past society's circumference to ensure the permanent rediscovery of its center.

Beyond Durkheim

It seems likely that Makarius herself might have reached this same conclusion if she had pressed Durkheim's insights a little harder. Still, she uses Durkheim creatively to interpret the trickster as Mary Douglas uses him to explore what the trickster exploits—social anomaly. Although Douglas realizes that Durkheim's understanding of society was too simple and his separation of the sacred and the profane too neat, she agrees that ritual both symbolizes and preserves social processes.[49] She insists that A. R. Radcliffe-Brown and the functionalist school have put this insight to faulty use. Durkheim's awareness that religion and the ritual forms expressive of it, Douglas believes, properly belong to "a social theory of knowledge" in which religious realities form a special language giving voice to certain personal and communal experiences.

Douglas is not calling for a "sociology of knowledge" that merely repeats the truism that thought and language have a sociohistorical context. Rather, she is claiming that the language which is religion, in all its mythic, ritual, and even "magical" forms, both responds to and is responsible for specific social ways of perceiving, labeling, and relating to the world.

49. Douglas, *Purity and Danger*, p. 34; see especially pp. 29–34.

Indeed, the very aim of *Purity and Danger* is to show "that rituals of purity and impurity create unity in experience"[50] by alternately defining the boundaries of social life and discovering ways of dealing with all that this definition renders anomalous. Her sense of the anomalous as a kind of metaphysical dirt—not only matter, but experience itself out of place—and her pursuit of the way in which the entire social enterprise is geared to recognize and then to incorporate anomaly immediately suggest a deeper way of looking at the intended meaning of the trickster's boundary-breaking character. His multiformity begins in this light to assume a theoretical and practical purposiveness that Lévi-Strauss's structuralism could not give it.

Douglas's work really rests on the necessary ambiguity with which people regard ambiguity itself. On the one hand, "our impressions are schematically determined from the start," if not by our senses, then by our concepts.[51] Yet, the "filtering mechanism" is imperfect, and its very imperfection compels us to try to organize what we perceive as unorganized, or, more subtly, invites us to contemplate the nature of both form and formlessness. Quoting Sartre's remarks on stickiness, she notes how viscosity repels us:

An infant, plunging its hands into a jar of honey, is instantly involved in contemplating the formal properties of solids and liquids and the essential relation between the subjective experiencing self and the experienced world. . . . The viscous is a state of half-way between solid and liquid. . . . It is unstable, but does not flow. It is soft, yielding and compressible. There is no gliding on its surface. Its stickiness is a trap, it clings like a leech, it attacks the boundary between myself and it. Long columns falling off my fingers suggest my own substance flowing into the pool of stickiness. Plunging into water . . . I remain a solid, but to touch stickiness is to risk diluting myself into viscosity.[52]

50. *Ibid.*, p. 13.
51. *Ibid.*, p. 49. Douglas differs from Lévi-Strauss in that the "schemas" that filter experience are not for her innate categories of the mind, but the internalized forms of perception and speech that all societies create.
52. *Ibid.*, pp. 50–51. See Jean-Paul Sartre, *L'Etre et le néant: Essai d'ontologie phénomenologique*, 3d ed. (Paris: Gallimard, 1943), pp. 696 ff.

"Aberrant fluid or melting solid": Sartre's conclusion is that honey's viscous ambiguity symbolizes an unpleasant, even disgusting mode of existence. Yet we can push his example even farther. Even as its viscosity dissolves the lines between solid and liquid, self and world, and challenges our scheme of reality itself, honey's sweetness attracts us. It may take the poetic genius of a Yeats to suggest the full implications of such a double ambiguity ("Honey of generation had betrayed": Does sweetness trap us? Does viscosity entice?), but society finds ways of treating the anomalous to fit it into some sort of pattern or to make use of its doubleness to enlarge the pattern. Cultures provide for anomalies by deciding that they fit one category and not another, by physically eliminating them, by rigidly avoiding them and labeling them as dangerous, or by using them "to enrich meaning or to call attention to other levels of existence," as, for example, "ritual, by using symbols of anomaly, can incorporate evil and death along with life and goodness, into a single, grand, unifying pattern."[53]

Such a pattern is achieved only after the other side of "dirt" has been recognized. "A by-product of the creation of order," dirt is created by the process of differentiation, and throughout that process it threatens the lines of distinction until "finally it returns to its true indiscriminable character. Formlessness is, therefore, an apt symbol of beginning and of growth as it is of decay."[54] In this sense, Douglas points to the parallel between dirt and water, which sweeps away and dissolves all forms, wipes out the past, and restores things to their unmarked beginnings. Yet even though dirt possesses this aspect of "creative formlessness," it differs from water as a symbol by reason of its passivity. Water flows, but dirt simply abides. However, as religion strives to harness the ceaseless movement of water for the work of regeneration, so too it seeks to capture for life that absolute immobility which earth both represents and is. "Those vulnerable margins and those attacking forces which

53. Douglas, *Purity and Danger*, pp. 52–53.
54. *Ibid.*, p. 190.

threaten to destroy good order represent the powers inhering in the cosmos,"[55] and if that pure potency is not made available for human life, then the longing for absolute clarity and permanence of form will end in total rigidity. If all that seems immalleable, anomalous, and therefore impure is simply excluded from society, then the sheer facticity of the formless, above all as it shows itself in death, will overwhelm the forms of human life. As William James saw, unless negations are claimed for society, unless anomalies are made "powerful for good . . . like turning weeds and lawn cuttings into compost,"[56] then the attempt to render the body social impermeable will be all too successful. Order will turn into immobility and differentiation into mere repetition. The "dirt" will be within, not without. But if a way can be found to embrace the anomalous, then anomaly, like the honey of generation, will both disrupt and regenerate order by immersing it more deeply in the ocean of the commonplace.

NAMING THE NAMELESS—IRONICALLY

One brief comment reveals why Douglas's sensitive enlarging of the insights of Durkheim is more helpful, finally, than structuralism in interpreting the trickster. Speaking of the temptation of the lapidary and the changeless to which all societies are subject as they "attempt to force experience into logical categories of noncontradiction," she notes the paradox that "experience is not amenable and those who make the attempt find themselves led into contradiction."[57] That is so evidently the case that one can only conclude that if traditional societies were simply engaged in a struggle to hold off time by the discovery of logical structures resolving contradiction, their efforts would not only fail, but would appear foolish and lead them to despair. But this does not happen. True, Lévi-Strauss can point to the mortality of all things human to but-

55. *Ibid.*, pp. 190–91.
56. *Ibid.*, p. 193. Cf. Eliade, *Patterns*, pp. 14–19.
57. Douglas, *Purity and Danger*, p. 192.

tress his conviction of the illusoriness of social meanings, but it is he who conveys world-weariness, not those living in "cool" societies. Their joy may be the fruit of ignorance—that is the theological question—but, as Lévi-Strauss himself knows well, it is not the result of stupidity. These societies do not believe that they have forced "experience into logical categories of noncontradiction," but that they have made contradiction, defeat, and death—anomaly in any form they know—a part of their lives, indeed compost for life itself. One must, I suppose, in the end call this belief "faith," but whatever one calls it, it has a more complex, a denser, a fleshier core than any purely cerebral structure.

The trickster, then, symbolizes the very manner in which traditional peoples try to seize the contradictory and the anomalous just as much as he embodies one mode of the seizure. His messiness and metaphysical ambiguity reveal that the "cool" society seeks to open itself to the wild, not to construct a pure and impermeable order. His presence—in story, dance, phallic image, divination, or "soul"—represents a ceaseless informing of structure with rawness and formlessness and a boundless confidence that such a process is truly constructive. Because the trickster pulls the most unyielding matter—disease, ugliness, greed, lust, lying, jealousy—into the orbit of life, and because, especially in divination, he links these anomalies in their most commonplace forms to the taxonomies of communal life, he reveals how it is precisely on the plane of the daily and the specific that time is cooled down, social order enlarged, and all experience opened to transformation.

Now in one sense to say that the trickster's peculiarly gross duality symbolizes the social embrace of anomaly in a way not adequately dealt with by Lévi-Strauss is to choose Anglo-American anthropology over its more theoretically inclined French counterpart and to make explicit what has long been tacitly plain: that the history of religions, whatever its quarrels with some versions of social anthropology, favors a method and a practice that stress the uncovering of a society's self-understanding more than the fitting of that self-understanding into an overall theory of human thought and behavior. It would be nonsense to maintain that Lévi-Strauss is unconcerned with the particularities of the societies he writes about; the massiveness of *Mythologiques* alone shows otherwise. Yet one has only to compare his work with Paul Mus's *Barabadur*, for example, to see that, where Lévi-Strauss has carried the formal concerns of the *sociologie française* of Hubert, Mauss, and Durkheim in the direction of Descartes, Rousseau, and Kant, Mus has taken them into the realm of history, seeking the key to the patterns of symbols that he finds not only in innate structures of the mind, but in the patterns themselves under the pressure of life within time.

For Lévi-Strauss "history" is itself a myth.[58] This conviction certainly prevents him from being trapped by the cant of evolutionism, paralyzed by lack of historical evidence, or embarrassed by superficial morphologies that are really the exotica of encyclopedism disguised as "phenomenology." Yet, to say it once again, the real issue is not the difficulty or the possibility of doing history, but the decision to accept or reject the language of religious symbolism as language in its own right. Of course it represents and gives access to deeper structures both within society and within the human mind; of course it can be summarized or broken down into segments of varying degrees of human universality. However, it cannot be reduced to its parts, any more than *Hamlet* can finally be reduced to a variant of the Oedipus myth, the Oedipus myth reduced to a series of logical oppositions, or the English and the Greek languages reduced to their phonemes, morphemes, and sememes. By choosing to handle religion as a kind of interpretable but irreducible language, the history of religions obviously leaves itself open to dilettantism when it treats the

58. See *Savage Mind*, pp. 245–69, where Lévi-Strauss insists that Sartre's notion of history is equivalent to the traditional notion of myth.

phenomena that are its subject without adequate sociological probing, and to philosophical confusion when it attempts to explain, without a realist epistemology on which to rely, the patterns it discovers. Yet in the struggle to define the relationship between the universal and the particular, the history of religions does well to align itself with those who are persuaded of the ultimately analogical character of life. If it thereby draws the fire of all those who, in Victor Turner's words, make a "Manichean separation" in religious studies either by "sociologistic reductionism" or by neglect of "contextual involvement,"[59] at least it has chosen the position with the greatest fidelity to that final ambiguity rightly called "mystery."

The logic of symbols

It is this ambiguity understood as mystery which the trickster's multiformity discloses. Moreover, by uniting "high" and "low" in a language of sacred ribaldry or serious triviality as well as in joining planes of being and centers of life-giving potency, the trickster embodies the very process of symbol creation lying at the heart of the "dialectic of hierophanies." Symbols, as Eliade says, always show forth "the basic oneness of several zones of the real," but "symbolism carries further the dialectic of hierophanies by transforming things into *something other* than what they appear to profane experience to be: a stone becomes a symbol for the center of the world, and so on; and then, by becoming symbols, signs of a transcendent reality, those things abolish their material limits, and . . . despite their precarious and fragmentary nature, they embody in themselves the whole of the system in question."[60] Each sacred symbol tends to embrace the whole transcendent order, but the trickster represents the creation of sacredness just because he is an image of that "symbol-making machine"[61]

59. Turner, "Passages, Margins, and Poverty," p. 492.
60. Eliade, *Patterns*, p. 452.
61. The phrase was suggested to me by Charles H. Long.

which is the mind of man in perpetual motion, even in sleep and in other subliminal states.

The trickster's embodiment of the symbolic process is what led Radin to interpret the Winnebago trickster cycle as a paradigm of the growth of human consciousness, and Ricketts to see the trickster as the emblem of man's mind in the process of mastering the earth. But the Dogon placement of Ogo-Yurugu's activity simultaneously within man's "souls" and on the boundaries of his life, in the present and in the deepest past, in solitary rebellion and in complex relationship with every other force suggest, rather, that the trickster represents man's imaginative participation in a "universe impregnated by sacredness."[62] Similarly, the phallic imagery of each of the four tricksters studied here shows that this impregnation is the work of men as well as of the gods. That organ which unmistakably links man's generation to the animals and all the powers of the wild also unites him to the transparent order of the High God.[63] In the trickster's movement between these two worlds the human world takes shape as the fruit of the dialectic of hierophanies, sacred both as given and as process, both as social enterprise and as divine creation. Divination, a fitting symbol of the human effort to learn the "real" patterns of existence, is the language of the trickster, and the sacred forms of myth and even ritual (e.g., Legba's "invention" of the dance and Ananse's knowledge of the "words" of the drum) also belong to him.

In short, the trickster is the image of man individually and communally seizing the fragments of his experience and *discovering* in them an order sacred by its very wholeness. Legba juggling his instruments, Ananse gathering and then spreading disease, Eshu fomenting quarrels, Ogo trying to create a world from a piece of his placenta—all symbolize man weaving a fabric of meaning through the transforming power of his

62. Eliade, *The Quest*, p. 157.
63. See Kerényi, "The Trickster," pp. 182–83.

imagination. Yet at the same time that the trickster discloses the radically human character of the whole cosmos, he shows the holiness of ordinary life. This is not an "antigod" secular holiness, but the sacredness that discloses itself when the world is seen to be more than meets the eye, "something other," a web of multidimensional planes of being, a Sigui dance where all beings, human and nonhuman, meet and move together in a single pattern.

It may seem that to speak of the trickster as a symbol of the transforming power of the human imagination is to yield to the post-Kantian assumption that religion, for good or ill, is nothing more than a human project. One might draw that conclusion; certainly, as Eliade says, the logic of symbols "goes beyond the sphere of religious history to rank among the problems of philosophy" [64] so that the debate must finally be carried to the metaphysical level. Nevertheless, "discovery" and "imagination" are not words that necessarily imply the projection of human yearning beyond an impermeable history.

Etymologically, "imagination" is related to both *imago*—a representation or imitation—and *imitor*, to imitate or reproduce. And for once, etymology is in accord with both psychological realities and spiritual truth. The *imagination imitates* the exemplary models—the Images— reproduces, reactualises and repeats them without end. To have imagination is to be able to see the world in its totality, for the power and the mission of Images is to *show* all that remains refractory to the concept; hence the disfavor and failure of the man "without imagination"; he is cut off from the deeper reality of life and from his own soul. [65]

Eliade's language may be rather Jungian, but his point is that the human mind is itself an epiphany of the structures hidden beneath the surface of thought as well as of matter. Thus a "mythology" of human life is not only possible but necessary in order to express the human situation according to the truth of our being.

64. Eliade, *Patterns*, p. 453.
65. Eliade, *Images and Symbols*, p. 20 (his emphasis).

Imagination as passio

Certainly this is the assumption of the "imaginers" of the trickster, and I believe that we can grasp much of the sense of this assumption even without being able to demonstrate it conclusively. In his analysis of the Dinka religion, Godfrey Lienhardt explored the self-awareness of the Dinka in an effort to understand their experience of *nhialic*, or "divinity." He realized that they do not regard themselves as divided from the world by their minds so that the world—that is, extrahuman reality—is only an object. Rather, they know it is an active subject. Thus the sacred "powers"—the High God, the "free-divinities," the "clan-divinities," and other transhuman beings—are, in effect, the images of human *passiones*. That is, they are the active reciprocals of those events in which men are acted upon by life in a way surpassing their understanding. Lienhardt chose the Latin word *passio* because the Dinka know "divinity" so frequently in their painful separation from it and also because the word carries the meaning of "experience" or "being acted upon." [66] It is important to realize that he is speaking, not of what we lightly term "subjective sentiment," but of events that have specific shape and meaning. To this specificity even the Dinka's most complex and subtle "images" answer. Therefore the Dinka are able to distinguish between those *passiones* whose answering images are the experience of social structure and those others which seem to them to transcend that structure by providing "the possibility of creating desirable experience and of freeing themselves from what they must otherwise passively endure." [67]

In this sense, the trickster is an "image," the reflection in the processes of the human mind not of a Jungian archetype, but of the world experienced as an active subject. And what is the specific experience out of which the image of the trickster

66. See Lienhardt, *Divinity and Experience*, pp. 149–56.
67. *Ibid.*, p. 170.

springs? What is the "active reciprocal" of that *passio* which is his imprint on the human imagination? It is the experience of the human mind in its imaginative operation as itself radically ambiguous, essentially anomalous, inescapably multivalent —facing both out and in, linking above and below, animal-like and godlike, social cog and individual solitude, shaped and shaping, part of all that is but only as a subject knowing its own apartness. The trickster is an image of that sort of self-awareness, but in the very sense that the *passio*, the inner experience of the imagination, would not exist if there were not a specific active subject to produce it. Even where that subject seems, as among the Ashanti, to reside only in the stories about him, still he is perceived to live side by side (not independently; nothing in the traditional framework is independent) with the minds that experience and imagine him, reflecting simultaneously an inborn quality of those minds and of every other plane of being—animal, transhuman, divine.

The language of irony

The one language befitting this image of the imagination in dialogue with all being is the language of irony. Such irony is "a distinctive paradigm or patterning of facts, a recomposing in which the fact (e.g., 'having nothing') is seen within the creative presence of a contrary ('and possessing all things')."[68] *"The task of the imagination,"* William Lynch says, *"is to imagine the real"* (his emphasis), above all when it works at giving body to the human relationship to the ultimately real. "We are accustomed to ask: what has this fey, transcendental, religious thing to do with the hustle and bustle, the burn and the iron of life? But it is there, as large and as hard as the everyday life of nations and human society."[69] This division between the sup-

68. William F. Lynch, *Images of Faith: An Exploration of the Ironic Imagination*, p. 14. Lynch suggests a way of dealing with religious language that is properly analogical and takes account of the epistemological gap between "experiencing" and "imagining," between "subjectivity" and "objectivity"; see pp. 15–19. Cf. D. C. Muecke, *The Compass of Irony*.

69. Lynch, *Images of Faith*, p. 63.

posed airiness of the sacred and the density of daily life Lynch dissolves in his "exploration of the ironic imagination," which is, in fact, a reimagining of the imagination. And it is this same division that the "primitive," the "archaic," or the "traditional" mind bridges with—among other ways, but symbolizing them all—the confident, grossly elegant irony of the trickster.

Irony, Lynch shows, has its own structure. The mere coexistence of opposites in a single subject, such as the one and the many, is not ironic, for it may belong to the nature of things in such a way that reason is comfortable with it, even if it cannot fully explain the coexistence. Nor is the "copresence of contradictory elements" necessarily ironic; that copresence may simply be a misunderstanding or fault of logic. Lynch insists, rather, that

the usual quality of irony is the unexpected coexistence, to the point of identity, of certain contraries [his emphasis]. Usually the words contraries and contrariety are employed in a metaphysical sense. The philosophical understanding is that contraries come in pairs and . . . are the two most widely separated members of the one species or class. . . . The very mad and the very wise among mankind would be a pair of contraries . . . that begins to be metaphysical. They are the most widely separated. But suddenly we realize ironically, that in man, and in one and the same man, they are not widely separated.

The shock of irony (and of recognition) comes not only from uniting them but also from seeing that the act of uniting them is not a mistake. . . . In Christianity there is more than fascinating coexistence of the low and the high. The lowliness is the very instrument to be passed through in order to reach the high. And there is more than paradox . . . involved. There is an actual transformation of being.[70]

Irony, then, lies in yoking together in a single figure the "most widely separated" opposites in such a way that they are seen to belong together, without losing their contrariness, in a dialectic expressing what is really so and capable of a transformation of the real, which is its fuller embodiment. Of course Lynch is finally thinking of Christ, but Socrates is also such a figure,

70. Ibid., pp. 84–85.

"the permanent ironic hero of Western civilization," ugly and beautiful, flexible and adamantine, managing the mind's life, but not his wife. And in the world of myth we have the figure of the trickster, in whom the anomalous and the ordered, the sacred and the profane, the absurd and the meaningful are joined to create, not merely an ironic symbol, but an image of irony and of the working of the ironic imagination itself.

Lynch is speaking of a process that is style, method, and decision all at once. He uses the word "composition" to convey the meaning of this process, which involves bringing into true relationship the hidden and the manifest elements of life, the low and the high, the particular and the cosmic.[71] Such composition also entails a correct seeing, a "double vision of reality," which rejects the one-eyed vision of things-as-they-are because of the inescapable interchange between reality and mind grappling with reality.[72] Thus that act of composition which works through mind and world to create both a larger and a finer image of what is will always bring about transformation, since it shatters and reforms both the too-neat structures of the world and the too-smooth images of the mind. This mode of thought, which builds on antagonism and finds a passage through one opposite to another ("the way down is the way up"), is the ironic mode, suspicious of all tidiness and insistent on the doubleness of all reality.

Composing the symbolic

We are back again to Ananse and Hate-to-be-contradicted. The latter symbolizes the one-eyed vision, intolerant of disorder, contemptuous of social density and biological necessity, the enemy of nature and its multiplicity. Ananse destroys him by composing images of the world apparently even more outrageous than those of Hate-to-be-contradicted, but actually

71. Cf. Erich Auerbach, *Mimesis: The Representation of Reality in Western Literature*, trans. Willard R. Trask (Princeton: Princeton University Press, 1953), pp. 29, 35–40.

72. See Lynch, *Images of Faith*, pp. 103–5.

more faithful to reality. His great penis, longer than seventy-seven poles and repairable by a blacksmith; his wife's feat of catching a falling pot on succeeding days; and the water that holds the impress of his polygynous family—these are images of social and biological process reified yet stretched beyond any possibility of truth, except the truth that human life unites both order and endless becoming. When Ananse caps his victory by cutting up his enemy to bring contradiction to the people, he thereby discloses both his real triumph, the ironic embrace of all antagonism, and his own nature, the embodiment of the dialectic making this embrace, and social life itself, possible. The whole collection of *anansesem* shows that this life is charged with sacredness and that Ananse endlessly both imagines and images the meeting of contraries which is the fullest expression of that sacredness,[73] yet this one story reveals, in miniature, his total mastery of the potencies of irony.

In language suited to their societies, Legba, Eshu, and Ogo exploit still deeper veins of irony. In divination, each of them composes individual and social disorder into new images of the entire network that is the sacred universe. Through them, society seizes opposition and antagonism to forge a pattern of life at once more stable and more permeable. However, the human representation of Eshu, along with Legba's and Ogo-Yurugu's unending composition and recomposition of the world within the human soul, discloses another meaning of the trickster's embodiment of man's imaginative interrelationship with the sacred. Because the trickster symbolizes both liminality and the human interaction with every other being that fashions all religious images, he also symbolizes the presence, within each human space, of that passage to recreated life which we call the limen. In short, the trickster reveals that man himself is a symbol.

Kerényi suggests just this when he calls the trickster "the exponent and the personification of the life of the body." But

---

73. Cf. Eliade, *The Two and the One*, pp. 80–81.

that life, in which he, like Makarius and Douglas, sees the symbolism of sacred violation and inclusion, has a larger significance, for the body, in the processes of symbolic thought, comes to represent and even to assimilate apparently incompatible planes of being. As Eliade says,

Magico-religious experience makes it possible for man himself to be transformed into a symbol. And only in so far as man himself becomes a symbol, are all systems and all anthropo-cosmic experiences possible. . . . Man no longer feels himself to be an "air-tight" fragment, but a living cosmos open to all the other living cosmoses by which he is surrounded. The experiences of the world at large are no longer something outside him . . . ; they do not alienate him from himself but . . . lead him towards himself, and reveal to him his own existence and his own destiny.[74]

The trickster, therefore, in juggling with his own body, in his manipulation of its parts, his toying with its wastes, his fascination with its orifices and their products, his confidence in its potencies, is the image of man in his openness to every other world and his readiness to meet and exchange with each, to be modified by each in turn.

Thus the trickster ironically symbolizes the symbolic reality of man, that "freak," as Pascal calls him, who is the "glory and refuse of the universe."[75] Freakily, the trickster can image man's openness to the sacred by lust, gluttony, lying, and flatulence. His satiric mimicry of shamanic rites and practices is not, as Radin and Ricketts believe, a sign of popular hostility to priestly arrogance.[76] Rather, like Ogo's rebellion against Amma or Legba's phallic dance, his satire affirms the doubleness of the real and denies every one-dimensional image of it. If he struggles with the High God and causes pain and death to enter the world, spoiling primordial bliss, his quarrel is not with the divine order as such, but with a false human image of the sacred, one that cannot encompass suffering, disorder, and

74. Eliade, *Patterns*, p. 455.
75. See Lynch, *Images of Faith*, p. 87.
76. See Radin, *The Trickster*, pp. 151–54; and Ricketts, "The North American Indian Trickster," pp. 336 ff.

the ultimate mess of death. If death is allowed to remain an anomaly lying outside all the taxonomies that make up life, then, immobilized by death's unyielding solidity, life will become stasis. Death seems static because it manifests—with breath leaving, bowels voiding, words escaping into silence, movement fleeing, spirit vanishing, flesh decaying—such a total centripetality, but if that centripetality is captured for the center and for the classifications of life, then death's absoluteness of movement will guarantee life's eternal reirruption.

Death and wit

Thus it is that so often the trickster's actions make death part of human life.[77] Ogo, for example, introduces death through his primordial incest; Legba does the same by his gift of magic to men. Unwittingly, Ananse lets loose the instrument of death, the Old Woman's magic knife, which brings death to all and becomes spear-grass, the symbol of the boundaries of life. Eshu's ironic use of dissension, disease, and even death to shatter incomplete order and renew the act of sacrifice that ends the starvation of the gods and their killing of men discloses the doubleness of the trickster's work. He uses death to stop death—social stasis or breakdown, cosmic rivalry and noncommunion. So too, Ogo's incest ultimately guarantees human life by fully separating male and female, while Legba and Ananse accept death as the price of cooked food and sex, the transformations that establish the human world.

Yet who is selling what to whom? Who is the fooler and who the fool? The image of man that the trickster composes is more than that of the shrewd bargainer who gets the better of a hard deal. Like Ananse trading a stinking corpse for a king's daughter, the trickster reveals man trading what is for him divine immobility for a human form of apparently equivalent immobility. But the dissolution that is death gives to man the possibility of new life. The other face of the centripetality of

77. Cf. Ricketts, "The North American Indian Trickster," p. 348.

death is the centrifugality of sex and cooked food, symbols—sacraments, really—of the life-giving openness that man receives when he allows himself to be penetrated by and to penetrate every force and mode of being surrounding him. In that experience which most completely dissolves and fragments man, he sees himself in the trickster laying hold of his own center—the transforming power of the ironic dialogic imagination whose true stability is its capacity to compose new images of life out of every form of death.

This ability of the trickster to turn on its head every idea and every event, and death above all, accounts for the humor he provokes as he embodies the radically metamorphic character of man and his imagination. His is the irony of "wit," in the old sense of a truth-seeking capacity that gives delight by its power to expose the sham of the obvious in the very act of uniting surface and depth. It has become a commonplace that humor involves the exploitation of the incongruous, but the trickster's role is to transform as well as to exploit—to recompose, not simply to expose. As Kenneth Lash points out,

Where the failure of the object to fit its archetype is *intentional*, as in the case of wit turning a value upsidedown, the incongruity is presented for the purpose of edification through the agency of the imagination. A new norm, to supplant or to modify the original, is suggested; a new point of view is invited. This twin-edged sword of wit . . . is patently dependent for its very existence upon . . . a common body of norms. Wit may often turn traditional norms topsyturvy, but in so doing does it not turn up to our vision the underside, perhaps hitherto unseen or else forgotten? [78]

Or, to put it more tricksterishly, when the trickster waves his excrement like the emblems of a shaman, slays elephants with his magnificent flatulence,[79] simultaneously purges and cuckolds a rival, he is not issuing a manifesto about the overthrow of shamanism, the superiority of the small, or the rightness of adultery. His mockery includes himself, for he literally makes

78. Kenneth Lash, "A Theory of the Comic as Insight," p. 119.
79. See van der Post, *The Heart of a Hunter*, pp. 170–71.

fun of the hidden underside of life, even his own. As the trickster exposes that dirty bottom, he invites man to contemplate what he shall become and to hope for what he already is—a world large in its intricacy, spiritual in its crude bodiliness, multiple in its ironic wholeness, and finally transcendent in the very absurdity of its pretensions.

Celebrating open-endedness

The trickster, then, shows that the task of imagining the real is an exercise in sacred irony because the "real" itself is more than incoherent dailiness or changeless sacredness. The trickster's playfulness links design and celebration by disclosing how the imagination both receives and shapes the multivalence of reality. Clifford Geertz insists that the Balinese cockfight, as W. H. Auden says of poetry in his elegy of Yeats, "makes nothing happen." It does not change social status, nor does it effect a more inward movement that compensates for the lack of social mobility. Rather, as an art, in a "particulate burst of form," the cockfight makes ordinary experience more deeply understandable by stripping it of its usual consequences so that its meanings "can be more powerfully articulated and more exactly perceived." Like the art of *King Lear* or *Crime and Punishment*, it seizes certain themes—

death, masculinity, rage, pride, loss, beneficence, chance—and, ordering them into an encompassing structure, presents them in such a way as to throw into relief a particular view of their essential nature. It puts a construction on them, makes them . . . meaningful—visible, tangible, graspable—"real," in an ideational sense. An image, a fiction, a model, a metaphor, the cockfight is a means of expression; its function is neither to assuage social passions nor to heighten them, . . . but, in a medium of feathers, blood, crowds, and money, to display them.[80]

The cockfight's eloquence, therefore, springs from its aptness as "metasocial commentary" on the density and elaboration of hierarchy in Balinese life. It has an interpretive function:

80. Geertz, "Deep Play," p. 23.

"it is a Balinese reading of Balinese experience; a story they tell themselves about themselves."[81] Like the trickster tale, the cockfight reveals the imagination's power to lay bare the real depths of social order.

In this sense tricksters are metasocial commentary. They are a language about every sort of language, and thus their extravagance, their "wandering beyond" the borders of ordinary discourse—whether ritual, cosmological, or familial—is an act beyond either repudiation or validation of that discourse since it encompasses both. Like Ogo-Yurugu bursting the confines of the primordial matrix and prowling beyond the fringes of human society, yet all the while engaging in unending conversation with Amma, Nommo, and the social order in the depths of the human personality, the trickster makes real the openness of each language to every other language. He embodies the translatability of divine, animal, astral, and geographical experience into human experience, and makes visible the fluid coherence and the structured movement of human life. He reveals the point at which web and dance become one.

Yet because that revelation takes place in a most particular sort of ritualized glee, the trickster shows that the societies that imagine him do not accept the distinction between word and event, art and reality, made by Auden, Geertz, and, indeed, our whole post-Cartesian culture. The laughter the trickster evokes is a laughter of truly disillusioned delight. Human dread begins with the suspicion that the project that is life will fail, that every human trajectory will fall short of its goal. Tragedy is the discovery that this failure has its own magnificence, while systems of salvation deny the finality of the failure. The trickster, however, launches himself beyond the boundaries and rules of all structure only to splash down again in the world he left with such boisterous nonchalance, a world he refashions both by his departure and by his return. He displays human order, then, as an enduring system precisely be-

81. *Ibid.*, p. 26.

cause it is an ironic language where every "surd-factor" can be woven into some sort of sentence. Just because the trickster is all synchronicity, he discloses that the irreversible diachronicity of the world, its relentless successiveness, is a symbol of dynamism and renewal, not death.

The meaning that the trickster reveals is not merely ideational, for in playing creatively with the radical untidiness of the world, he shows that its incongruities are a form of anti-entropic energy. His scatological bent is more than a metaphor. As Mary Douglas says, the trickster "exploits the symbol of creativity which is contained in a joke, for a joke implies that anything is possible." [82] But for the premodern mind, the possibility of anything is in itself a threat, not a promise. Human life is seen to be so porous, so vulnerable to forces that may dissolve it like so much food turned into feces, that only carefully maintained social structures can arrest and control this wasting process. However, the structure too becomes clogged with waste, and thus the trickster lays hold of the structure and shakes the stuffing—or whatever—out of it. He celebrates its porosity, reveals its open-endedness to be hilarious. Anything is *possible*: even feces can be turned into treasure.

In this composting of the products of open-endedness, the trickster acts very much like Thomas Kuhn's scientist faced with anomalies, or simply new experiences, that challenge his received paradigms. Both seek to befriend the strange, not so much striving to "reduce" anomaly as to use it as a passage into larger order. There are differences, of course, for the scientist's concerns are more specialized and the trickster's paradigms more all-inclusive. Still, Kuhn's work suggests that not only in "the realm of primitive hypothesis" is there "a certain freedom to juggle with the factors of existence," [83] but that

82. Douglas, "The Social Control of Cognition," p. 373.
83. Turner, *Forest of Symbols*, p. 106. See Thomas Kuhn, *The Structure of Scientific Revolutions*; and Barry Baines, "The Comparison of Belief-Systems: Anomaly versus Falsehood," in *Modes of Thought: Essays on Thinking in Western*

something in human self-awareness drives the human mind to seek, even more than continuity, order, closure, or meaning, the encompassing of the unencompassable.

Moreover, like the scientist the trickster always yokes just *this* world to a suddenly larger world. His stories and myths are always particular, and the deeper order into which the passages he opens up lead is always just *here*. Even as he embodies a universal quality of human consciousness, his work is inescapably specific. Thus Ananse comments on a world carefully balanced between Nyame and Asase Yaa, a balance that the Golden Stool makes manifest. Legba translates the purposes of Mawu and her offspring to enable the Fon to change and discard form as well as content without ceasing to be Fon. Eshu shatters and reforms the complex image of the divine order that is Yoruba society so that it may move through both mythical and historical time, while Ogo-Yurugu challenges Amma and Nommo to speak the world according to its proper Dogon specifications.

T. O. Beidelman's excellent studies of Kaguru trickster-figures support this view of the trickster's ability to link meta-social commentary with a specific social-religious order.[84] As Hare especially makes fools of the other animals, he displays key Kaguru concerns—the way food-sharing images both kinship and sexuality, conflicts between youth and age, tensions created by matrilineal order, and the meaning of certain verbal symbols and moral evaluations. Beidelman believes that Hare is a folkloric "metaphor" for various issues of social organization, but his reference to the use of the dung of hares "to stanch the flow of blood from wounds, especially at male circumcision,"[85] implies a more subtle Kaguru understanding of meta-

and Non-Western Societies, ed. Robin Horton and Ruth Finnegan (London: Faber & Faber, 1973), pp. 182–98.

84. See especially "Hyena and Rabbit: A Kaguru Representation of Matrilineal Relations," "Further Adventures of Hyena and Rabbit: The Folktale as a Sociological Model," and "Ambiguous Animals: Two Theriomorphic Metaphors in Kaguru Folklore."

85. Beidelman, "Ambiguous Animals," p. 183.

phor than he has, perhaps, perceived. That is, while Hare, like the other trickster-figures we have discussed, may well reflect the psychic anxieties and the social decisions of a community that is both tightly ordered and innately porous, he also embodies the power of the ironic imagination to use waste as medicine. He reassures precisely because he reveals how human vulnerability at moments of radical change is, in truth, liminal openness. Through it dissolution itself is dissolved, and formlessness becomes the passage to new form.

Although E. E. Evans-Pritchard never analyzed the Zande trickster tales he published toward the end of his life in the light of his earlier writings about the Azande, his introduction to the tales contains many shrewd observations. In suggesting that Ture has "imposed his image on his creators,"[86] he touches the power of the trickster, speaking extravagantly in the specific language of the people who know him, to trigger the recognition that cultural creativity springs from joining the energies of the individual imagination to the expressiveness of the transcendent. If the reality of the human word in symbol, ideal, ritual, or custom is necessarily many-faced and ironic, then, says the trickster, so is the word of the "really real." The trickster is neither a god nor a man, neither human nor animal; he is all of them. In that "ensemble of texts, themselves ensembles,"[87] which is the culture of any people, the trickster is only one text among many, yet as master of all language, he is the ensemble of ensembles, the meeting-place of all words. If, then, he is the image of the ironically imaginative mind of polymorphous man, he is equally the image of the adaptability of transcendence, for which no material thing is too trivial to become a hierophany, not even that little gust of tongue-shaped breath known as the human word.

That word may seem too puny to make anything as large as a

86. Evans-Pritchard, *The Zande Trickster*, p. 29. For a recent study of the way in which the trickster both embodies and fashions cultural self-understanding, see Lawrence W. Levine, " 'Some Go Up and Some Go Down': The Meaning of the Slave Trickster."

87. Geertz, "Deep Play," p. 29.

world happen, yet in the end it is as the master of language—possessor of all stories, linguist of the gods, agent of Ifa, embodiment of the "word of the world," metaphor of social conversation—that the trickster reveals the human world itself to be language. Thus as "image, fiction, model, metaphor," or, more abstractly, as active reciprocal of the human capacity to converse with every other mode of being, the trickster reveals man in his inmost and most daily reality. He is a composition of the human juggling and flip-flopping needed to hold in balance the words arising from all the conversations in which man is engaged. As the trickster's myths are told, his dances danced, his twisted word unraveled, and his hidden presence discerned, his multiformity insists that the words of all dimensions meet in man. His synchronicity discloses that life as it is and as it ought to be are ironically joined in the present—a now which is never finally imagined.

It is the *quality* of that permanently uncompleted now which is the trickster's greatest revelation. Peter Berger sees that humor is ultimately rooted in the immense incongruity that is the "discrepancy between man and the universe." The tragic vision is one response to this discrepancy, yet, as Berger says, laughter, the other response, "relativizes" that vision and suggests that "the seemingly rocklike necessities of this world" can not only be transcended, but even transformed.[88] The trickster so incarnates discrepancy that it finally evokes laughter, yet this incarnation does more than provide a comic alternative to tragedy. By reveling in contingency itself—in clasping the broken word, the contradictory relationship, the deal gone wrong, the food that never fills—the trickster welds together necessity and brokenness in a composition displaying the underlying "energetics" of the ordinary. His sleight-of-form insists that the necessity of the present is really a necessary incompleteness that is always open to a movement at once gross and subtle enough to carry man beyond what he sees

88. See Berger, *A Rumor of Angels*, pp. 87–89.

and knows. Eshu's penis breaks, the travelers fall into the river, and the people shout with glee: the destination is never reached—and therefore it is here.

SOME CONCLUSIONS

The tricksters of hunters and growers

We may not have enough evidence to determine what historical changes the trickster pattern has undergone, but to see the trickster as a symbol of man imagining his world in its daily joining of opposed experiences is, I believe, to possess the key that will unlock the problem of his many guises at different times and places. Thus I think it likely that hunters have imagined their tricksters differently from agriculturalists and that the more complex civilizations made possible by agriculture have found still other ways to express the ironic modes of transformation that the trickster embodies. Ricketts, therefore, is probably right to see in North American Indian cultures a kind of violent competition between the trickster and the High God that is simply not present in agricultural societies. However, instead of attributing either the earlier competition or the later harmony to an evolutionary process or to the wiliness of priests, I find it more probable that the differences spring from the styles of imagination appropriate to each type of culture.

Each has its harmonies, but all cultures imagine these harmonies in ways faithful to the widely differing conditions of their lives.[89] If hunters and agriculturalists had not both experienced the ambivalence of the world and the sacred, they would not both have used trickster-figures to image their experiences. Yet the hunter in his very embeddedness in the wild, by his very kinship with the animals, feels most vividly his distance from "nature." Knowing his dependence on all

89. See van der Post, *The Heart of a Hunter*; Paul Shepard, *The Tender Carnivore and the Sacred Game* (New York: Charles Scribner's Sons, 1973); and Colin M. Turnbull, *The Forest People: A Study of the Pygmies of the Congo* (New York: Simon and Schuster, 1961). These recreations of the worlds of hunting peoples show that their imaginations work differently from those of agriculturalists.

that is nonhuman, he knows also his remoteness from it. The imaginative act that expresses both closeness and distance joins them with a crude power and exuberant pleasure which owes nothing to a presumed inability to differentiate and everything to an ever-present awareness of differentiation. The grower, on the other hand, knows harmony as an imaginative achievement holding in balance a whole network of opposing forces. For him, the trickster becomes responsible for disclosing the denseness of these relationships and the possibility of sustaining them by stretching their inner boundaries. In the end, both kinds of tricksters, unlike the mediatorial figures that spring from a less ironic vision of the sacred, show a similarly witty response to the question of our human ties to all that surrounds us, a response that sees us as most ourselves when, in ceaseless conversation with everything nonhuman, we seize everything for human life by hook or by crook, without confusing identities or priorities.

This sort of imagining is a program neither for polytheism nor for pragmatism. It is, rather, as Victor Turner has said, a constant movement from "indicative to subjunctivity," where anything is possible because man himself is so much unexploited symbolic material.[90] Thus the trickster incarnates in every culture the oxymoronic imagination at play, literally "fooling around" to discover new paradigms and even new logics. As such, he reveals man's freedom to shape the world just because it actively offers itself to him—even if he must trick it to make it come across.

The trickster and West Africa

It is plain enough that such an entity as West Africa exists, if not as an isolated geographical and cultural unit like Australia, then as a loose congeries of related languages and historically interacting societies held in a rough framework of geography and climate. Most scholars believe that certain patterns of reli-

90. In personal communication.

gion and society have assumed there a recognizable combination of forms, none of them unique to the area, but as a whole suggestive of a special way of looking at human life.[91] These forms include the elaboration of kinship structures and ancestral relationships with an unusual sense of historical time; a playful way of handling social and cosmic bipolarity that focuses on the issue of determination and freedom; an exploration of the meanings of such political and economic structures as kingship/queenship and the market; a remarkable development of the plastic arts; and, finally, that inner rendering of African life shown in the joking relationship and dance, a rendering used for so many centuries by nonblacks to caricature and condescend to African civilization, but which has lately come to be known, aptly, under the rubric of "soul."[92] Still, it seems to me that it would require a work of the linguistic and cultural magnitude of Georges Dumézil's studies to place these forms in more than extrinsic relationship and to prove why they reveal an anatomy and not a mere physiognomy.

Nevertheless, this study does suggest that whoever may undertake such a work would do well to consider what seems to me the most distinctive feature of the West African trickster: his association with divination. Divination touches each of the "forms" that seem to give West African life a distinctive shape. As the I Ching both rests and comments on a uniquely Chinese cosmology, sociology, and anthropology, and as the development of the stupa recapitulates the inner growth of Buddhism, so West African divination offers a deliberately intended image of social life, religious thought, and psychic makeup. Because divination binds kinship, every sort of polarity, political and

91. See, for example, Daryll Forde, "The Cultural Map of West Africa: Successive Adaptations to Tropical Forests and Grasslands," *Transactions of the New York Academy of Sciences*, ser. 2, vol. 15, no. 6 (1953); and Meyer Fortes, *Oedipus and Job in West Africa*.

92. See Gustave E. von Grunebaum, *Medieval Islam: A Study in Cultural Orientation*, 2d ed. (Chicago: University of Chicago Press, 1961), pp. 209–11, 354. He quotes Ibn Butlan (d. after 1063): "Dancing and beating time are engrained in their nature. They say: were the Negro to fall from heaven to the earth he would beat time in falling" (p. 211).

economic institutions, and plastic art to the more elusive forms of thought, dance, and inner style, it is a fit topic for comparative and historical study. It is language and document, institution and vision all at once, so that a comparative study should reveal the presence—or absence—in West Africa of related patterns of thought and social order such as Dumézil found from India to Ireland.

The trickster's association with divination already suggests some of the possibilities of these patterns as creative forms of the imagination. If Chinese divination is a marvelous type of linguistic iconography, West African divination discloses both a passion for sociotherapy and a conviction that such therapy is the creation of that mode of social, personal, and cosmic composition which, following William Lynch, I have been calling the work of the ironic imagination. Indeed, the imaginative energy poured into divination demonstrates the depth of the West African passion to discover how life blooms out of the compost of contradiction and antagonism. And if the trickster possesses the language of divination, does it not mean that the inner dialectic of West African life is his own oxymoronic process—absurdly wise, seriously playful, transcendently ordinary, savagely social—imaging and shaping West African man in confident pursuit of a synchronous movement through history?

Although he may have relied too heavily on that aspect of historical research which is empirical science, Franz Boas was certainly, almost prophetically, right to conclude, after discussing the trickster, "that mythological worlds have been built up, only to be shattered again, and that new worlds were built from the fragments."[93] The trickster reveals that just such a work of shattering and rebuilding is the achievement of the West African imagination. In his West African guises the endless dialectic of hierophanies is seen to be an outward, social process as well as an inner, individual one, the labor of com-

93. Introduction to *Traditions of the Thompson River Indians*, p. 18.

munal as well as personal composition, and a witty game as well as a historical project. If the trickster in West Africa provides a way of dealing with discontinuity and change so that human movement through time may become not merely repetition, but an enlargement of sacred frontiers, he does so by linking the acts of re-vision and re-membering in divination, in myth, in dance, in sacrifice. As he teaches West Africans, again and again, how to see, he instructs them over and over how to piece together their experience and to discover in that new whole the same open-ended order that they have always known as the source of transcendent ordinariness.

Nothingness and transformation

In himself, then, the trickster is an anamnesis. He is the riddle that, once posed, brings the healing of the memory and the liberation of the imagination. Ruthless as Eshu, persistent as Ogo, ingratiating as Ananse, cocksure as Legba: he is a question that cannot be put down once picked up. Like the kind of society he symbolizes, the trickster cannot easily be forgotten because he conjures up that startling vision of man which de Tocqueville was given a century and a half ago:

I need not traverse earth and sky to discover a wondrous object woven of contrasts, of infinite greatness and littleness, of intense gloom and amazing brightness, capable at once of exciting pity, admiration, terror, contempt. I have only to look at myself. Man springs out of nothing, crosses time, and disappears forever in the bosom of God; he is seen but for a moment, wandering on the verge of the two abysses, and there he is lost. [94]

Man's imagination, de Tocqueville says, is driven restlessly onward, pushed by what he does see of himself, pulled by what he does not, a vast darkness "in which he gropes forever, and forever in vain, to lay hold on some completer notion of his being." Just so not only West Africans, but most traditional

94. Alexis de Tocqueville, *Democracy in America*, trans. Henry Reeve, ed. Phillips Bradley (New York: Alfred A. Knopf; Vintage Books, 1954), vol. 2, p. 80.

peoples, see themselves in their tricksters—a set of amazing contraries pushing and pulling them in unchanging process along the thinnest possible boundary between past and future, nothingness and death.

Just so, and yet not quite so, for in his nature woven of contrasts, in the mixed reaction he provokes, in his wandering and groping, the trickster is what de Tocqueville saw man to be, but in his assurance and his gaiety he is not. He is an image, not of stoic nobility and final defeat, but of a hope so bold that it becomes a self-fulfilling prophecy. The source of the hope lies in the composition of the image. The Fon, Yoruba, Dogon, and Ashanti see the trickster, and themselves, as embodying that boundary as well as wandering on it. Moreover, they see that boundary as a threshold between states of being—static and formless, wholly actualized and wholly potential, transparent and opaque, nothingness and death; call them what you will —which are known as meeting *now* and are therefore experienced in their meeting as life. Nothingness and death become ancestry and progeny; the boundary between them is endlessly erased. The liminal state that the trickster discloses to be man's most ironic reality never ceases to transform those very elements which seem most adamantine and impervious to life. How can he not be carefree and cocksure, then, when his every movement carves life out of death?

In large measure, this image seems the language of paradox, perhaps of sheer nonsense, to the contemporary ear. Yet it must be remembered that the body in which the trickster composes the life of man is an open body, a body that is also the whole social order experienced as perduring and renewing itself throughout time and by means of time. The transforming limen that the trickster is and that has its real root within the human soul has also a twin root within communal life, itself an image of a divine and cosmic order truly, if not merely, human. This image, then, is neither the language of paradox and nonsense nor the nonlanguage of a great pantheistic broth. It is the language of analogy, of corresponding levels of being yoked together in an irony that demonstrates its own truth by its capacity to engender life, to realize life's doubleness in society and history as well as in the mind.

We need to remember that such a language is known to us by its very absence. We can say, "A rose is a rose is a rose," or "Hail to thee, blithe spirit! Bird thou never wert"; but we cannot find a way to see the rose's ultimacy or the skylark's feathers simultaneously. Such an inability we know as a terrible loss, for even as we dream of integrity, of becoming single, "a success of a person, something firm and fixed," we yearn, like the heroine of *Them*, for the possibility of transformation: "I only want to escape the doom of being *Maureen Wendall* all of my life. I dream of a world where you can go in and out of bodies, changing your soul, everything changing and not fixed forever, becoming men and women, daughters, children again, even old people, feeling how it is to be them."[95] We cannot imagine such fixedness joined to such flux. Our culture has been unable to achieve that act of imagination at least since the moment in the sixteenth century when *Hoc est enim corpus meum* became "hocus-pocus."[96] And so the best that Joyce Carol Oates's heroine can do is to be alternately passionate for transformation and ravenous for fixity, her anxiety only a feeble sign of a terrible cultural desire to discover a new language of communion.

Certainly Marx and Freud have probed the substructures of human life to find the meeting-place between theory and praxis, objectivity and ego, between what Vico called "the

95. Joyce Carol Oates, *Them* (Greenwich, Conn.: Fawcett World Library, 1970), pp. 409, 317–18.
96. In 1927 Reinhold Niebuhr had this to say about the debate in the Church of England over the nature of Christ's presence in the Eucharist: "How can one be tolerant of medievalism without playing traitor to the best in the modern day? . . . Think of the spiritual leaders of a torn and bleeding world debating learnedly on whether and how God can be magically localized . . . in a capsule." *Leaves from the Notebook of a Tamed Cynic* (Cleveland: World Publishing Co., 1965), pp. 182–83. But as Kafka's *Metamorphosis* implies, if sacred transformations are absurd, then other, and even more absurd, transformations will inevitably take place.

verum (the truth of things) and the *factum* (that which is made
. . . by man himself)."[97] Yet no matter how persuasive have
been the secularized languages of transformation and communion that these geniuses have devised, even so sympathet-
ic a student of Marx as Lévi-Strauss knows that they have not
found the juncture between the given and the image where
alone life passes both into and out of death. Lévi-Strauss, of
course, would agree with Marx and Freud that to seek such a
juncture is an alienation and an illusion. For them it exists only
as a false image of a nothingness that man must acknowledge
inwardly, even as he moves toward its outer form in death, so
that he might at least live authentically. This is the final vision
of *Tristes Tropiques*: that the human race is a kind of massive, if
courageous, amoeba, devouring the earth and rendering it inert, as it slides like all species toward extinction; that the insight of Buddhism bursts like a flare to disclose that darkness
extends infinitely and that all we have is one another; that the
blessing of Marx is to hold out some hope, however modest, of
slowing the rate of historical entropy.[98]

Yet it seems to me that Lévi-Strauss has only asked the next-
to-last question—"What is there, then?"—and received only
the next-to-last answer: "Nothing." That is what the two most
persistent images of the trickster—his youthfulness and his
glee—suggest would be the response of those societies who
imagine their own meeting with death in him. They hint, in
the trickster, that Lévi-Strauss has not lacked faith so much
as irony. Ogo, Eshu, and Legba are all in some sense youngest children, while Ananse is more "childish" than his children. On the other hand, each is in some way the master of
his people's wisdom. Too complex to be dismissed as mere
light entertainment, too dense with cultural detail to be simply structural catechesis, too bawdy for cautionary tales—the
trickster's stories are an ironic yoking of foolishness and wis-

97. Lynch, *Images of Faith*, p. 54.
98. See Claude Lévi-Strauss, *Tristes Tropiques*, pp. 393–98.

dom, littleness and significance, a celebration of the boundless potential for form that the unformed possess.

If we can see the storyteller, for the moment at least the repository of all that his or her people know, as the youngest of all, the readiest to make-believe, then we begin to grasp how the trickster does indeed train children to be adults—and adults to be children. They are not meant to imitate the trickster by rebelling, lying, or cheating, in greed, lust, irreverence, or incest, but they are meant to learn from him what a human really is: an imaginer of life. The purpose of the stories is to put an adult mind in a child's heart and a child's eye in an adult head. They mean to shape the imagination by revealing this image of the human power to mold the world by language and to compose human life by the willingness to engage every reality in intimate conversation. Certainly Fon, Ashanti, Dogon, and Yoruba children learn docility and obedience, but from the trickster they learn that there is no question that cannot be asked because every answer, even "I don't know," produces a larger world. For adults the trickster remains a life-long instructor in the uses of language, reminding them that childhood—in its structurelessness and verbal naiveté—is a permanent symbol of liminality, where true wisdom and authentic speech come into being in the amazing union of plain word and ordinary thing.

Like divination, the trickster's myths reveal the world as human process, indeed as a story whose many-sidedness requires it to be never-endingly reimagined. The trickster and his tales, then, are an education in wit. They invest the plastic imagination of the child with adult irony and remind the adult consciousness that social barriers are boundaries of the mind that only a child's expectancy can break through. It is there, within, that death will rule if the imagination cannot find a way to question nothing, which is both the absolute of formlessness and the silence of perfection. Only the discovery of a language bold and subtle enough to ask the question and frame the answer brings sacred wholeness and profane multiplicity together in that intricate exchange of words which is human life.

The film *2001: A Space Odyssey* opens with a shot of a great African plain suffused with the warm, still pale light of dawn. Over the flat grassland, distant trees, and growing brightness lies a mantle of silence. All is still. There is no sound in all this vast, waiting world. Yet in that moment, before the birth of man, surely the earth was filled with the noises of animals —barking, roaring, snorting, warbling, crooning, snarling, screaming, sighing, even chattering. But despite that clamor the world was silent because it lacked the one sound that gives it its true shape: the human voice in simple conversation. Only that voice, first questioning the animals and thus giving them too a voice, and then, in male and female wholeness, enclosing the entire earth in language, breaks the silence. The human voice rises like the sun to give the world a face, and always it retains, no matter how complex its grammar and its imagery become, something of this primal simplicity. The human voice remains the voice of a child—filling the universe with names, questioning its silence, itself demanding to be heard and answered—even as it achieves the adult wit to spell out both question and answer in ever more elaborate webs of language.

The trickster, then, embodies that voice asking and answering the last question: "What is nothing?" His answer is double. Its first part is this: "I do not know, but when I went there, I found myself back here." The humor of the trickster's stories and myths rests finally on his disclosure of the potency, and thus the sacredness, of all that is, now. Legba pushes the sacred center away from the earth so that he might penetrate, through that very separation, its nearness in every daily space. Ananse reveals that the corners of human life are not culs-de-sac, but interstices in a web of purpose—always expanding, always drawing tighter—into which all beings are woven. Eshu overcomes the threat of change and denies its apparently essential link to chaos by claiming it for the humanness of the world. Moving each day and each year to bring the light, he turns Andrew Marvell's conceit into a boast: "Thus, though we cannot make our sun/Stand still, yet we will make him run." If there were only stasis, there could be no transformation, and thus Ogo's shattering of primordial androgyny brings forth the communion of sex even as Yurugu's random wanderings assimilate dailiness to transcendence.

The trickster soars into heaven, forages in the wild, goes out to capture disease, death, and contradiction for human life, not heroically, but simply as the agent of a sovereign irony. Ecologists are the most recent students of the world to discover that the system holding all creatures in mutually sustaining life is itself held together by change and sustained by death. But those who know the trickster understand that if the system of life embraces change and death, it is because its boundaries are ceaselessly enlarged by him—the image of a mind subtle enough and a heart playful enough to seize and affirm all that is negative and anomalous. That affirmation discloses the holiness of what is, as all of it, man's own anomalous being especially, becomes a vessel of the mysterious dynamism that continues always to make being *be*. In reaching into nothing the trickster touches the ultimate pollution that threatens every something, and in discovering that nothing's power only thrusts him back into what is present, he transforms every potential avenue of corruption into a passageway of rebirth. The least thing, then, like the worst thing, becomes a possible place for the revelation of what is greatest.

The second part of the answer thus completes the first: "I do not know what nothing is, but when I touched it, it caught me, and filled me with joy." If the trickster's opponent is Hate-to-be-contradicted, is he not therefore Love-to-contradict? He can speak all languages and embrace every form. Why should he fear nothingness, formlessness, death? Why should he not instead revel in the passage of old forms into new? Indeed, he does. Ananse plays so that the elephant can dance, teaches the sun the words of the drum, dances himself at the center of the world in Nyame's court; Legba invents the dance to celebrate the victory of sexual communion; Eshu is all agility as he fosters every means of exchange; Ogo-Yurugu moves in a sacred spiral in his womb and dances each day across the divining tables. Sir James Frazer would surely think that such insouciance was as doomed as it was brave, but the trickster's dance leaps beyond the tragic mode and even farther beyond mere humor. His extravagant glee is the revelation that to be stuck in the sweet viscosity of the world is sheer delight because that world—in the ambiguity of its sweetness as much as in its unyielding, unclassifiable ambivalence—is the image of a transcendence as inexhaustibly fluid as water, as wholly present as air, as immovable as earth.

In the debate set off by Victor Turner's monograph on the Chihamba initiation rite among the Ndembu, only Mary Douglas seems to have grasped his central point: that the *kind* of demythification contained in this attempt to disclose "the inadequacy of the categories of thought for expressing the nature of existence" by means of a laughter-provoking "mock-killing" of the god at the most solemn moment of the ritual is, in fact, "an apotheosis of wit."[99] Turner was taken to task for using Thomistic language to explore this summit of Ndembu irony, but, as Douglas sees, he has listened to African laughter keenly enough to hear in it a specifically African way of saying the unsayable. If he is right, and this entire book witnesses to my belief that he is, then it seems likely that Africans have indirectly, almost offhandedly, developed a metaphysics of delight, a way of reaching into the ungraspable and describing its nature by the laughter that greets the reacher as he slowly opens his clenched fist to reveal—nothing.

In this metaphysics the trickster is neither first cause nor last end. He is an exemplar of wit in action, the most practical joke of all as he pulls the chair out from under the system to keep it moving, as he bounces back from beyond every beyond

99. Douglas, "Social Control of Cognition," p. 375. See Victor Turner, *Chihamba, The White Spirit*; and Robin Horton, "Ritual Man in Africa." Cf. di Nola, "Demythicization."

with a gleeful shout that there is really here. Other peoples have made similar discoveries, of course. The Buddha's smile, Zen masters' pranks, Heidegger's ponderous linguistic somersaults, and especially Jesus's cross—all in various ways proclaim that no-thingness will never have the last word because it is the last laugh. But with a unique clarity the trickster reveals that the active reciprocal of the apparently bottomless *passio* of human yearning that he embodies is no-thing—so huge, so dense, so resilient, so *real* that it turns bottomlessness inside-out to a fullness that is pure joy.

Thus the delight that the trickster both creates and is finally springs from an intuition of the force driving the ironic dialectic of the imagination, which enables man himself to become a sacred world and human yearning to become the earthly synonym for that same force—this no-thingness that is the very antithesis of nothing. In touching nothing and finding joy the trickster reveals that this most supple energy of all is by its very adaptability the ultimate holiness made the moving power of ordinary human life. In the trickster's myths this energy appears as a passion for intercourse that looks like lust, but lust is a word too puny by far for a power so far-reaching. Concupiscence too lacks sufficient weight for this passionate insistence on purpose, this ironic attachment to the earthy, this restless composition of the most intricate meanings. Freud knew what this force was and how it alone could wrest life out of death's grasp, and his word, Eros, describes well the trickster's seizure of life.[100]

Yet the joy that the trickster gives and receives in penetrating nothingness and contradicting contradiction, in shaping and reshaping man's life without end, rises from an even deeper source than Freud knew of—tougher, gentler, far more ironic. The trickster is wonderful because he is the image of that yearning—that driving energy of inclusion which is itself an image of final boundlessness—which sets the social order in

100. See Freud, *Civilization and Its Discontents*, pp. 143–44.

motion and keeps it spinning, which holds heaven and earth in balance, which names the nameless and speaks the unspeakable. The figure of Loki bears witness that this force, in its mythic as in its fleshly embodiments, can run amuck, can choose a nothing that is not no-thing, that is chaos. But where the trickster continues to instruct in every form of wit, can we not say that the mysterious power shaping him is the same power shaping all that is deepest in human delight? And can we not name it, then, remembering how Ananse named himself to Akwasi, with the word grown ever more oxymoronic over the centuries, too ambivalent for even Freud to use, too ironic for Marx, and say that this love to contradict, this passion to rise and make love, which finds in the trickster an image of transforming joy as he weaves his web of purpose and dances his dance of delight, is nothing less simple and more complex than love?

Appendix

WESTERN interpreters have found it difficult to grasp the meaning of divination chiefly because its practice, like that of most forms of folk-medicine, assumes the active reality of a spirit-world that Greek, Jewish, and Christian thought has regarded as demonic, false, or both. Even when diviners were not accused of sorcery or charlatanry, many commentators have supposed them to possess extrasensory gifts enabling them to diagnose and treat the ills of their clients.[1] Although anthropologists and historians of religion have insisted on the systematic rationality and the symbolic depths of divination, only a few years ago Morton Smith chastised Eliade for ignoring the sham in shamanism.[2] Those who have studied divination in the last generation, however, do not believe that the shamanic personality, vocation, and technique are the basis of divination. They have discovered that forms of divination are, as the Fon state explicitly, languages complete with their own units of meaning, inner structures, and social purposes. Insofar as divination is indeed a process for transformation,

1. See Bascom, *Ifa Divination*, pp. 24–25.
2. See Morton Smith, "Historical Method in the Study of Religion," in *On Method in the History of Religions*, ed. J. S. Helfer, pp. 14 ff.

enough mystery remains to fuel many debates, as our own culture's experience with psychotherapy would lead us to expect, but the scholarly consensus that has emerged reveals a social process designed to *combat* darkness by bringing to light the causes of disorder, no matter to what other uses that process has been or might be put.

Bascom's work on Ifa divination and the comments of Herskovits on its Fon counterpart show how mundane and nondramatic are the procedures of Yoruba and Fon diviners. A climate for mystification is lacking since everyone present at a divination ceremony knows the patterns of the sixteen basic figures and the 256 derivative figures, while the verses recited by the diviner are familiar to all.[3] These verses consist of phrases, proverbs, and brief tales linked to certain casts. Clients would not know the full set, of course, but the wider knowledge of the diviner is not any more deceptive than a doctor's ability to recite the names of his patient's bones and muscles and to detect a certain pathology from a given pattern of symptoms. The diviner, like the doctor, has a specialized language and an expert's skills, yet he shares with his clients a mental universe in which names, symbols, methods, and problems are mutually recognized, if not equally understood.

The *bokono*, or Fon diviner, casts with palm nuts in almost precisely the same manner as does the Yoruba *babalawo*. He holds sixteen nuts in one hand and "casts" by bringing them quickly into the other hand, where either one or two nuts are left for an instant before being picked up again. As he glances at the nut or nuts left, he marks on the powdered clay or meal before him a single line for two nuts or a double line for one nut.[4] After eight casts, the diviner has two vertical columns, each consisting of four double or single lines. Each column has sixteen possible combinations (e.g., 1111, 1112, 1121, 1211, 2111, 2211, etc.), and thus the total number of figures possible is 256.

3. See Bascom, *Ifa Divination*, pp. 76–90.
4. Herskovits, *Dahomey*, vol. 2, p. 210; cf. Bascom, *Ifa Divination*, pp. 40–50.

However, there are only sixteen figures in which the first and second columns match, and if one compares the Fon names of these figures with their Yoruba counterparts, one sees that the Fon have only slightly modified their names.[5] Both the Fon and the Yoruba emphasize the significance of the verses connected to the sixteen major *odu* (Fon, *du*) and to the 240 lesser ones to create an intricate network of analysis and prescription.

As a psychiatrist may use the Rorschach inkblots to elicit the psychic patterns of a patient's mind, so Bascom believes that a diviner offers his client a series of verses from which the client chooses the one suited to his case. He admits, however, that the Yoruba insist that "it is the diviner rather than the client who selects the appropriate verse."[6] Recent studies agree that this is the case, and show that such a selection is not so mysterious as it might seem. Richard Werbner, for example, has reported that among the Kalanga of Botswana diviners choose the proper verses just as much because of the casts that were *not* thrown as because of those that were.[7] The point is that the choice is part of a sequence. That sequence may be a series of divinatory casts, or it may be the unfolding of a person's life, in which a single cast, as at the time of receiving the partial *fa*, is a privileged moment offering an especially crucial choice. Yet the aim is always to discern the pattern of a client's life and to disclose it to him. Like the inkblot, the divinatory cast hints at a hidden pattern. Unlike that associative, projective technique, however, divination provides a shape objective as well as flexible, capable of manifesting a whole system of outward relationships in their inward, personal arrangement.

Victor Turner's study of Ndembu divination suggests how the divinatory process joins personal revelation, sociotherapy, and cosmic renewal. In striving to uncover "the causes of misfortune or death," the Ndembu diviner seeks "to make known

5. See Herskovits, *Dahomey*, vol. 2, p. 210, and Bascom, *Ifa Divination*, pp. 42–46, 50.

6. Bascom, *Ifa Divination*, p. 69.

7. See Werbner, "Superabundance of Understanding," pp. 1425–26.

and intelligible in Ndembu terms what is unknown and unintelligible." [8] In working to discover, name, and deal with some troublesome ancestor or spirit who is provoking conflict or to find and root out a sorcerer or a witch, diviners try to lay bare not only the workings of an individual life, but the inner structure of the community. They seek, as Turner says, "to grasp consciously and bring into the open the secret, and even unconscious, motives and aims of human actors in some situation of social disturbance." [9] Members of traditional societies sense how porous are the boundaries between individual and communal, visible and invisible worlds, and thus in time of affliction they consult a diviner with the hope that he will prepare them to receive a "word" that will unite these worlds once again in a single, many-leveled design. For this reason diviners are expected, before casting, to perform a delicate social analysis, "to elicit from their clients responses which give them clues to the pattern of current tensions in their groups of origin." [10] As divination, then, maps uncharted social terrain, it heals personal or communal ills by assimilating momentary chaos to the unchanging, and therefore changelessly life-giving, cosmic order that individual and society are meant to image.

It is this sense of the divinatory moment as cosmic iconography that Carl Jung has caught so brilliantly in his introduction to the Wilhelm edition of the *I Ching*. Certainly too blithe in his assessment of the Chinese attitude toward the principles of causality as the West knows them, Jung nevertheless pierces to the heart of divination with his insight that a given moment, more nearly the creation of chance than the product of scientific law, exists as a revelation of the interplay of all the beings and powers of the universe. As a system, the I Ching was thought to map this interplay so thoroughly that each "hexagram worked out in a certain moment coincided with [it] in quality no less than in time . . . inasmuch as the hexagram was

8. Turner, *Ndembu Divination*, p. 14.
9. *Ibid.*, p. 15.
10. *Ibid.*, p. 17.

understood to be an indicator of the essential situation prevail-
ing in the moment of its origin."[11] This vision of the singularity
of each moment, based on the "synchronic" focusing of the
forces of the cosmos, is not unknown to Western thought. Certainly Duns Scotus's notion of *hicceitas*, "thisness," explores
the same quality of experience, while Gerard Manley Hop-
kins's "inscape" and "instress" advocate the notion poetically
against the blearing abstractions of the industrial age. However, Jews and Christians, convinced of the freedom of a divine
omnipotence that orders history through human choice into a
pattern at once more transcendent and more intimate than that
of a divinatory cast, have rejected divination because it substitutes a human technique for submission to the sovereign Word
of that freedom. Such, of course, is not the intention of traditional societies. They too seek obedience—obedience to an
order they know as sacred because it has brought them life.
How amazingly large that order is, how charged with both
danger and delight, how opposed to the mindless tinkering
with mystery so fashionable in the secularized West, the trickster reveals, ironically: as he grasps for the ungraspable and
spells out the unsayable, he shows forth divination's power to
redraw in the plain earth of daily life the icon of all that truly is.

11. Jung, Introduction to the *I Ching*, p. xxiv.

Selected Bibliography

GENERAL

Africa

Beattie, John H. M. "Consulting a Diviner in Bunyoro: A Text." *Ethnology* 5 (1966): 202–17.

Davidson, Basil, and Bush, F. K. *A History of West Africa.* Garden City, N.Y.: Doubleday & Co., 1966.

Evans-Pritchard, E. E. *Witchcraft, Oracles, and Magic among the Azande.* Oxford: Clarendon Press, 1937.

Finnegan, Ruth. *Oral Literature in Africa.* Oxford: Clarendon Press, 1970.

Forde, Darryl, ed. *African Worlds: Studies in the Cosmological Ideas and Social Values of African Peoples.* London: Oxford University Press for the International African Institute, 1954.

Forde, Darryl, and Kaberry, Phyllis M., eds. *West African Kingdoms in the Nineteenth Century.* London: Oxford University Press for the International African Institute, 1967.

Fortes, Meyer. *Oedipus and Job in West Africa.* Cambridge: Cambridge University Press, 1959.

Fortes, Meyer, and Dieterlen, Germaine, eds. *African Systems of Thought.* Oxford: Clarendon Press, 1965.

Herskovits, Melville J. "The Culture Areas of Africa." *Africa* 3 (1930): 59–77.

Horton, Robin. "Ritual Man in Africa." *Africa* 34 (1964): 85–104.

Levtzion, Nehemia. *Ancient Ghana and Mali*. London: Methuen and Co., 1973.

Lienhardt, Godfrey. *Divinity and Experience: The Religion of the Dinka*. Oxford: Clarendon Press, 1961.

Murdock, George P. *Africa: Its People and Their Cultural History*. New York: McGraw-Hill, 1959.

Park, George K. "Divination and Its Social Contexts." *Journal of the Royal Anthropological Institute* 93 (1963): 165–86.

Ray, Benjamin. "African High Gods: A Study of the Concept of Supreme Being in Six African Societies." Ph.D. dissertation, University of Chicago, 1971.

Smith, Edwin W., ed. *African Ideas of God: A Symposium*. 3d ed. London: Edinburgh House Press, 1966.

Turner, Victor W. *Ndembu Divination: Its Symbolism and Techniques*. The Rhodes-Livingstone Papers, No. 31. Manchester: Manchester University Press, 1961.

———. *Chihamba, the White Spirit*. The Rhodes-Livingstone Papers, No. 33. Manchester: Manchester University Press, 1962.

———. *The Forest of Symbols: Aspects of Ndembu Ritual*. Ithaca, N.Y.: Cornell University Press, 1970.

van der Post, Laurens. *The Heart of a Hunter*. London: Hogarth Press, 1961.

Werbner, Richard P. "The Superabundance of Understanding: Kalanga Rhetoric and Domestic Divination." *American Anthropologist* 75 (1973): 1414–40.

Interpretation

Berger, Peter L. *A Rumor of Angels: Modern Society and the Rediscovery of the Supernatural*. Garden City, N.Y.: Doubleday & Co., 1969.

Caquot, André, and Leibovici, Marcel, eds. *La Divination*. 2 vols. Paris: Presses Universitaires de France, 1968.

di Nola, Alfonso M. "Demythicization in Certain Primitive Cultures: Cultural Fact and Socioreligious Integration." Translated by Robert D. Pelton. *History of Religions* 12 (1972): 1–27.

Douglas, Mary. "The Meaning of Myth." In *The Structural Study of Myth and Totemism*, edited by Edmund Leach. A.S.A. Monographs, No. 5, pp. 49–69. London: Tavistock Publications, 1967.

———. "The Social Control of Cognition: Some Factors in Joke Perception." *Man (Journal of the Royal Anthropological Institute, n.s.)* 3 (1968): 361–76.

———. *Purity and Danger: An Analysis of Concepts of Pollution and Taboo*. London: Penguin Books, 1970.

Dundes, Alan. "Metafolklore and Oral Literary Criticism." *The Monist* 50 (1966): 505–16.

Durkheim, Emile. *The Elementary Forms of the Religious Life*. Translated by Joseph Ward Swain. New York: The Free Press, 1965.

Eliade, Mircea. *Images and Symbols*. Translated by Philip Mairet. New York: Sheed & Ward, 1961.

———. *Patterns in Comparative Religion*. Translated by Rosemary Sheed. Cleveland: World Publishing Co., 1963.

———. *The Quest: History and Meaning in Religion*. Chicago: University of Chicago Press, 1969.

——— *The Two and the One*. Translated by J. M. Cohen. New York: Harper & Row, 1969.

Eliade, Mircea, and Kitagawa, Joseph M., eds. *The History of Religion: Essays in Methodology*. Chicago: University of Chicago Press, 1959.

Erikson, Erik H. *Childhood and Society*. 2d ed. New York: W. W. Norton, 1958.

———. "The Ontogeny of Ritualization." In *Proceedings of the Royal Society* (1966), pp. 601–21.

———. *Identity: Youth and Crisis*. Austen Riggs Monograph, No. 7. New York: W. W. Norton, 1968.

Evans-Pritchard, E. E. *Theories of Primitive Religion*. Oxford: Clarendon Press, 1965.

Fink, Eugen. *Spiel als Weltsymbol*. Stuttgart: Kohlhammer, 1960.

Freud, Sigmund. *Civilization and Its Discontents*. Translated by Joan Riviere. London: Hogarth Press, 1930.

Geertz, Clifford. "Religion as a Cultural System." In *Anthropological Approaches to the Study of Religion*, edited by Michael Banton. A.S.A. Monographs, No. 3, pp. 1–46. London: Tavistock Publications, 1966.

———. "Deep Play: Notes on the Balinese Cockfight." *Daedalus* 101 (1972): 1–37.

Gluckman, Max. *Closed Systems and Open Minds: The Limits of Naivety in Social Anthropology*. Chicago: Aldine Publishing Co., 1964.

Hayes, E. Nelson, and Hayes, Tanya, eds. *Claude Lévi-Strauss: The Anthropologist as Hero*. Cambridge, Mass.: M.I.T. Press, 1970.

Helfer, J. S., ed. *On Method in the History of Religions*. History and Theory, Beiheft 8. Middletown, Conn.: Wesleyan University Press, 1968.

Huizinga, J. *Homo Ludens*. Translated by R. F. C. Hull. London: Hunt, Barnard & Co., 1949.

Hux, Samuel. "Culture and the Abyss." *Commentary* 58 (August 1974): 54–59.

Hyers, M. Conrad, ed. *Holy Laughter: Essays on Religion in the Comic Perspective*. New York: Seabury Press, 1969.

Jung, Carl G. Introduction to *The I Ching*. Translated by Richard Wilhelm and Cary F. Baynes. 3d ed. Princeton: Princeton University Press, 1970.

Kuhn, Thomas. *The Structure of Scientific Revolutions*. 2d ed. Chicago: University of Chicago Press, 1970.

Lash, Kenneth. "A Theory of the Comic as Insight." *Journal of Philosophy* 45 (1948): 113–21.

Lévi-Strauss, Claude. *Tristes Tropiques*. Translated by John Russell. New York: Atheneum, 1963.

———. *The Savage Mind*. Translated by George Weidenfeld and Nicolson, Ltd. The Nature of Human Society Series. Chicago: University of Chicago Press, 1966.

———. *Structural Anthropology*. Translated by Claire Jacobson and Brooke Grundfest Schoepf. Garden City, N.Y.: Doubleday & Co., 1967.

———. *The Raw and the Cooked: Introduction to a Science of Mythology*. Translated by John Weightman and Doreen Weightman. 2 vols. New York: Harper & Row, 1969.

Lynch, William. *Images of Faith: An Exploration of the Ironic Imagination*. Notre Dame: Notre Dame University Press, 1973.

Montagu, Ashley, ed. *The Concept of the Primitive*. New York: The Free Press, 1968.

Muecke, D. C. *The Compass of Irony*. London: Methuen and Co., 1969.

Penner, Hans. "Is Phenomenology a Method for the Study of Religion?" *Bucknell Review* 38 (1970): 29–54.

———. "The Poverty of Functionalism." *History of Religions* 11 (1971): 91–97.

Pettazoni, Raffaele. *The All-knowing God: Researches into Early Religions and Cultures*. Translated by H. J. Rose. London: Methuen and Co., 1956.

Radcliffe-Brown, A. R. "The Comparative Method in Anthropology." *Journal of the Royal Anthropological Institute* 81 (1951): 15–22.

Radin, Paul. "The Religion of the North American Indians." *Journal of American Folklore* 27 (1914): 335–73.

Read, H. E. *Icon and Idea: The Function of Art in the Development of Human Consciousness*. Cambridge, Mass.: Harvard University Press, 1955.

Redfield, Robert. *The Primitive World and Its Transformations*. Ithaca, N.Y.: Cornell University Press, 1953.

Smith, Jonathan Z. "Adde Parvum Parvo Magnus Acervus Erit." *History of Religions* 11 (1971): 67–90.

———. "I Am a Parrot (Red)." *History of Religions* 11 (1972): 391–413.

———. "When the Bough Breaks." *History of Religions* 12 (1973): 342–71.

Thompson, Stith. *The Folktale*. New York: Holt, Rinehart, & Winston, 1946.

Turner, Victor W. *The Ritual Process: Stucture and Anti-structure*. Chicago: Aldine Publishing Co., 1969.

———. "Passages, Margins, and Poverty: Religious Symbols of Communitas." *Worship* 46 (1972): 390–412, 482–94.

van Gennep, Arnold. *The Rites of Passage*. Translated by Monika B. Vizedom and Gabrielle L. Caffee. Chicago: University of Chicago Press, 1960.

Welsford, Enid. *The Fool: His Social and Religious History*. London: Faber & Faber, 1935.

Trickster

Babcock-Abrahams, Barbara. " 'A Tolerated Margin of Mess': The Trickster and His Tales Reconsidered." *Journal of the Folklore Institute* 11 (1975): 147–86.

Beidelman, T. O. "Hyena and Rabbit: A Kaguru Representation of Matrilineal Relations." *Africa* 31 (1961): 61–74.

———. "Further Adventures of Hyena and Rabbit: The Folktale as a Sociological Model." *Africa* 31 (1961): 250–57.

———. "Ambiguous Animals: Two Theriomorphic Metaphors in Kaguru Folklore." *Africa* 45 (1975): 183–200.

Bianchi, Ugo. "Pour l'histoire du dualisme: Un Coyote africain, le Renard pâle." In *Liber Amicorum: Studies in Honour of Professor Dr. C. J. Bleeker*, pp. 27–43. Leiden: E. J. Brill, 1969.

———. "Seth, Osiris et l'ethnographie." *Revue de l'histoire des religions* 179 (1971): 113–35.

Boas, Franz. "The Growth of Indian Mythologies." *Journal of American Folklore* 9 (1896): 1–11.

———. Introduction to *Traditions of the Thompson River Indians*, by James Teit. Memoirs of the American Folklore Society, vol. 6. New York: Houghton Mifflin & Co., 1898.

Brelich, Angelo. "Il Trickster." *Studi e Materiali di Storia delle Religione* 29 (1958): 129–37.

Brinton, Daniel. *The Myths of the New World*. Philadelphia: David McKay Co., 1868.

Brown, Norman O. *Hermes the Thief: The Evolution of a Myth*. New York: Vintage Books, 1969.

Dumézil, Georges. *Loki*. Paris: Maisonneuve, 1948.

Evans-Pritchard, E. E., ed. *The Zande Trickster*. Oxford: Clarendon Press, 1967.

Greenway, John. *Literature among the Primitives*. Hatboro, Pa.: Folklore Associates, 1964.

Jung, Carl G. "On the Psychology of the Trickster Figure." Translated by R. F. C. Hull. In *The Trickster*, by Paul Radin, pp. 195–211. New York: Greenwood Press, 1969.

Jung, Carl G., and von Franz, M. L., eds. *Man and His Symbols*. London: Aldus Books, 1964.

Kerényi, Karl. "The Trickster in Relation to Greek Mythology." Translated by R. F. C. Hull. In *The Trickster*, by Paul Radin, pp. 173–91.

Layard, John. "Critical Notice of *The Trickster*, by Paul Radin." *Journal of Analytical Psychology* 2 (1957): 106–11.

———. "Note on the Autonomous Psyche and the Ambivalence of the Trickster Concept." *Journal of Analytical Psychology* 3 (1958): 21–28.

Levine, Lawrence W. " 'Some Go Up and Some Go Down' : The Meaning of the Slave Trickster." In *The Hofstadter Aegis: A Memorial*, edited by Stanley Elkins and Eric McKitrick, pp. 94–124. New York: Alfred A. Knopf, 1974.

McKean, Philip Frick. "The Mouse-deer (*Kantjil*) in Malayo-Indonesian Folklore: Alternative Analyses and the Significance of a Trickster Figure in South-East Asia." *Asian Folklore Studies* 30–31 (1971): 71–84.

Makarius, Laura. "Le Mythe du 'Trickster'." *Revue de l'histoire des religions* 175 (1969): 17–46.

———. "The Magic of Transgression." *Anthropos* 69 (1974): 537–52.

Metman, Philip. "The Trickster Figure in Schizophrenia." *Journal of Analytical Psychology* 3 (1958): 5–20.

Pelton, Robert D. "The Web of Purpose, the Dance of Delight: A Study of Four West-African Trickster-Figures in Their Social and Mythological Settings." Ph.D. dissertation, University of Chicago, 1974.

Radin, Paul. *The Trickster: A Study in American Indian Mythology*. New York: Greenwood Press, 1969.

Ricketts, Mac Linscott. "The Structure and Religious Significance of the Trickster-Transformer-Culture Hero in the Mythology of the North American Indians." Ph.D. dissertation, University of Chicago, 1964.

———. "The North American Indian Trickster." *History of Religions* 5 (1965): 327–50.

Varty, Kenneth. *Reynard the Fox: A Study of the Fox in Medieval English Art*. Leicester: Leicester University Press, 1967.

ASHANTI

Barker, W. H., and Sinclair, Cecilia. *West African Folk-Tales*. London: George G. Harrap, 1917. Reprint. Northbrook, Ill.: Metro Books, 1970.

Busia, Kofi A. "The Ashanti of the Gold Coast." In *African Worlds*, pp. 190–209.

Christensen, James B. "The Role of Proverbs in Fante Culture." *Africa* 28 (1958): 232–43.

Danquah, Joseph B. *The Gold Coast Akan*. London: Lutterworth Press, 1945.

———. *The Akan Doctrine of God*. 2d ed. London: Frank Cass & Co., 1968.

Field, Margaret J. *Search for Security: An Ethno-Psychiatric Study of Rural Ghana*. London: Faber & Faber, 1960.

Frobenius, Leo. *The Childhood of Man*. Translated by A. H. Keane. London: Seeley & Co., 1909.

Kaye, Barrington. *Bringing up Children in Ghana*. Legon: Institute of Education, 1960.

King, Noel Q. *Religions of Africa: A Pilgrimage into Traditional*

Religions. New York: Harper & Row, 1970.

Manoukian, Madeline. *Akan and Ga-Adangme Peoples*. Ethnographic Survey of Africa, Western Africa, part 1, edited by Daryll Forde. London: Oxford University Press for the International African Institute, 1950.

Nketia, J. H. K. *Funeral Dirges of the Akan People*. Achimota: Gold Coast, 1955.

Rattray, R. S. *Ashanti Proverbs*. Oxford: Clarendon Press, 1916.

————. *Ashanti*. Oxford: Clarendon Press, 1923.

————. *Religion and Art in Ashanti*. Oxford: Clarendon Press, 1927.

————. *Ashanti Law and Constitution*. Oxford: Clarendon Press, 1929.

————. *Akan-Ashanti Folk-Tales*. Oxford: Clarendon Press, 1930.

Sarpong, Peter K. "The Sacred Stools of Ashanti." *Anthropos* 62 (1967): 1–60.

van Dyck, Charles. "An Analytic Study of the Folktales of Selected Peoples of West Africa." Ph.D. dissertation, Oxford University, 1967.

Ward, William E. F. *A History of Ghana*. 4th rev. ed. London: George Allen & Unwin, 1967.

FON

Alapini, Julien. *Les Noix sacrées: Étude complète de Fa-Ahidégoin-Génie de la sagesse et la divination au Dahomey*. Monte Carlo: Regain, 1950.

Argyle, W. J. *The Fon of Dahomey: A History and Ethnography of the Old Kingdom*. Oxford: Clarendon Press, 1966.

Bertho, Jacques. "La Science du destin au Dahomey." *Africa* 10 (1937): 335–41.

Burton, Richard F. *A Mission to Gelele, King of Dahomey*. 2 vols. 2d ed. London: Tinsley Bros., 1864.

Cornevin, R. *Histoire du Dahomey*. Paris: Presses Universitaires de France, 1965.

Foà, Edouard. *Le Dahomey*. Paris: A. Hennuyer, 1895.

Hazoumé, P. *Doguicimi*. Paris: Larose Editeurs, 1938.

Herskovits, Melville J. "Some Aspects of Dahomean Ethnology." *Africa* 5 (1932): 267–85.

———. *Dahomey. An Ancient West African Kingdom*. 2 vols. 2d ed. Evanston: Northwestern University Press, 1958.

Herskovits, Melville J., and Herskovits, Frances S. *Dahomean Narrative: A Cross-cultural Narrative*. Evanston: Northwestern University Press, 1958.

Le Herissé, A. *L'Ancien royaume du Dahomey*. Paris: Emile Larose, 1911.

Maupoil, Bernard. *La Géomancie à l'ancienne Côte des Esclaves*. Travaux et Mémoires de l'Institut d'Ethnologie, vol. 42. Paris: Institut d'Ethnologie, 1943.

Mercier, Paul. "The Fon of Dahomey." In *African Worlds*, Darryl Forde, ed., pp. 210–34.

Parrinder, Geoffrey. *West African Religion*. London: Epworth Press, 1949.

Skertchly, J. A. *Dahomey As It Is: Being a Narrative of Eight Months' Residence in That Country*. London: Chapman & Hall, 1874.

Trautmann, René. *La Divination à la Côte des Esclaves et à Madagascar; Le Vôdoû Fa-Le Sikidy*. Mémoires de l'Institut Français d'Afrique Noire, vol. 1. Dakar: Institut d'Afrique Noire, 1940.

YORUBA

Abimbola, Wande. "An Exposition of Ifa Literary Corpus." Ph.D. dissertation, University of Lagos, 1970.

Babalola, S. A. *The Content and Form of Yoruba Ijala*. Oxford Library of African Literature. New York: Oxford University Press, 1966.

Bascom, William. "The Sanctions of Ifa Divination." *Journal of the Royal Anthropological Institute* 71 (1941): 43–54.

———. "The Relationship of Yoruba Folklore to Divining." *Journal of American Folklore* 56 (1943): 127–31.

————. "Urbanization among the Yoruba." *American Journal of Sociology* 60 (1955): 446–54.

————. "Odu Ifa: The Names of the Signs." *Africa* 36 (1966): 408–21.

————. *Ifa Divination: Communication between Gods and Men in West Africa*. Bloomington, Ind.: Indiana University Press, 1969.

————. *The Yoruba of Southwestern Nigeria*. New York: Holt, Rinehart & Winston, 1969.

Beier, Ulli. "Before Oduduwa." *Odu* 3 (1956): 25–32.

————. "Oshun Festival." *Nigeria* 53 (1957): 170–87.

Carroll, Kevin. *Yoruba Religious Carving*. London: Geoffrey Chapman, 1967.

Clarke, J. D. "Ifa Divination." *Journal of the Royal Anthropological Institute* 69 (1939): 235–56.

Delano, Isaac O. *Owe l'Esim Oro: Yoruba Proverbs*. New York: Oxford University Press, 1966.

Forde, Daryll. *The Yoruba-Speaking Peoples of South-Western Nigeria*. Ethnographic Survey of Africa, Western Africa, part 4. London: Oxford University Press for the International African Institute, 1957.

Fraser, Douglas. *Village Planning in the Primitive World*. New York: George Braziller, 1968.

Frobenius, Leo. *The Voice of Africa*. Translated by Rudolf Blind. 2 vols. New York: Benjamin Blom, 1913. Reissued, 1968.

Fuja, Abayomi. *Fourteen Hundred Cowries*. New York: Oxford University Press, 1962.

Gbadamosi, Bakare, and Beier, Ulli. *Yoruba Poetry*. Ibadan: General Publications Section, Ministry of Education, 1959.

Idowu, E. Bolaji. *Olódùmare: God in Yoruba Belief*. London: Longmans, Green & Co., 1962.

Jaulin, Robert. *La Géomancie—Analyse formelle*. Cahiers de l'Homme, Ethnologie-Géographie-Linguistique, N.S., vol. 4. Paris: Mouton, 1966.

Krapf-Askari, Eva. *Yoruba Towns and Cities: An Enquiry into the*

Nature of Urban Phenomena. Oxford: Clarendon Press, 1969.

Lloyd, Peter C. "Yoruba Myths: A Sociological Interpretation." *Odu* 2 (1955).

———. "Sacred Kingship and Government among the Yoruba." *Africa* 30 (1960): 221–37.

Mabogunje, A. L. *Yoruba Towns*. Ibadan: Ibadan University Press, 1962.

McClelland, E. M. "The Significance of Number in the Odu of Ifa." *Africa* 36 (1966): 421–30.

Morton-Williams, Peter M. "The Yoruba Ogboni Cult in Oyo." *Africa* 30 (1960): 362–74.

———. "An Outline of the Cosmology and Cult Organization of Oyo Yoruba." *Africa* 32 (1962): 336–53.

Ojo, G. J. Afolabi. *Yoruba Culture: A Geographical Analysis*: London: University of Ife and University of London Press, 1966.

———. *Yoruba Palaces: A Study of the Afins of Yorubaland*. London: University of London Press, 1966.

Parrinder, Geoffrey. *Religion in an African City*. London: Oxford University Press, 1953.

Pemberton, John. "Eshu-Elegba: The Yoruba Trickster God." *African Arts* 9 (1975): 21–27, 66–70, 90–91.

———. "A Cluster of Sacred Symbols: Orișa Worship Among the Igbomina Yoruba of Ila-Orangun." *History of Religions* 17 (1977): 1–28.

Prince, Raymond. *Ifa: Yoruba Divination Sacrifice*. Ibadan: Ibadan University Press, 1963.

———. "Indigenous Yoruba Psychiatry." In *Magic, Faith, and Healing*, edited by Ari Kiev, pp. 84–118. New York: The Free Press, 1964.

Stevens, Phillips. "Orisha-Nla Festival." *Nigeria* 90 (1966): 184–99.

Verger, Pierre. *Notes sur le culte des Orisa et Vodun à Bahia, la Baie de tous les Saints, au Brésil et à l'ancienne Côte des Esclaves en Afrique*. Mémoires de l'Institut Français d'Afrique Noire, vol. 51. Dakar: Institut Français d'Afrique Noire, 1957.

Westcott, Joan. "The Sculpture and Myths of Eshu-Elegba, the Yoruba Trickster." *Africa* 32 (1962): 336–53.

Westcott, Joan, and Morton-Williams, Peter M. "The Symbolism and Ritual Context of the Yoruba *Laba Shango*." *Journal of the Royal Anthropological Institute* 92 (1962): 23–37.

Willett, Frank. *Ife in the History of West African Sculpture*. London: Thames & Hudson, 1967.

Williams, Denis. "The Iconology of the Yoruba *Edan Ogboni*." *Africa* 34 (1964): 139–63.

DOGON

Calame-Griaule, Geneviève. "Esotérisme et fabulation au Soudan." *Bulletin de l'Institut Français d'Afrique Noire* 16 (1954): 307–21.

———. Review of *Die Weissen Denken Zuviel: Psychoanalytische Untersuchungen bei den Dogon in Westafrika* by Paul Parin et al. *Africa* 34 (1964): 281–82.

———. *Ethnologie et langage: la parole chez les Dogon*. Paris: Editions Gallimard, 1966.

Dieterlen, Germaine. *Les âmes des Dogon*. Travaux et Mémoires de l'Institut d'Ethnologie, vol. 40. Paris: Institut d'Ethnologie, 1941.

———. "Parenté et mariage chez les Dogon." *Africa* 27 (1957): 107–48.

———. "Le rire chez les Noirs d'Afrique." In *Colloque sur le Rire*, pp. 17–25. Paris: Institut des Relations Humaines, 1958.

———. "Les Cérémonies soixantenaires du Sigui chez les Dogon." *Africa* 41 (1971): 1–11.

Douglas, Mary. "Dogon Culture—Profane and Arcane." *Africa* 38 (1968): 16–25.

Griaule, Marcel. "Note sur la divination par le chacal (Population dogon de Sanga)." *Bulletin du Comité d'études historiques et scientifiques de l'Afrique occidentale française* 20 (1937): 113–41.

————. *Jeux dogons*. Travaux et Mémoires de l'Institut d'Ethnologie, vol. 32. Paris: Institut d'Ethnologie, 1938.

————. "Nouvelles recherches sur la notion de personne chez
les Dogon (Soudan français)." *Journal de psychologie nor-
male et pathologique* 40 (1947): 405–31.

————. "L'alliance cathartique." *Africa* 18 (1948): 242–58.

————. *Conversations with Ogotemmêli: An Introduction to Dogon
Religious Ideas*. Translated by Ralph Butler, Audrey I.
Richards, and Beatrice Hooke. London: Oxford Univer-
sity Press for the International African Institute, 1965.

Griaule, Marcel, and Dieterlen, Germaine. "The Dogon of the
French Sudan." In *African Worlds*, Darryl Forde, ed.,
pp. 83–110.

————. *Le Renard pâle*, vol. 1, *Le Mythe cosmogonique*. Part 1, "La
Création du Monde." Travaux et Mémoires de l'Institut
d'Ethnologie, vol. 72. Paris: Institut d'Ethnologie, 1965.

Leiris, Michel. *La langue secrète des Dogon de Sanga (Soudan français)*. Travaux et Mémoires de l'Institut d'Ethnologie, vol.
50. Paris: Institut d'Ethnologie, 1948.

Lifchitz, Deborah, and Paulme, Denise. "Les animaux dans le
folklore dogon." *Revue de folklore français et de folklore colo-
nial* 7 (1963): 282–92.

Palau-Marti, Montserrat. *Les Dogon*. Monographies ethnolo-
giques africaines. Institut Africain International. Paris:
Presses Universitaires de France, 1957.

Parin, Paul; Morgenthaler, Fritz; and Parin-Matthau, Goldy.
*Die Weissen Denken Zuviel: Psychoanalytische Untersuchun-
gen bei den Dogon in Westafrika*. Zurich: Atlantis Verlag,
1963.

Paulme, Denise. *Organisation sociale des Dogon*. Institut de Droit
Comparé, Études de Sociologie et d'Ethnographie juri-
diques, vol. 32. Paris: Domat-Montchrestien, 1940.

Tait, David. "An Analytical Commentary on the Social Structure of the Dogon." *Africa* 20 (1950): 175–99.

Zahan, Dominique. "Aperçu sur la pensée théogonique des
Dogon." *Cahiers internationaux de Sociologie* 6 (1949): 113–33.

Index

Compositor:	G&S Typesetters
Printer:	Maple-Vail Book Manufacturing Group
Binder:	Maple-Vail Book Manufacturing Group
Text:	VIP Palatino
Display:	VIP Palatino